Ugaritic Narrative Poetry

Writings from the Ancient World
Society of Biblical Literature

Volume 9

Ugaritic Narrative Poetry

Translated by Mark S. Smith, Simon B. Parker,
Edward L. Greenstein, Theodore J. Lewis, David Marcus

Edited by Simon B. Parker

Ugaritic Narrative Poetry

Translated by
Mark S. Smith
Simon B. Parker
Edward L. Greenstein
Theodore J. Lewis
David Marcus

Edited by
Simon B. Parker

Society of Biblical Literature
Writings from the Ancient World Series

Scholars Press

UGARITIC NARRATIVE POETRY

Translated by Mark S. Smith, Simon B. Parker, Edward L. Greenstein, Theodore J. Lewis, David Marcus

The Society of Biblical Literature gratefully acknowledges a grant from the National Endowment for the Humanities to underwrite certain editorial and research expenses of the Writings from the Ancient World series. Published results and interpretations do not necessarily represent the view of the Endowment.

Library of Congress Cataloging-in-Publication Data

Ugaritic narrative poetry / translated by Mark S. Smith . . . [et al.].
p. cm. — (Writings from the ancient world ; no. 09)
Includes bibliographical references and indexes.
ISBN 0-7885-0336-7 (cloth ; alk. paper). — ISBN 0-7885-0337-5 (pbk ; alk. paper)
1. Ugaritic poetry—Translations into English. I. Smith, Mark S., 1955– . II. Series.
PJ4150.Z95E5 1997
892'.67—DC21 96-54717
CIP

Printed in the United States of America
on acid-free paper.

Contents

Series Editor's Foreword

Writings from the Ancient World is designed to provide up-to-date, readable, English translations of writings recovered from the ancient Near East.

The series is intended to serve the interests of general readers, students, and educators who wish to explore the ancient Near Eastern roots of Western civilization, or compare these earliest written expressions of human thought and activity with writings from other parts of the world. It should also be useful to scholars in the humanities or social sciences who need clear, reliable translations of ancient Near Eastern materials for comparative purposes. Specialists in particular areas of the ancient Near East who need access to texts in the scripts and languages of other areas will also find these translations helpful. Given the wide range of materials translated in the series, different volumes will appeal to different interests. But these translations make available to all readers of English the world's earliest traditions as well as valuable sources of information on daily life, history, religion, etc. in the preclassical world.

The translators of the various volumes in this series are specialists in the particular languages and have based their work on the original sources and the most recent research. In their translations they attempt to convey as much as possible of the original texts in a fluent, current English. In the introductions, notes, glossaries, maps, and chronological tables, they aim to provide the essential information for an appreciation of these ancient documents.

Covering the period from the invention of writing (by 3000 B.C.E.) down to the conquests of Alexander the Great (ca. 330 B.C.E.). the ancient Near East comprised northeast Africa and southwest Asia. The cultures represented within these limits include especially Egyptian, Sumerian, Babylonian, Assyrian, Hittite, Ugaritic, Aramean, Phoenician, and Israelite. It is hoped that Writings from the Ancient World will eventually produce translations of most of the many different genres attested in these cultures: letters—official and private, myths, diplomatic documents, hymns, law collections, monumental inscriptions, tales, and administrative records, to mention but a few.

The preparation of this volume was supported in part by a generous grant from the Division of Research Programs of the National Endowment for the Humanities. Significant funding has also been made available by the Society of Biblical Literature. In addition, those involved in preparing this volume have received financial and clerical assistance from their respective institutions. Were it not for these expressions of confidence in our work, the arduous tasks of preparation, translation, editing, and publication could not have been accomplished or even undertaken. It is the hope of all who have worked on these texts or supported this work that Writings from the Ancient World will open up new horizons and deepen the humanity of all who read these volumes.

Simon B. Parker
Boston University School of Theology

List of Maps and Illustrations

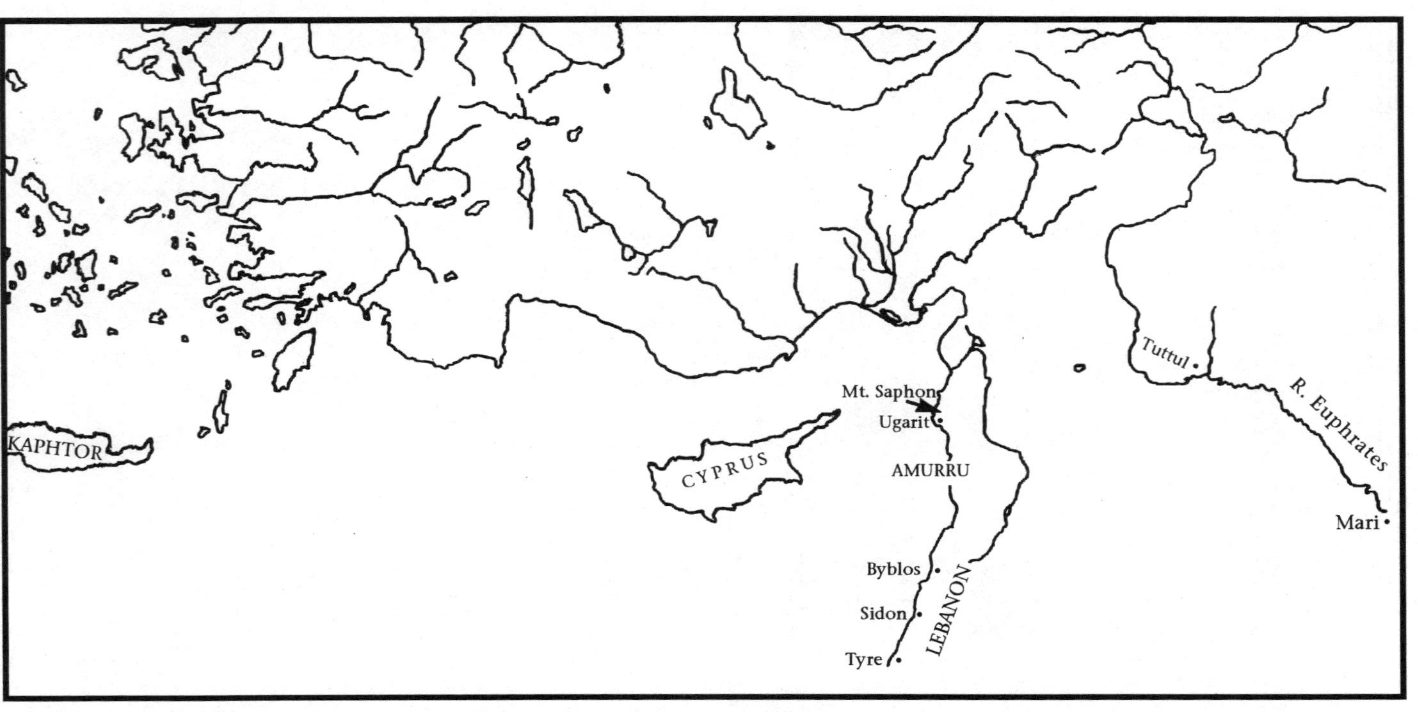

The Eastern Mediterranean and Western Asia

Abbreviations

ANET J. B. Pritchard (ed.), *Ancient Near Eastern Texts Relating to the Old Testament,* 3d ed. (Princeton: Princeton University Press, 1969)

BDFSN J.-L. Cunchillos and J.-P. Vita, *Banco de Datos Filológicos Semíticos Noroccidentales. Primera Parte: Datos Ugaríticos. I. Textos Ugaríticos* (Madrid: CSIC, 1993)

CAT M. Dietrich, O. Loretz, and J. Sanmartín (eds.), *The Cuneiform Alphabetic Texts from Ugarit, Ras Ibn Hani and Other Places* (Münster: Ugarit-Verlag, 1995)

CTA A. Herdner (ed.), *Corpus des tablettes en cunéiformes alphabétiques découvertes à Ras Shamra-Ugarit de 1929 à 1939* (Paris: Imprimerie Nationale, 1963)

KAI H. Donner and W. Röllig, *Kanaanäische und Aramäische Inschriften,* 3 vols. (Wiesbaden: Harrassowitz, 1964)

KTU M. Dietrich, O. Loretz, and J. Sanmartín (eds.), *Die Keilalphabetischen Texte aus Ugarit. Teil 1 Transkription,* Alter Orient und Altes Testament 24/1 (Kevelaer: Butzon und Bercker; Neukirchen-Vluyn: Neukirchener Verlag, 1976)

UF *Ugarit-Forschungen.*

UT C. H. Gordon, *Ugaritic Textbook.* Analecta Orientalia 38 (Rome: Pontifical Biblical Institute, 1965)

Explanation of Signs

[ ]	Single brackets enclose gaps (sometimes with restorations).
< >	Angle brackets indicate text presumably omitted by the scribe.
{ }	Braces indicate text presumed to be erroneously written by the scribe.
/	In the transcription, a slash indicates the end of a line on the tablet. This is not used at the end of a verse and only inconsistently when the end of a line on the tablet and the end of a poetic line coincide.
.	A single dot between the words of the transcription indicates a word divider (a very small cuneiform wedge) in the original.
...	A row of dots indicates text insufficiently preserved or understood for translation.
!	Within the transcription, an exclamation point indicates a correction of a mistake by the original scribe.
Italics	In the transcription, italics indicate Ugaritic text. In the English translation, italics within parentheses indicate comments by the translator.
CAPS	A succession of capital letters in the translation represents the Ugaritic letters of a name of unknown vocalization.
BOLD	Rubrics in boldface type are contributed by some translators to help the reader perceive the structure and progress of the narrative.
(?)	A question mark in parentheses follows doubtful readings in the transcriptions and doubtful renderings in the translations.

Introduction

THE UGARITIC NARRATIVE POEMS all come from the ancient city of Ugarit, which lies half a mile inland from the Syrian coast opposite the eastern tip of Cyprus. The city was discovered after a farmer's accidental exposure of an ancient tomb nearby in 1928 and has been excavated almost annually since 1929. The excavators have uncovered a large palace; an acropolis with two temples, the house of the high priest, and the house of a divination priest; and numerous other large and small buildings, both sacred and secular. These all date from the fourteenth and thirteenth centuries B.C.E. The levels from this period lie closest to the surface, have been most extensively excavated, and have yielded several archives and libraries. The uninscribed and inscribed remains together disclose many aspects of the city's culture during the Late Bronze Age.[1]

Ugarit was well situated for trade. Trade routes extended by land eastward to the other major cities of Syria, to Mitanni, and to Assyria; by sea westward to Cyprus and the Aegean; by land and by sea northward and westward to Asia Minor and the territory of the Hittites; and southward to Palestine and Egypt. Through economic and cultural contacts with these various regions, Ugarit became a rich and cosmopolitan city in the Late Bronze Age.

Excavators have found in the city the scripts and languages of several of the cultures with which it had relations. Two languages and scripts predominate, however. Akkadian, the language of the Assyrians and Babylonians, was the international language of the period and was used especially for communications between states, including Egypt. (Ugarit was predominantly under Egyptian influence in the first part of the Late Bronze Age but after ca. 1350 B.C.E. was dominated by the Hittite state to the north.) Akkadian was written in the complex cuneiform writing system, in which each of several hundred signs consisted of a cluster of wedge-shaped impressions on soft clay and represented a syllable, word, or indicator of a semantic category. But Ugarit also had its own native language, related to several Semitic languages, but generally classified as Northwest Semitic, reflecting its proximity to the hypothetical ancestor of the first-millennium languages of Syria-Palestine: Aramaic, Hebrew, Phoenician, and so on. To write this language, the scribes of Ugarit devised their own script. They exploited the alphabetic principle that had already inspired the invention of the Canaanite alphabet farther south, but devised signs using cuneiform impressions on clay, as for Akkadian. The Ugaritic alphabet consists of thirty simple cuneiform signs, each one representing a consonant (except for three which represent the same consonant—a glottal stop—with three different vowels[2]). In this script the scribes of Ugarit wrote numerous internal administrative records of the city government, many letters and religious texts, and a few literary texts.

The Ugaritic texts include the only collection outside of the Bible of native poetry and narratives[3] from pre-Roman Syria-Palestine. These narrative poems are of unique value as a source of information about Syro-Palestinian poetry, narrative, and mythology toward the end of the Bronze Age. As such, they also provide us with a sample of the traditional background of some of the poetic, narrative, and mythological material in the Hebrew Bible. We find in the Ugaritic narrative poems representatives of a developed poetic tradition that lies behind the poetic achievement now preserved in the prophetic, liturgical, and wisdom books of the Hebrew Bible; versions of traditional tales or motifs that are later recast in Hebrew prose narratives; and a world of gods, with their conflicts and assemblies and interventions in human affairs, that is still dimly reflected in the surviving Hebrew literature.

The Ugaritic narratives are all apparently poetic; that is, they consistently use parallelism and/or poetic formulas. Parallelism, familiar from most biblical poetry, refers to the juxtaposition of phrases or clauses in usually two, sometimes three, and occasionally more, poetic cola of similar syntactic structure and/or semantic import. Poetic formulas include standard epithets for common characters, including gods; standard expressions for the introduction of direct speech, for a character's arrival at or departure from a place, for the passage of time, and so on; and standard pairs of words or phrases used in parallel cola. Many formulas constitute a complete colon and even appear in pairs or larger clusters of cola. While a prose translation that did away with these features would offer a more fast-paced and engaging narrative to the modern reader, we have retained them in the interest of giving a sense of the traditional, poetic character of narratives that would have been not read silently but recited orally.

The various Ugaritic narrative poems draw on and adapt in different ways a common stock of material: accounts of births and arrangements of marriages, of journeys and banquets, of appeals and of conflicts (physical, political, and verbal). Within the individual stories too, there are recurring blocks of material (commonly called epic repetition)—the word-for-word repetition of instructions given and then acted upon, of messages entrusted to someone and then delivered, and so on. Appreciation of these works evidently depended on delight in recognition of the familiar and in the playing off of one version of a statement, speech, or episode against another—more analogous to the aesthetics of modern Western music than narrative literature.

The plots of the larger works are episodic, one crisis being resolved and then followed by another. Only *Aqhat* seems to have a progressive large structure in which each part plays a necessary role. Of course, an episodic plot is no bar to a unified theme, and the episodes of both *Baal* and *Kirta* contribute to overarching interests. Despite the common narrative material, the episodic structure, and the frequent use of epic repetition and formulaic language, however, the passions of the characters, human and divine, are often still apparent to the sympathetic reader.

The first three narratives translated here, *Kirta, Aqhat,* and *Baal*—stories of a king, a patriarch, and the gods respectively—are recognizably literary works, whatever the social purposes they served. Several of the other, shorter narratives, however, appear to have some more immediate, practical use, as is suggested by references to ritual acts, prescriptions, or social circumstances in conjunction with which the narratives were recited. This suggests the immediate power of specific narratives in relation to specific situations.

The world of the gods, in which the action of *Baal* and the shorter texts takes place, is also prominent in the story of Daniel and his son Aqhat, and is clearly in the background of the story of *Kirta.* The patriarch of the gods is El,[4] who presides over the divine assembly in *Baal* and *Kirta.* It is to him that individual gods turn with requests or for final approval of their plans.

Sometimes the best way to El's favor is through his consort, Asherah, the mother of the gods.[5] Kirta, however, having been already assured of El's intervention on his behalf, makes a vow to Asherah to get *additional* support. Despite this, on the evidence of *Kirta,* El is also the patron of kings. Another side of El appears in texts 19 and 23, where we see his drunkenness and sexual activity.

The most prominent deity in the preserved narratives is the god known as Baal, "Lord" (the title of the Syrian storm god, Hadad).[6] Baal resides on the mountain north of Ugarit, Mt. Saphon, where his thunder and lightning can be seen; and he is the protagonist for monarchic rule among the gods, challenging Yamm, "Sea," and Mot, "Death," in the episodic *Baal* myth. His strongest supporter is his sister, Anat, a fierce and tender young woman—indeed, in modern terms, a young teenager or girl—here operating outside the normal sphere of family, and so, as a woman, unmonitored by father or husband (Walls 1992; P. Day 1991; 1992). Baal and Anat cooperate also in text 15, in which Baal fathers a bull. In *Aqhat,* however, the two seem to be working at cross-purposes: Baal supports Daniel in his initial request for a son; Anat later arranges the killing of Aqhat; and Baal then responds to Daniel's appeals for assistance in his attempts to recover Aqhat's remains.

Other deities play more specialized roles. Kothar (and Khasis), for example, is the craftsman of the gods, who produces Baal's palace and Aqhat's bow. Horon is an underworld deity, associated with snakes in text 25. The sun goddess Shapsh, who travels across the sky during the day and through the underworld at night, keeps an eye on all that happens and assists Anat in finding Baal. Text 24 concerns the arrangement of the marriage of the West Semitic moon god Yarikh with the Mesopotamian moon goddess Nikkal.

Unfortunately, almost none of the narratives is preserved in its entirety. Further, even where a text is perfectly preserved, we often encounter individual words or lines whose meaning still escapes us. One or both of these facts limit our understanding of almost every work included here, even of the apparently complete and clear portions (since to some extent understanding of the parts depends on understanding of the whole). Thus there are significant limits to the adequacy of any translations of these texts, and we are aware that our versions are no exception.

The first three works are best known and have been translated several times. The other, shorter texts have in many cases not been included in the standard translations of Ugaritic texts, and the translations that are available sometimes exhibit the translator's creativity and imagination where a sound basis for determining the meaning of the original is lacking. The more fragmentary and obscure texts are included because of their obvious relations with those that are better preserved and understood and also because they have been used in some bold hypotheses concerning Ugaritic mythology and religion. Other fragmentary and ill-understood texts have been omitted altogether. The reader's patience will be sufficiently tried by the gaps in the present translations. We have generally tried to restrain ourselves from speculative reconstructions and to limit our imaginations and creativity to the task of converting what is preserved of the poetry of these ancient texts into a contemporary English that also has some literary qualities. This has been a more realistic aim in the case of the larger and better understood narratives. The more fragmentary and less understood texts demand, for the time being, a more cautious, plodding approach.

I wish to thank the contributors for their patience with the editor, who, while largely leaving judgment about the meaning of the texts to each translator, has pressed for a version that observes English usage and rhythms.

The textual basis of the transcriptions is the various epigraphic studies of particular texts or passages, the standard editions of the texts (*CAT/KTU* and *CTA*), and especially the macro-photographic record being compiled by West Semitic Research. Many of the photographs were taken especially for this project with funding from the National Endowment for the Humanities. We are grateful to the Endowment for funding; to the Louvre, the Syrian Department of Antiquities, and the British Museum for permission to photograph; to the photographers: Bruce and Kenneth Zuckerman of the University of Southern California, Wayne Pitard of the University of Illinois, Theodore Lewis of the University of Georgia, Andrew Vaughn of Princeton University, and Marilyn Lundberg of West Semitic Research; and to Kathryn Campbell for the photographic reproductions.

Finally, thanks are due to Beth Bidlack, who compiled the indexes and assisted me with the glossary.

Notes

1. For a convenient overview of the material and written remains from Ugarit, see Yon, Pardee, and Bordreuil 1992.

2. The transcription in this volume follows the current convention of transliterating each of these three letters by the appropriate vowel alone.

3. There are few poetic texts from Ugarit that are not narratives.

4. "El" is also the basic word for "god."

5. On Asherah, see Wiggins 1993.

6. Cf. the use of *Adonay,* "my Lord," as a substitute for the divine name Yahweh in ancient Judah.

Translations

Kirta

Translated by Edward L. Greenstein

THE EPIC OF KIRTA begins with the story of the near extinction of a royal house and narrates how it is restored with the help of the creator god El. The present text of the epic was copied from a master text by a well-known scribe of mid-fourteenth-century Ugarit; and although the text originated somewhat earlier, its language suggests that *Kirta* is the youngest of the three large epic texts in Ugaritic.

Our epic lacks certain critical markings of time, and the only place-names that can be identified with relative certainty are the Phoenician coastal cities of Sidon and Tyre. The action would seem to be set in Syria (modern Syria and Lebanon), in the mid-second millennium B.C.E., at a time when the Mitanni Empire, dominated by Indo-European Hurrians, ruled northern Syria. Kirta is a known Hurrian name, and several other names of the protagonists are probably Hurrian. From the fact that Kirta is blessed in association with Ditanu, who is among the venerated deified kings of Ugarit, one might deduce that the Kirta Epic is native to Ugarit. However, there is no mention of Ugarit in the text, and Kirta's town is called Khubur. Although some scholars have assumed that the story has a historical basis, the tale is more likely a legend about a royal hero whose specific identity is unknown. The routine interactions of humans and gods in the narrative recall the mythic stories of bygone days in Genesis more than the more mundane stories of relatively recent events in Kings.

The narrative is formed of a number of interlocking action sequences and motifs familiar from mythology and folktales; several have parallels in the Hebrew Bible, and there is a strong parallel in the Hittite tale of Appu as well. The story begins with a disaster the hero must reverse. A king is bereft of family, his dynasty threatened with extinction. This is, as scholars often remark, a concern endemic to dynastic kingship. The disaster is described step by step, like the fateful series of announcements to Job that his estate and children have been destroyed. And just as the name Job (*ʾIyyōb*) is interpreted in the biblical text in the light of his situation—as the apparent "enemy" (*ʾōyēb*) of God (see Job 13:24)—the name Kirta would seem to be played upon according to a Semitic derivation: the man "cut off" (*karūtu* or *karītu*) from progeny.

Kirta cries himself to sleep, perhaps with the intent of contacting his god, and the fatherly El does indeed appear to him in a dream. He instructs Kirta to appeal for support to the rain god, Baal, and then mount a march of the entire population of his town to fetch the beautiful princess bride who would bear him another family. The plan works like a charm: with the blessings of El, Kirta gets eight children. There the story might have ended, but for one hitch: for some reason Kirta had made an unscheduled stop in Phoenicia at the shrine of the goddess Asherah, a consort of El. There Kirta attempted to enlist the goddess's aid by vowing a generous gift should his mission succeed. But he forgets to fulfill his vow to Asherah. The goddess remembers the vow and afflicts Kirta with a fatal illness. The blessed king's disability is reflected in nature, which suffers a drought.

El solves Kirta's problem once again, creating a healer, a female golem, who removes the disease. Kirta returns to his throne. There too the story could end, but ironically, the healing of Kirta leads to another near disaster. The seeds of this conflict were, like the roots of his illness, sown in the first cycle of episodes.

El, in a manner reminiscent of the biblical God's favoring of younger siblings, had declared the youngest of Kirta's new children—Thitmanit or "Octavia," a daughter—to have firstborn status. She and the sympathetic younger son of Kirta are particularly solicitous of their father, while Kirta's older son, in an act that recalls Adonijah's revolt against David in 1 Kings 1–2, seeks to overtake Kirta's throne, oblivious to the fact that his father has been cured. Kirta, once desperate for a son and heir, now brings down a curse on his arrogant firstborn, and there the text as we have it concludes. Some scholars think the tale is not over, but it may, in fact, end on this sobering lesson on life's ironies.

Kirta's children note another irony too. The divinely blessed Kirta, who is intimate with gods, whose illness impacts upon nature, is nonetheless mortal. How, they innocently inquire, can that be? Scholars discuss whether kingship was divine and how the king ritually mediated between the gods and our world. But it is the tension between the benevolence manifested by the creator god El and the seeming malevolence of the fact that people die that lends the story of Kirta broad human interest. Scenes of crying pervade the narrative, inducing a constant sense of existential vulnerability.

Lest we distort the narrative by understating its theological cast, let us observe one final feature of the plot. Kirta gets in trouble when he deviates from his divine instructions, and his older son plays with fire when he follows his own heart. In the final analysis, it's a gods' world—beyond our control—and it is their rules by which the game of life is played.

The text of the Kirta Epic was pieced together from larger and smaller fragments discovered in 1930–1931 and published in sections by Charles Virolleaud between 1934 and 1945. Several sections are missing, and the condition of the preserved fragments is uneven. Advances in philology—the edition published by H. L. Ginsberg in 1946 in particular—and technology—especially the new photographs by West Semitic Research—have led to improvements in reading the text. At the same time, the condition of the tablets has deteriorated over the years. For that reason, earlier scholars have sometimes seen more text than scholars today can. On the other hand, the new, transparent photographs made by West Semitic Research often allow us to read, or trace, formerly illegible signs.

Accordingly, our transcription of the text closely follows the edition of 1963 by A. Herdner (*CTA*) and departs from it, as a rule, only on the basis of the new photographs. The recently revised edition of the text by M. Dietrich, O. Loretz, and J. Sanmartín (*CAT*) has been routinely compared. Important differences with *CTA* and *CAT* are indicated in our notes. In conformity with the guidelines of the *WAW* series, partly legible signs are transcribed without brackets.

Acknowledgments

I completed a large part of my work on this project while enjoying a sabbatical and research leave from the Jewish Theological Seminary of America in 1991–1993, spent as Visiting Scholar in the Institute of Jewish Studies, the Hebrew University of Jerusalem. During that period I was supported by fellowships from the National Endowment for the Humanities, the John Simon Guggenheim Memorial Foundation, and the Memorial Foundation for Jewish Culture. I am grateful to all of the above, and I also thank Simon Parker for valuable editorial advice, David Marcus for discussing some problems with me, Bruce Zuckerman for providing the photographs and for some tutelage in reading them, and Wayne Pitard for making the newest photographs and performing some collations at my request. I dedicate this effort to the memory of Professor H. L. Ginsberg, for many years my teacher, for several years my colleague, in later years my friend.

1. *CAT* 1.14		1. First Tablet
Column I		Column I
1	*[lk]rt*	[Belonging to K]irta[1]
(Five lines almost entirely missing.)		*(The first five, broken lines seem to consist of exposition concerning King Kirta.)*
7–9	*bt / [m]lk . itbd*[2] *dšbʿ / [a]ḫm . lh .* *ṯmnt . bn um /*	The house of a king has perished: A house with seven brothers, Even eight mother's sons!
10–11	*krt . ḫtkn . rš/* *krt . grdš. mknt /*	Kirta—his progeny's ruined! Kirta—his line is sundered!
12–13	*aṯt . ṣdqh . lypq /* *mtrḫt . yšrh /*	A proper wife he'd found, Yes, and rightly wed.
14–15	*aṯt . trḫ . wtbʿt /* *ṯar um . tkn lh /*	He wed a wife, she "departed." She'd had a mother's brood.
16–17	*mṯlṯt . kṯrm . tmt /* *mrbʿt . zblnm /*	A third[3] died in health; A quarter by disease.
18–20	*mḫmšt . yitsp / ršp [.]* *mṯdṯt . ġlm / ym .*	A fifth was gathered by Rashap[4]; A sixth by the Lad of Yamm.[5]
20–21	*mšbʿthn . bšlḥ / ttpl .*	A seventh part— By the sword it was felled.[6]
21–23	*yʿn . ḫtkh / krt* *yʿn . ḫtkh rš /* *mid . grdš . ṯbth /*	He sees his progeny, Kirta, He sees his progeny ruined, His dynasty utterly sundered.
24–25	*wbklhn . špḥ . yitbd /*	So all his descendants have perished,

	wb . pḫyrh . yrṯ /	In sum, the lot of his heirs.
26–27	*yʿrb . bḥdrh . ybky /* *bṯn . ʿgmm . wydmʿ /*	He enters his chamber, he cries; An inner alcove (?), and weeps.
28–30	*tntkn . udmʿth /* *km . ṯqlm . arṣh /* *km ḫmšt . mṭth /*	His tears are poured forth Like shekels[7] on the ground, Like five-weights on the couch.
31–32	*bm . bkyh . wyšn /* *bdmʿh . nhmmt /*	As he cries, he falls asleep; As he weeps, there's slumber.
33–35	*šnt . tluan*[8] */ wyškb .* *nhmmt / wyqmṣ .*	Sleep overwhelms him, he lies down; Slumber, and he crumples.
35–37	*bḥlmh / il. yrd .* *bḏhrth / ab . adm [.]*	Now in his dream, El comes down; The Father of Man, in his vision.[9]
37–38	*wyqrb / bšal . krt .*	Now El approaches, asking Kirta:
38–41	*mat*[10] */ krt . kybky /* *ydmʿ . nʿmn . ġlm / il.*	"What ails Kirta, that he cries? That he weeps, the Pleasant, Lad of El?
41–43	*mlk . kabh*[11] */ yarš .* *hm . drk[t] / kab . adm* *[...]*	Is it kingship like his Father[12] he wants? Or dominion like the Father of Man?"
(Ca. seven lines missing.)		*(Ca. seven lines missing. El offers Kirta diverse tokens of wealth and privilege, the very items that Kirta refuses.)*
Column II		Column II
51–Col. II 2	*[. . . lm / ank . ksp .* *wyrq / ḫrṣ .]* *yd . mqmh /* *[wʿb]d .ʿlm .*	["What to me is silver, or even yellow gold,] Together with its land, and slaves forever mine?
2–3	*ṯlṯ / [ssw]m . mrkbt* *btrbṣ / bn .amt*	A triad of chariot horses From the stable of a slavewoman's son?

4–5	*[tn .]*[13] *bnm . aqny /* *[tn . ṯa]rm*[14] *. amid /*	[Let] me procreate sons! [Let] me produce a brood!"
6	*w[yʿn] . ṯr . abh . il/*	Bull his Father, El, an[swers]:
7–9	*d[y]k*[15] *. bbk . krt /* *bdmʿ . nʿmn . ǵlm / il .*	"Enough of crying, O Kirta! Of weeping, the Pleasant, Lad of El!
9–11	*trtḥṣ . wtadm /* *rḥṣ [. y]dk . amt /* *uṣb[ʿtk .] ʿd . ṯkm /*	Wash yourself, and rouge yourself too: Wash your hands to the elbow, [Your fin]gers as far as the shoulder.
12	*ʿrb [. bẓl . ḫmt] /*	Enter [a shaded pavilion].
13–16	*qḥ . im[r . byd]k /* *imr . d[bḥ . bm] . ymn /* *lla . kl[atn]m /* *klt . l[ḥmk .] dnzl /*	Take a lamb [in your hands]: A lamb of sa[crifice in] your right, A kid in them both— All your available (?) [food].
17–18	*qḥ . ms[rr .] ʿṣr / dbḥ .*	Take a pig[eon], bird of sacrifice.
18–19	*ṣ[q . bg]l . ḥtṯ / yn .* *bgl [. ḫ]rṣ . nbt /*	Pour wine into a silver basin; Into a gold basin, honey.
20–22	*wʿl . lẓr . m[g]dl .*[16] *rkb / ṯkmm . ḥmt .*	Ascend to the top of the lookout; Mount the city-wall's shoulder.
22–24	*ša . ydk / šmm .* *dbḥ . lṯr / abk . il.*	Raise your hands toward the sky. Sacrifice to Bull El, your Father.
24–26	*šrd . bʿl / bdbḥk .* *bn . dgn / bmṣdk .*	Adore Baal with your sacrifice, Dagon's Son with your offering.
26–27	*wyrd / krt . lggt .*	Then let Kirta descend from the rooftops.
27–29	*ʿdb / akl . lqryt /* *ḥtt . lbt . ḫbr /*	Ready rations for the city, Wheat for the whole house of Khubur.[17]
30–31	*yip . lḥm . dḫmš /* *mǵd [.] <d>ṯdṯ . yrḫm /*	Have bread for five months baked, Provisions for as many as six.

32–33	*ᶜdn [.] ngb . wyṣi /* *ṣbu . ṣbi . ngb /*	Then let the army, supplied (?), go forth, The host of hosts, supplied (?).
34	*wyṣi . ᶜdn . mᶜ /*	Then let the escorting (?) army go forth.
35–36	*ṣbuk . ul . mad /* *ṯlṯ . mat . rbt /*	Let your host be a very large force, As many as three hundred myriads!
37–38	*ḫpṯ . dbl . spr /* *ṯnn . dbl . hg /*	Soldiers beyond number, Archers beyond count!
39–40	*hlk . lalpm . ḫḏḏ /* *wlrbt . kmyr /*	They'll march by the thousand, in rows, In myriads, by rank arrayed.
41–42	*[a]ṯr . ṯn . ṯn . hlk /* *aṯr . ṯlṯ . klhm /*	After two, two will march; After three, all of them.
43–45	*yḥd . bth . sgr /* *almnt . škr / tškr .*	The sole survivor'll shut his house.[18] The widow'll hire on for a fee.
45–47	*zbl . ᶜršm / yšu .* *ᶜwr . mzl / ymzl .*	Even the ill will be carried in bed. Even the blind will blink his way.
47–50	*wyṣi . trḫ / ḥdṯ .* *ybᶜr . lṯn / aṯth .* *lm . nkr / mddth .*	The new-wed groom will go forth; To another man he'll drive his wife; To a stranger, his own true love.

Column III		Column III
50– III 1	*kirby / tškn . šd /*[19] *km . ḥsn . pat . mdbr /*	Like a locust swarm, they'll inhabit the steppe; Like crickets, the desert's edge.
2–3	*lk . ym . wṯn .* *ṯlṯ . rbᶜ . ym /* *ḫmš . ṯdṯ . ym .*	March a day, and then a second; A third day, and a fourth; A fifth day, and a sixth.
3–4	*mk . špšm / bšbᶜ .*	Then, at sunrise, on the seventh:

4–5	*wtmǵy . ludm / rbt*[20] . *wludm . trrt /*	When you arrive at Udum the great, Arrive at Udum majestic,
6–7	*wgr . nn . ʿrm .* *šrn / pdrm .*	Attack its outlying towns, Assault the surrounding villages!
7–8	*sʿt . bšdm / ḥṭbh*[21] . *bgrnt . ḥpšt /*	Sweep from the fields[22] the men cutting wood, From the threshing-floors the women picking straw!
9–10	*sʿt . bn<p>k*[23] . *šibt .* *bmqr*[24] */ mmlat .*	Sweep from the well the women drawing water, From the spring, the women filling jars!
10–12	*dm . ym . wṯn /* *ṯlṯ . rbʿ . ym .* *ḫmš*[25] */ ṯdṯ . ym .*	Then halt, a day and a second, A third day, and a fourth, A fifth day, and a sixth.
12–14	*ḥẓk . al . tšʿl / qrth .* *abn . ydk / mšdpt .*	Fire none of your arrows into the city, None of your hand-flung stones.
14–15	*whn . špšm / bšbʿ .*	Then, at sunrise, on the seventh,
15–16	*wl . yšn . pbl / mlk .*	King Pabuli will sleep no more,
16–17	*lqr . ṯigt . ibrh /* *lql . nhqt . ḥmrh /*	For the noise of his stallion's neighing, For the sound of his ass's braying,
18–19	*lgʿt . alp . ḥrṯ .* *zǵt / klb . ṣpr .*	For the lowing of the plow-ox, The barking of the watch-dog.
19–21	*wylak / mlakm . lk .* *ʿm . krt / mswnh .*	Then he'll send two messengers, To Kirta in the night-camp (?):
21	*tḥm . pbl . mlk /*	'Message of King Pabuli:
22–23	*qḥ . ksp . wyrq . ḫrṣ /* *yd . mqmh . wʿbd . ʿlm /*	"Take silver and take yellow gold, Its land, and slaves forever;

24–25	*ṯlṯ . sswm . mrkbt /* *btrbṣ . bn . amt /*	Take a triad of chariot-horses From the stable of a slavewoman's son.
26–27	*qḥ . krt . šlmm /* *šlmm .*	Take, O Kirta, offerings—offerings of peace!
27–29	*wng . mlk / lbty .* *rḥq . krt / lḥẓry .*	But fly, O king, from my palace, O Kirta, far from my court!
29–30	*al . tṣr / udm . rbt .* *wudm ṯrrt /*	Do not harass Udum the great, Do not harass Udum majestic.
31–32	*udm . ytnt*[26] *. il .* *wušn / ab . adm .*	For Udum is a gift of El, A grant from the Father of Man."'
32–33	*wṯṯb / mlakm . lh .*	Return to him two messengers:[27]
33–34	*lm . ank / ksp .* *wyrq . ḫrṣ /*	'What to me is silver, or even yellow gold,
35–36	*yd . mqmh .* *wʿbd / ʿlm .*	Together with its land, and slaves forever mine?
36–37	*ṯlṯ . sswm . mrkbt /* *btrbṣt*[28] *. bn . amt /*	A triad of chariot horses From the stable of a slavewoman's son?
38–40	*pd . in . bbty . ttn* *tn . ly. mṯt . ḥry /* *nʿmt . špḥ . bkrk /*	What is not in my house you must give me: You must give me Lady Huraya, The Fair One,[29] your firstborn child!
41–42	*dk . nʿm . ʿnt . nʿmh /* *km . tsm . ʿṯtrt . ts[mh]*	Who's as fair as the goddess Anath, Who's as comely as Astarte;
43–44	*dʿqh . ib . iqni .* *ʿpʿ[p]h / sp . ṯrml .*	Whose eyes are lapis lazuli, Eyeballs, gleaming alabaster;
44–45	*tḥgrn . […]*[30] */* *ašlw . bṣp . ʿnh /*	Who'll transfix (?) me [...]; I'll repose in the gaze of her eyes;
46–47	*dbḥlmy . il . ytn /*	Whom El has given in my dream,

	bd̲rty . ab . adm /	The Father of Man in my vision;
48–49	*wld . šph . lkrt /* *wǵlm . lʿbd . il /*	Who will bear a child for Kirta, A lad for the Servant of El.'"
50–51	*krt . yḫt . wḥlm /* *ʿbd . il . whdrt /*	Kirta awakes—it's a dream! The Servant of El—a vision!
52–54	*yrtḥṣ . wyadm /* *yrḥṣ . ydh . amth /* *uṣbʿth . ʿd . t̲km /*	He washes himself, and rouges too: Washes his hands to the elbow, His fingers as far as the shoulder.
55	*ʿrb . bẓl . ḫmt .*	He enters a shaded pavilion.
55–58	*lqḥ / imr . {dbḥ .}*[31] *bydh /* *<imr . dbḥ . bm . ymn>* *lla . klatnm /* *klt . lḥmh . dnzl /*	He takes a lamb in his hands: <A lamb of sacrifice in his right,> A kid in them both— All his available (?) food.
59	*lqḥ . msrr . ʿṣr . db[ḥ] /*	He takes a pigeon, bird of sacrifice.

Column IV

Column IV

1–2	*yṣq . bgl . ḥt̲t. yn /* *bgl. ḫrṣ . nbt .*	Pours wine into a silver basin; Into a gold basin, honey.
2–4	*wʿly / lẓr . mgdl .* *rkb / t̲kmm . ḥmt .*	Ascends to the top of the lookout; Mounts the city-wall's shoulder.
4–6	*nša / ydh . šmmh .* *dbḥ / lt̲r . abh . il .*	Raises his hands toward the sky; Sacrifices to Bull El, his Father.
6–8	*šrd / [b]ʿl . bdbḥh .* *bn dgn / b[m]ṣdh .*	He adores Baal with his sacrifice, Dagon's Son with his offering.
8–9	*yrd . krt / [lg]gt .*	Kirta descends from the rooftops.
9–10	*ʿdb . akl . lqryt /* *ḥtt . lbt . ḫbr /*	He readies rations for the city, Wheat for the whole house of Khubur.

11–12	*yip . lḥm . dḫmš/* *m[ġ]d . tdṯ . yr[ḫm] /*	He has bread for five months baked, Provisions for as many as six.
13–14	*ʿdn . ngb . w[yṣi .* *ṣbu] / ṣbi*[32] *. ng[b .*	The army, supplied (?), goes [forth, The host] of hosts, supplied (?).
14–15	*wyṣi . ʿdn] / mʿ [.*	[The] escorting (?) [army goes forth].
15–16	*ṣ]buh [.] u[l . mad] /* *ṯl[ṯ] . mat . rbt /*	His host is a very [large force], As many as three hundred myriads!
17–18	*hlk . lalpm . ḫḏḏ /* *wl . rbt . kmyr /*	They march by the thousand, in rows, In myriads, by rank arrayed.
19–20	*aṯr . ṯn . ṯn . hlk /* *aṯr . ṯlṯ . klhm /*	After two, two march; After three, all of them.
21–23	*aḥd . bth . ysgr /* *almnt . škr / tškr .*	The sole survivor shuts his house. The widow hires on for a fee.
23–25	*zbl . ʿršm / yšu .* *ʿwr / mzl . ymzl /*	Even the ill is carried in bed. Even the blind blinks his way.
26–28	*wyṣu*[33] *. trḫ . ḥdṯ /* *ybʿr . lṯn . aṯṯh /* *wlnkr . mddt<h>*[34] */*	Then the new-wed groom goes forth; To another man he drives his wife; To a stranger, his own true love.
29–31	*km irby tškn / šd .* *kḥsn . pat / mdbr .*	Like a locust swarm, they inhabit the steppe; Like crickets, the desert's edge.
31–32	*tlkn / ym . wṯn .*	They march a day, and a second.
32–33	*aḫr / šp[š]m . bṯlṯ /*	Then at sunrise on the third,
34–36	*ym[ġy .] lqdš / a[ṯ]rt ṣrm .* *wlilt / sdynm .*	He[35] arrives at the shrine of Asherah of Tyre, At the shrine of the Goddess of Sidon.
36–37	*ṯm / ydr [.] krt . ṯʿ /*	He there makes a vo[w, Ki]rta the Noble:

38–39	*iiṯt . aṯrt . srm /* *wilt . sdynm /*	"As Asherah of Tyrians lives, The Goddess of the Sidonians,
40–42	*hm . ḥry . bty / iqḥ .* *ašʿrb . ǵlmt / ḥẓry .*	If I take Huraya into my palace, And have the girl enter my court,
42–43	*ṯnh . kspm*[36] */ atn .* *w . ṯlṯth . ḫrṣm /*	Her two parts I'll make silver, Her third part I'll make gold!"[37]
44–45	*ylk ym . wṯn /* *ṯlṯ . rbʿ . ym*	He marches a day, and a second, A third day, and a fourth.
46	*aḫr . špšm . brbʿ /*	Then at sunrise on the fourth,[38]
47–48	*ymǵy . ludm . rbt /* *wudm [. ṯr]rt /*	He arrives at Udum the great, At Udum [the majestic].
49–50	*grnn . ʿrm /* *šrnn*[39] *. pdrm /*	He attacks its outlying towns, Assaults the surrounding villages.
51–52	*sʿt . bšdm . ḥṭb<h>*[40] */* *wbgrnt*[41] *. ḥpšt /*	Sweeps from the fields the men cutting wood, From the threshing-floors the women picking straw.

Column V		Column V
1–2	*sʿt . bnpk . šibt .* *wb / mqr . mmlat /*	Sweeps from the well the women drawing water, From the spring, the women filling jars.
3–5	*dm . ym . wṯn*[42] */* *ṯlṯ . rbʿ . ym*[43] */* *ḫmš . ṯdṯ . ym /*	He halts, a day and a second, A third day, and a fourth, A fifth day, and a sixth.
6	*mk [.] špšm . bšbʿ /*	Then, at sunrise, on the seventh,
7–8	*wl [.] yšn [.] pbl /* *mlk .*	King Pabuli sleeps no more,
8–10	*lql*[44] *ṯiqt*[45] */ ibrh .* *lql . nhqt / ḥmr[h .*	For [the noise] of his stallion's neighing, For the sound of his ass's braying,

10–12	*lg]ʿt*[46] *. alp / ḥrṯ [.* *l]zġt . klb / [ṣ]pr [.]*	[For the lowing] of the plow-ox, The barking of the watch-dog.
12–14	*a[p]nk / [pb]l . m[lk .* *gm . laṯt / [h . y]ṣ[ḥ*[47] *.]*	Thereupon K[ing Pa]buli Loudly ca[lls out] to his wife:
14–17	*šmʿ . mʿ / [l(?)ʿ(?)* *]m[y(?)]*[48]*. aṯty /* *[… …] tḥm / [… k(?)r(?)]t* *ttn*[49] *[…]*	"Hear now, […], my wife! […] message [to Kir]ta […]"
(Lines 18–29 very fragmentary.)[50]		*(Twelve lines very fragmentary. Pabuli, observing that Kirta has not yet assaulted Udum, instructs two messengers:)*
29–31	*[…id]k*[51] */ pn[m . al. ttn]* *ʿm . [krt . msw]n*[52]	"[Now], proceed [directly] To [Kirta, in the night-camp (?)];
32	*wr[gm . lkrt .] ṯʿ /*	And s[ay to Kirta] the Noble:
33	*tḥm [. pbl mlk] /*	'Message [of King Pabuli]:
34–36	*qḥ . [ksp . wyr]q / ḫrṣ [.* *yd . mqm]h / ʿbd [. ʿlm .*	"Take [silver and take yell]ow gold, [Its land,] and slaves [forever];
36–38	*ṯlṯ] / ss[wm . mrkbt] /* *bt[rbṣ . bn . amt] /*	[Take a triad of chariot-ho]rses From [the stable of a slave-woman's son].
39–40	*[qḥ . krt . šlmm] /* *[šlmm .*	[Take, O Kirta, offerings—offerings of peace!]
40–42	*al . tṣr] / [udm . rbt .* *wudm] / [ṯrrt .*	[But do not harass Udum the great, Do not harass Udum majestic.]
42–43	*udm . ytnt] / [il .* *wušn . ab . adm] /*	[For Udum is a gift of El, A grant from the Father of Man.]
44–45	*[rḥq . mlk . lbty] /* *[ng . kr]t . lḥ[ẓ]ry /*	[Fly, O king, from my palace, O Kir]ta, [far] from my court!"'"

	Column VI	Column VI
	(Four lines missing but partly restorable.)[53]	*(Four lines missing.)*
	[... ttbʿ] / [mlakm . lyṯb] /	[The two messengers leave right away.
	[idk . pnm . lytn] /	They now proceed directly]
1	*[ʿ]m [. krt . mswnh]/*	To [Kirta, in the night-camp (?).]
2	*tša[n . ghm . wtṣḥn] /*	They ra[ise their voices, proclaiming:]
3	*tḥm [. pbl . mlk] /*	"Message [of King Pabuli]:
4–6	*qḥ [.] k[sp . wyrq] / ḫrṣ . [yd . mqmh] / wʿbd [. ʿlm .*	'Take si[lver and take yellow] gold, [Its land,] and slaves [forever];
6–8	*ṯlṯ] / sswm . m[rkbt] / btrbṣ . [bn . amt] /*	[Take a triad of chari]ot-horses From the stable [of a slave-woman's son.]
9–10	*q[ḥ . kr]t [. šlmm] / šl[mm .]*	[Take, O Kirta, offerings]—offerings of [peace]!
10–12	*al . t[ṣr] / udm [.] rbt [.] wu[dm] / [ṯ]rrt [.]*	But do not ha[rass] Udum the great. Do not harass U[dum] majestic.
12–13	*udm . ytn[t] / il [.] ušn [.] ab [. ad]m /*	For Udum is a gift of El, A grant from the Father [of Ma]n.
14–15	*rḥq [.] mlk [.] lbty / ng [.] krt [.] lḥẓ[ry] /*	Fly, O King, from my palace, O Kirta, far from my cou[rt]!'"
16	*wyʿn[y . k]rt [.] ṯʿ /*	[Ki]rta the Noble answers:
17–18	*lm . ank . ksp / wyrq [. ḫ]rṣ /*	"What to me is silver, or even yellow [gold],
19–20	*yd . mqmh . wʿbd / ʿlm .*	Together with its land, and slaves forever mine?

20–22	*ṯlṯ . sswm / mrkbt .* *btrbṣ / bn . amt .*	A triad of chariot horses From the stable of a slavewoman's son?
22–25	*pd . [i]n / bbty . ttn [.]* *tn / ly . mṯt. ḥry /* *nʿmt . šbḥ . bkrk /*	What is not in my house you must give me: You must give me Lady Huraya, The Fair One, your firstborn child!
26–28	*dknʿm . ʿnt / nʿmh .* *km . tsm / ʿṯtrt . tsmh /*	Who's as fair as the goddess Anath, Who's as comely as Astarte;
29–30	*dʿqh . ib . iqni /* *ʿpʿph . sp . ṯrml /*	Whose eyes are lapis lazuli, Eyeballs, gleaming alabaster;
31–32	*dbḥlmy . il . ytn /* *bdrty . ab . adm /*	Whom El has given in my dream, The Father of Man in my vision;
33–35	*wld . špḥ . lkr{k}/t*[54] *.* *wġlm . lʿbd / il .*	Who will bear a child for Kirta, A lad for the Servant of El."
35–36	*ttbʿ . mlakm / lyṯb .*	The two messengers leave right away.
36–38	*idk . pnm / lytn .* *ʿmm . pbl / mlk .*	They now proceed directly To Udum, to King Pabuli.
38–39	*tšan / ghm . wtṣḥn /*	They raise their voices, proclaiming:
40–41	*tḥm . krt . ṯ[ʿ] /* *hwt . nʿmn . [ġlm . /* *il ...]*	"Message of Kirta the Noble, Word of the Pleasant, [Lad of El:]..."

2. *CAT* 1.15 / 2. Second Tablet

Column I

(Ca. forty lines missing.)

(Ca. forty lines missing. The missing portion surely included the messengers' delivery of Kirta's response, followed by Pabuli's reply. Pabuli evidently acquiesced to Kirta's demand for the fair Huraya, but not without expressing his city's collective distress at having to part with the virtuous princess.)

1–2	*mr[ǵ]b . yd . mṯkt /* *mẓma . yd . mṯkt /*	"The hungry she'd take by the hand; The thirsty she'd take by the hand.
3–4	*tṯkrn . [ ]tddn*[55] */* *ʿm . krt . mswn*[56]	(...) To Kirta in the night-camp (?).
5–7	*arḫ . tzǵ . lʿglh /* *bn . ḫpṯ . lumhthm /* *ktnḥn . udmm /*	Like a cow calls to her calf, Like soldiers cry for their mothers, So the Udumians mourn."
8	*wyʿny . krt . ṯʿ*[57] */*	Then Kirta the Noble answers:

Column II

(Ca. twenty lines missing. Lines 1–2 almost entirely broken.)[58]

(Ca. twenty lines missing. Lines 1–2 almost entirely broken. Kirta has brought Huraya home to Khubur and would seem to be holding a reception for the gods to honor the occasion.)

3–5	*[aliy]n . bʿl /* *[ ] yrḫ . zbl /* *[kṯ]r wḫss /*	[... Almigh]ty Baal, [...] Prince Yarikh, [... Kutha]r Wa-Khasis.
6–7	*[ ] . rḥmy . ršp zbl /* *[wʿ]dt . ilm . ṯlṯh /*	[...] Rahmay,[59] Prince Rashap,[60] [A pa]rty of gods, a third (?).
8–9	*[a]pnk . krt . ṯʿ .* *ṯ[ǵ]r*[61] */ [ ]bbth . yšt .*	Right then Noble Kirta Puts a doorman at his house.
9–10	*ʿrb / b[t]h . ytn .* *wyṣu . lytn /*	To enter his house he allows, To exit his house he does not.[62]
11–12	*[aḫ]r . mǵy . ʿ[d]t . ilm /* *[w]yʿn . ali[yn .] bʿl /*	Once the party of gods has arrived, Up speaks Almighty Baal:
13–14	*[ ] tbʿ . llṭpn / [il . d]pid .*	"[Do not], Kind [El] the Compassionate, depart!
14–16	*ltbrk / [krt .] ṯʿ .* *ltmr . nʿmn / [ǵlm .] il .*	Won't you bless the Noble Kirta? Prosper the Pleasant, [Lad] of El?"

16–18	*ks . yiḫd / [il . b]yd .* *krpn . bm / [ym]n .*	[El] holds a cup in his hand, A chalice he holds in his right.
18–20	*brkm . ybrk / [ʿbdh] .* *ybrk . il . krt / [ṯʿ .* *ymr]m . nʿm[n] . ǵlm .* *il /*	He blesses, yes, blesses [his servant]; El blesses Kirta [the Noble, Prosp]ers the Pleasant, Lad of El:
21–23	*a[ṯt . tq]ḥ . ykrt .* *aṯt / tqḥ . btk .* *ǵlmt . tšʿrb / ḥẓrk .*[63]	"The w[ife you have tak]en, O Kirta, The wife to your palace you've taken, The girl you've brought into your court,
23–25	*tld . šbʿ . bnm . lk /* *wṯmn tṯmnm*[64] */ lk .*	Seven children to you she will bear, Eight, she will bear to you eight!
25	*tld . yṣb . ǵlm /*	She will bear you the Lad, Yassib,[65]
26–28	*ynq . ḥlb . ʿṯtrt*[66] */* *mṣṣ . ṯd . btlt . [ʿnt] /* *mšnq[t . ilm]*[67]	Who'll draw on the milk of Astarte, And suck at the breast of Maid [Anath], The wet-nurses [of the gods]."

Column III	Column III
(Ca. fifteen lines missing. Line 1 almost entirely broken.)	*(Ca. fifteen lines missing. Line 1 almost entirely broken. In the missing portion, El named a second son to be born to Kirta, Ilha'u. El goes on to name six daughters, bringing the total, as he said he would, to eight children. The stanza that follows may well have first appeared at the conclusion of the first son's birth announcement, as it closes the birth announcements of the second son and the six daughters.)*

2–4	*[mid . rm .] krt /* *[btk . rpi .] arṣ /* *[bpḫr] . qbṣ . dtn /*[68]	"[May you be much exalted,] O Kirta, [Among] the Netherworld's [shades],

		[In the midst] of Ditana's company![69]
5–6	*[wt]qrb . wld / [b]nt .*[70] *lk /*	Then she'll[71] conceive and bear to you daughters:
7–8	*tld . pǵt . t[ ]t /* *tld . pǵt . [ ] /*	She'll bear the girl [...] She'll bear the girl [...]
9–10	*tld . pǵ[t .] /* *tld . pǵ[t .] /*	She'll bear the girl [...] She'll bear the girl [...]
11–12	*tld . pǵ[t .] /* *tld . p[ǵt . ṯtmnt]*[72] */*	She'll bear the girl [...] She'll bear the gi[rl Thitmanit].[73]
13–15	*mid . rm [. krt] /* *btk . rpi . ar[ṣ] /* *bpḫr . qbṣ . dtn /*	May you be much exalted, [O Kirta,] Among the Netherworld's shades, In the midst of Ditana's company!
16	*ṣǵrthn . abkrn /*	The youngest of them I name first-born!"[74]
17–19	*tbrk . ilm . tity /* *tity . ilm . lahlhm /* *dr il . lmšknthm /*	The gods offer blessing, they go; The gods go home to their tents, The circle of El to their dwellings.
20–21	*wtqrb . wld bn lh /* *wtqrb . wld bnm lh /*	She conceives and bears him a son; She conceives and bears to him two sons.
22	*mk . bšbˁ . šnt /*	Then, when seven years have passed:
23–25	*bn . krt . kmhm . tdr /* *ap . bnt . ḥry / kmhm .*	The sons of Kirta are as many as vowed; Huraya's daughters are just as were vowed.
25–26	*wtḥss . aṯrt / ndrh .* *wilt . p[lih]*[76] */*	But Asherah—she remembers his[75] vow, The Goddess, [what he promised].
27	*wtšu . gh . w[tṣḥ] /*	She raises her voice and [cries]:

28–29	*ph mʿ . ap . k[rt ṯʿ] /* *uṯn . ndr [. . . .] /*	"Can it be so,[77] O Ki[rta the Noble!]? Is reciting a vow [...]?[78]
30	*apr . i[...]*[79]	I'll rupture (?) [....]"

(One line illegible and ca. seven lines missing.)

(Ca. seven lines missing. Asherah punishes Kirta for failing to remember and fulfill the vow he made to the goddess on the third day of his march to Udum. Kirta's dire illness prompts him to summon his nobles.)

Column IV

(Ca. five lines missing.)

(Ca. five lines missing.)

1–2	*p[ʿnh . lhdm . yṯpd]*[80] / *gm . l[aṯth . kyṣḥ] /*	[Resting his feet on his footstool,] Loudly [he calls to his wife]:
3	*šmʿ . lmṯt . ḥry /*	"Listen, [O Lady Huraya!]
4–5	*ṭbḫ [.] šmn . mrik /* *ptḥ . [rḥ]bt . yn /*	Prepare your fattest of livestock; Open the broad vats of wine!
6–7	*ṣḥ . šbʿm [.] ṯry /* *ṯmnym . ẓbyy /*	Summon my seventy captains,[81] Summon my eighty chiefs[82]—
8–9	*ṯr . ḫbr [. rb]t /* *ḫbr [.] ṯr[r]t /*	The captains of Khubur the [gr]eat, Of Khubur the magnificent!"

(Lines 10–13 very fragmentary.)[83]

(Lines 10–13 very fragmentary.)

14	*tšmʿ . mṯt . [ḥ]ry /*	She listens, Lady Huraya:
15–16	*tṭbḫ . šmn . [m]rih /* *tptḥ . rḥbt . yn /*	Prepares her fattest of livestock, Opens the broad vats of wine.
17–18	*ʿlh . ṯrh . tšʿrb /* *ʿlh . tšʿrb . ẓbyh /*	She brings in his captains to see him,[84] To see him she brings in his chiefs—

19–20	*ṯr . ḫbr [.] rbt /* *ḫbr . ṯrrt /*	The captains of Khubur the great, Of Khubur the magnificent.
21–23	*bt . krt . tbun /* *lm . mṯb [… ..] /*[85] *wlḫm mr . tqdm /*	Kirta's palace they enter; [They go (?)] to the area for sitting, Proceed to the festal (?) pavilion (?).
24–25	*yd . bṣʿ . tšlh /* *ḥrb . bbšr . tštn /*	She[86] herself handles the drinking bowl, She herself slices the meat.
26	*[wt]ʿn . mṯt . ḥry /*	Up speaks Lady Huraya:
27–28	*[llḥ]m . lšty . ṣḥtkm /* *[k?dbḥ . l]krt . bʿlkm /*[87]	"[For ea]ting, for drinking, I've summoned you. Your lord Kirta's having [a feast]."[88]
(Ca. fifteen lines missing.)		*(Ca. fifteen lines missing. Huraya must have explained that Kirta is ill, but she may have said more than that. Since Huraya repeats her gestures of hospitality in the next column, it would seem that another group of Kirta's nobles or other subjects [see lines 18–20] are being welcomed to the palace.)*

Column V

Column V

(One or two lines missing.)		*(One or two lines missing.)*
1–2	*[t]ṭb[ḫ . šm]n . [mrih] /* *tp[tḥ . r]ḥbt . [yn]*[90] */*	[She[89] prepares her fat]test [of livestock], [Opens the broad] vats [of wine].
3–4	*[ʿlh . ṯ]rh . tšʿr[b] /* *[ʿlh . tšʿ]rb*[91] *[. ẓb]y[h]*[92]	[She brings in] his [captains (?) to see him], [To see him she brin]gs in [his chiefs (?)].
(Lines 5–6 very fragmentary.)[93]		*(Lines 5–6 very fragmentary. This group of visitors proceeds to their seats.)*

7–8	*yd . bṣʿ . t[šl]ḥ /* *[ḥrb . b]bš[r] . tštn /*	She herself handles the drinking bowl; She herself [slices the m]eat.
9	*[wtʿn] . mṯt . ḥry /*	[Up speaks] Lady Huraya:
10	*[llḥ]m . lšty . ṣḥtk[m] /*	"[For ea]ting, for drinking, I've summoned you.
11–12	*[ ]brk . t[brkn]*[94] */* *[ʿl .] krt . tbkn*[95] */*	[...] bless, you [will bless]. [Over] Kirta will you weep.
13–14	*[km .] rgm . ṯrm /* *[rg]mtm .*	[As] the captains spoke have you sp[oken].
14	*tbkn / ...*	You will weep [....]"
(Lines 15–16 somewhat broken and unintelligible.)		*(Lines 15–16 somewhat broken and unintelligible. The visitors are now speaking.)*
17	*[k]rt . šrk . il /*	"Kirta, devotee of El.
18–20	*ʿrb . špš . lymǵ / krt .* *ṣbia . špš / bʿlny .*	Kirta is reaching the sunset,[96] Our lord, the niche of the sun.
21–22	*wymlk / yṣb ʿln .* *wy[ʿ]ny*[98] */ [kr]t ṯʿ .*	Therefore let Yassib[97] reign over us, And [Kir]ta the Noble [....]!
22–24	*ʿln . bḫr / [...] . aṯtk .* *ʿl / [.....] yšṣi /*	Over us (...) [...] your wife; Over [...] let him produce!
25–26	*[....] ḫbr . rbt /* *[wḫbr . ṯrr]t*	[...] Khubur the great, [Even Khubur the magnifi]cent!"
26–27	*il d/[pid . ...] . banšt /*	El the Com[passionate ...] company (?).
(Lines 28–29 almost entirely broken. Ca. eighteen lines missing.)		*(Lines 28–29 almost entirely broken. Ca. eighteen lines missing. A third group of visitors, possibly Kirta's children [see VI 4–5], are about to be addressed by Lady Huraya.)*

Column VI		Column VI
1–2	*šmʿ . l[ ]mt[ ]m*[99] *l[. .]ṯ?nm*[100]/ *ʿdm . <t>[lḥ]m*[101] *. tšty /*	Listen [. . . .] Still (?), they eat, they drink.
3	*wtʿn . mṯt ḥry /*	Up speaks Lady Huraya:
4–5	*ll[ḥ]m . lš[t]y . ṣḥtkm /* *db[ḥ] . lkrt . adnkm /*	"For eating, for dri[nking], I've summoned you; Kirta, your father,[102] is having a feast."
6–7	*ʿl . krt [.] tbkn*[103] *.* *km / rgm . ṯrm [.] rgm . hm /*	Over Kirta they weep; As the captains spoke do they speak.
8	*bškm*[104] *[. . . .]*[105] *krt /*	(. . .) [. . .] Kirta.
(Line 9 almost entirely broken. Ca. forty lines missing.)		*(Line 9 almost entirely broken. Ca. forty lines missing.)*

3. *CAT* 1.16 — 3. Third Tablet

Column I		Column I
1	*[l]krt*	[Belonging to] Kirta[106]
		(Ilha'u is receiving [from his mother?] or rehearsing [at his own prompting] the words he will address to his ailing father, Kirta.)
2–3	*k[kl]b . bbtk . nʿtq .* *kinr / ap . ḫštk .*	"Like a [do]g you pass into your tomb;[107] Like a cur, even into your grave.
3–5	*ap . ab . ikmtm / tmtn .* *uḫštk . lntn / ʿtq .* *bd . aṯt . ab ṣrry /*	How can you, father, die like a mortal? Your grave—will it pass into dirges?— To a woman's song, Father of Heights (?)?

6–9	*tbkyk . ab . ǵr . bʿl /* *ṣpn . ḥlm . qdš/* *n!ny*[109] *. ḥlm . adr .* *ḥl / rḥb . mknpt .*	Baal's mountain will weep for you, father— Mount Saphon,[108] the holy domain, Mount Nani,[110] the mighty domain, A domain stretched as wide as a wingspan.[111]
9–11	*ap . / krt . bnm . il .* *špḥ / lṭpn . wqdš.*	But Kirta's a scion of El— Son of the Gentle and Holy One!"
11–12	*ʿl / abh . yʿrb!*[112] *.*	He[113] enters his father's presence.
12–14	*ybky / wyšnn .* *ytn . gh / bky .*	He cries, bitterly cries; He utters his voice as he cries:
14–15	*bḫyk . abn . n!šmḫ*[114] */* *blmtk . ngln .*	"In your living, O father, we're happy! In your not-dying we can rejoice!
15–17	*kklb / bbtk . nʿtq .* *kinr / ap!*[115] *. ḫštk .*	Like a dog you pass into your tomb; Like a cur, even into your grave.
17–19	*ap . ab . kmtm / tmtn .* *uḫštk . lntn / ʿtq .* *bd . aṯt ab . ṣrry /*	How can you, father, die like a mortal? Or your grave—will it pass into dirges— To a woman's song, Father of Heights (?)?
20–22	*ikm . yrgm . bn il / krt .* *špḥ . lṭpn / wqdš .*	Is Kirta not called scion of El, Son of the Gentle and Holy One?
22–23	*uilm tmtn /* *špḥ . lṭpn . lyḥ /*	Gods, after all—do they die? The Gentle One's son—won't he live?"
24	*wyʿny . krt . ṯʿ /*	Noble Kirta answers:
25–26	*bn . al . tbkn .* *al / tdm . ly .*	"Cry for me not, O my son! Do not your tears shed[116] for me!
26–28	*al . tkl . bn / qr . ʿnk .*	Spend not the flow of your eyes,

	mḫ[117] *. rišk / udmʿt .*	Nor the wellsprings of your tears!
28–30	*ṣḥ . aḫtk / ṯtmnt .* *bt . ḥmḥ<m>h / dan*[118] *.*	Summon your sister, Thitmanit, A daughter whose passion is strong (?).
30–31	*tbkn . wtdm . ly [...] /* *ǵ?z?r?*[119] *. al . trgm . laḫtk /*	Let her cry and bewail me [...]! But, Valiant One, don't tell your sister.
32–33	*[.....] l[t]dm .* *aḫtk / ydʿt . krḥmt /*	[...] not bewail. Your sister, you[120] know how she loves me.
34–35	*al . tšt . bšdm . mmh /* *bsmkt . ṣat . npšh /*	She must not waste her tears in the field, Nor her precious breath on the steppe.
36–38	*tmtn . ṣba . rbt / špš .* *wtgh . nyr / rbt .*	Wait, then, till Lady Sun sets, And Lady Lamp[121] starts to shine.
38–39	*wrgm . laḫtk / ṯtmnt .*	Tell then Thitmanit, your sister:
39–41	*krtn . dbḥ / dbḥ .* *mlk . ʿšr / ʿšrt .*	'Kirta is having a feast; The king is making a banquet.
41–42	*qḥ . tpk*[122] *byd /* *[m]rqṣtk*[123] *. bm . ymn /*	Take in your hand your timbrel, Your dance-drum in your right.
43	*lk . šr . ʿl ṣrrt /*	Go, sing on the heights (?)!
44–45	*ndr*[124] *. šqrb [.] ksp /* *bmgnk . wḫrṣ . lkl /*	Make a vow and offer up silver; Your donation—gold for all!'"
46	*apnk . ǵzr ilḥu /*	Right then the Valiant Ilha'u:
47–49	*[m]rḥh / yiḫd . byd /* *grgrh . bm . ymn /* *[w]yqrb . trẓzh /*	His lance he grasps in his hand, His spear he takes in his right, And sets out on his run.

50–51	*[aḫ]r . mǵyh . wǵlm /* *[a]ḫth . šib . yṣat .*	By the time he arrives, it's grown dark; His sister's gone out to draw water.
51–53	*mrḥh . ltl [.] yṣb .* *pnh . ṯǵr / yṣu .*	His lance he stands up on the threshold; Its radiance shines in the doorway.
53–55	*hlm . aḫh . tph /* *[ksl]h*[125] *. larṣ . ṯṯbr /* *ʿ[l . . . .] aḫh . tbky /*	Just as her brother she sees, Her tendons go lax, she collapses;[126] On her brother's [. . .][127] she falls crying.
56–57	*m[rṣ .] mrṣ mlk /* *[hm dw.]*[128] *krt . adnk /*	"Is the king, then, direly sick? Is Kirta, your father, then, [ill]?"
58	*[wyʿn]. ǵzr . ilḥu /*	Valiant Ilha'u an[swers]:
59–60	*[lmrṣ .] mrṣ . mlk /* *[ldw . k]rt . adnkm /*[129]	"[No,] the king's [not direly] sick; Kirta your father's [not ill].
61–62	*[krt .] dbḥ . dbḥ /* *[m]l[k*[130] *. ʿ]šr . ʿšrt /*	[Kirta] is having a feast; [The king] is making [a ba]nquet."

Column II	Column II
(Only the very beginnings of the first sixteen lines are preserved.)	*(From what is preserved of the very broken sixteen lines that begin the column, including terms for serving drink, it would appear that Thitmanit visits her father, discovers he is ill, and begins catering to him.)*

17	*tqrb . aḫ[h . . . .] /*	She approaches her brother [and cries out]:
18	*lm . tbʿrn [. . . .] /*	"Why have you deceived (?) me [. . .]?
19–20	*mn . yrḫ . kmr[ṣ] /* *mn . kdw . kr[t] /*	He's been sick how many a month? How many has Kirta been ill?"
21	*wyʿny . ǵzr[. ilḥu] /*	Valiant [Ilha'u] answers:

22–23	*tlṯ . yrḫm . km[rṣ] /* *arbᶜ . kdw . k[rt] /*	"For three months has he been s[ick]; For four has Ki[rta] been ill.
24–25	*mndᶜ . krt . mǵ[y…]*[131] */* *wqbr . tṣr . q[…] /*	It seems Kirta's reaching [the sunset],[132] The grave (…) […]."
26–28	*tṣr . trm . tnq[th]*[133] */* *km . nkyt . tǵr […] /* *km . škllt . [… . . .] /*	She bellows (?), she raises a wa[il]; Like a cripple (?), she […] the door, Like a (…) […].
29–31	*ᶜrym . lbl […] /* *b[…. wt]ᶜny*[135] *[…] / lbl . sk .*	Stripped down, without […],[134] […] (…), […] without makeup (?).[136]
31–33	*w[…]h / ybmh . šbᶜ* *[…]/ ǵzr . ilḥu .*	[…] her brother[137] (…), […] Valiant Ilha'u.
33–34	*t[… q]l / trm [.]* *tṣr . trm [. t]nqt /*	She raises her [voi]ce, she [bellows (?)]; She raises up a [wa]il.
35–36	*tbky . wtšnn /* *ttn / gh . bky .*	She cries, bitterly cries; She utters her voice as she cries:
36–37	*bḥyk [.] abn / nšmḫ .* *blmtk . ngln /*	"In your living, O father, we're happy! In your not-dying we can rejoice!
38–39	*kklb . bbtk . nᶜtq /* *kinr [. ap .] ḫštk /*	Like a dog you pass into your tomb; Like a cur, even into your grave.
40–42	*ap . ab . kmtm . tmtn /* *uḫštk . lbky [.] ᶜtq /* *bd . aṯt ab . ṣrry /*	How can you, father, die like a mortal? Or your grave—will it pass into weeping— To a woman's song, Father of Heights (?)?
43–44	*uilm . tmtn .* *špḥ / [l]ṭpn . lyḥ .*	Gods, after all—do they die? The [Ge]ntle One's son—won't he live?

44–46	*tbkyk / ab . ǵr . bʿl .* *ṣ[p]n . ḥlm / qdš .*	Baal's mountain will weep for you, father— Mount Sa[ph]on, the holy domain,
46–47	*nny . ḥ[l]m . adr /* *ḥl . rḥb . mk[npt] /*	Mount Nani, the mighty do[ma]in, A domain stretched as wide as a win[gspan].
48–49	*ap . krt bn[m . il] /* *špḥ . lṭpn [. wqdš] /*	But Kirta's a scion [of El]— Son of the Gentle [and Holy One]!"
50–51	*bkm . tʿrb [. ʿl . abh] /* *tʿrb . ḥd[r krt]*[138]	She enters [her father's presence], She enters the cham[ber of Kirta].

(Lines 52–58 very fragmentary; another three lines are almost entirely damaged.)[139]

(Seven lines very fragmentary, and three lines missing. From what is preserved, it seems Thitmanit performed certain rituals to promote her father's healing.)

Column III

Column III

(Ca. thirty lines missing.)

(Ca. thirty lines missing. The illness of the blessed King Kirta leads to a sympathetic drought in the land. Some individual—possibly a god—would seem to be addressed—possibly by El, bidden to investigate the extent of the drought.)[140]

1	*yṣq . šmn [...]*	"Pouring oil [...].
2–4	*ʿn . tr . arṣ . wšmm /* *sb . lqšm . arṣ /* *lksm . miyt*[141] *.*	Look, scout, both earth and sky; Scan the far reaches of earth, For emmer (...)!
4–6	*ʿn / larṣ . mṭr . bʿl /* *wlšd . mṭr . ʿly /*	Look to the earth for Baal's rain, To the field, for the Most High's rain!
7–8	*nʿm . larṣ . mṭr . bʿl /* *wlšd . mṭr . ʿly /*	So good for the earth is Baal's rain, And for the field, the Most High's rain!
9–11	*nʿm [.] lḥṭt . bʿn /* *bm [.] nrt . ksmm /*	So good for the wheat in the plow-land,

ʿl . tl[m]k ʿṭrtrm /

For the emmer in the furrows,
For the wheat-crowns (?) in the til[th]!"

12–13 *nšu . riš . ḥrṯm /*
lẓr [.] ʿbd . dgn

They raise their heads, the plowmen do,
Up toward the Servant of Dagon:[142]

13–16 *kly / lḥm . bmʿdnhm*[143] .
kly / yn . bḥmthm .
k[l]y / šmn b[...]

"The food is all spent from its storage;
The wine is all spent from its skins;
The oil is all spent from its [casks]."

17 *bt krt . t[...]*[144]

They [...] the house of Kirta.[145]

(Ca. eighteen lines missing.)

(Ca. eighteen lines missing.)

Column IV

(Ca. sixteen lines missing.)

(Ca. sixteen lines missing. El is responding to an individual's appeal to end the drought by curing Kirta. The same individual whom El had charged with investigating the drought may have proposed a remedy.)

1–2 *il . šmʿ . amrk ph[n]*[146] */ kil .*
ḥkmt . kṯr . lṭpn /

"The god El's heard your word—it['s] like El's!
You have wisdom like Bull, the Gentle One.[147]

3–4 *ṣḥ . ngr . il . ilš*
il[š] <ngr . bt . bʿl>[148]
waṯth . ngrt [.] ilht /

Summon the herald-god, Ilish—
Ilish, the herald of Baal's house,
And his wives, herald-goddesses, too!"

5 *kḥṣ . kmʿr [...]*

(...) [...]

6–8 *yṣḥ . ngr il . ilš/*
ilš. ngr . bt . bʿl /
waṯth . ngrt . ilht /

He summons the herald-god, Ilish,
Ilish, the herald of Baal's house,
And his wives, herald-goddesses, too.

9	*kyʿn . lṭpn [.] il dpi[d] /*	Up speaks Kind El, the Compassio[nate]:
10–12	*šmʿ . lngr il il[š] /* *ilš. ngr bt bʿl /* *waṯtk . ngrt . ilht /*	"Listen, O herald-god Ilish, Ilish, the herald of Baal's house, And your wives, herald-goddesses, too!
13–14	*ʿl . lṯkm . bnwn /* *lnḫnpt . mšpy /*	Ascend to a tall building's shoulder, To the parapet (?) of a watchtower (?).
15–16	*ṯlṯ kmm ṯrry /* *[...] lǵr . gm . ṣḥ /*	Three (...), [...] to the mountain (?) loudly cry:"

(Line 17 very fragmentary; the next ca. twenty-seven lines missing.)

(One line mostly broken, the next ca. twenty-seven lines missing.)

Column V

Column V

(In the first eight, very broken lines, what is clear is that gods, evidently summoned, assemble in the presence of El.)

1–3	*ʿr[b...] /* *ʿr[b...] /* *ʿrb [...]/*	
4–5	*wyb[...] /* *bʿd[t...] /*	
6–7	*yaṯr [...] /* *bdk . b[...] /*	
8–9	*ṯnnth [...] /* *ṯlṯth [...]*	
9–10	*[wyʿn] / lṭpn . i[l . dpid .]*	[Up speaks] Kind E[l the Compassionate]:

10–12	*[my] / bilm . [ydy . mrṣ] / gršm . z[bln .]*	"[Who] of the gods [removes ill- ness]? Who can dispel a di[sease]?"
12–13	*[in . bilm] / ʿnyh .*	[None of the gods] will answer him.
13–14	*yṯ[ny . yṯlṯ] / rgm .*	He says it a sec[ond, a third time]:
14–15	*my . b[ilm . ydy] / mrṣ . grš[m . zbln]/*	"Who of [the gods removes] illness? Who can disp[el a disease]?"
16	*in . bilm . ʿ[nyh .]*	None of the gods will an[swer him].
16–17	*[yrbʿ] / yḫmš . rgm .*	He says it [a fourth,] and a fifth time:
17–18	*[my . bilm] / ydy . mrṣ . g[ršm . zbln] /*	"[Who of the gods] removes illness? Who can di[spel a disease]?"
19	*in . bilm . ʿn[yh .]*	None of the gods will ans[wer him].
19–20	*yṯdṯ / yšbʿ . rgm [.]*	He says it a sixth, and a seventh time:
20–21	*[my .] bilm / ydy . mrṣ . gršm . zbln /*	"[Who] of the gods removes illness? Who can dispel a disease?"
22	*in . bilm . ʿnyh /*	None of the gods will answer him.
23	*wyʿn . lṭpn . il . dpid*[149] /	So answers Kind El the Compassion- ate:
24–25	*ṯb . bny . lmṯbtkm / lkḥt . zblk[m .]*	"Stay seated, my sons, on your seats, On your elevated thrones.
25–28	*ank / iḫtrš . waškn / aškn . ydt . [m]rṣ gršt / zbln .*	As for me, I'll use skills and create! I'll create a Remover of Illness,[150] A Dispeller of Disease!"
28–29	*rḥt[h . rṯ] . ymlu / nʿm . rṯ . [uṣbʿth]*[151]	He fills his hands [with soil], With good soil fills his [fingers].
29–30	*yqrṣ / dm*[152] *. bpḫ[r .*	He pinches off some clay.

(Through line 32 fragmentary; lines 33–36 missing; lines 37–38 very fragmentary.)		*(In the nine lines either broken or missing, El completes his creation of a female Remover of Illness. He is about to name and commission her over a cup of wine.)*
39–40	*ks [. yqḥ . bdh] /* *kr[pn . bm . ymn]*[153] */*	A cup [he takes in his hand], A cha[lice he holds in his right].
41	*at . š[ʿtqt…]*	"You are Sh[ataqat…][154]
(Lines 42–46 very fragmentary.)		*(Five lines very broken.)*
47–48	*ʿrm . [di . mi .]* *[pdrm] / di . š[rr]*[155]	"[Swoop like a kite (?) over] villages, Swoop like a fl[yer (?) over towns]!
48–50	*[ḫṭm . tʿ]/mt p[ṭr .]*[156] */* *[km] zb[ln . ʿl . rišh] /*	[With a wan]d, un[bind the knot (?)]— [Thus] the dis[ease from his head]![157]
51–52	*t[ṯb . rḥṣ . nn .] / b[dʿt …]*[158]	Re[turn, and wash him clean of sweat]!"
(Eight lines missing.)		*(Eight lines missing.)*

Column VI

Column VI

1–2	*[m]t . dm . ḫt .* *šʿtqt dm!*[159] */ li .*	"[Dea]th, be shattered! Shataqat, triumphant!"
2–3	*wttbʿ . šʿtqt /* *bt . krt . bu . tbu /*	Shataqat then departs, The house of Kirta she enters.
4–5	*bkt . tgly . wtbu /* *nṣrt . tbu . pnm /*	(…) she penetrates and enters. (…) she enters, all the way in.
6–7	*ʿrm . tdu . mi /* *pdrm . tdu . šrr /*	She swoops like a kite (?) over villages, Swoops like a flyer (?) over towns.
8–9	*ḫṭm . tʿmt . pṭr .* *km / zbln . ʿl . rišh /*	With a wand she unbinds the knot (?)— And thus the disease from his head.

10	*wtṯb . trḥṣ . nn . bdᶜt /*	She returns and washes him clean of sweat.
11–12	*npšh . llḥm . tptḥ /* *brlth . lṯrm /*	She opens his throat up for eating, She opens his gullet to dine.
13–14	*mt . dm . ḫt .* *šᶜtqt / dm . lan .*	Death—is shattered, Shataqat, triumphant!
14–16	*wypqd / krt . ṯᶜ .* *yšu . gh / wyṣḥ .*	He gives a command, Noble Kirta, He raises his voice and proclaims:
16–17	*šmᶜ . lmṯt / ḥry .*	"Listen, O Lady Huraya!
17–18	*tbḫ!*[160] *. imr / wilḥm .* *mgṯ . wiṯrm /*	Prepare a lamb I might eat, Mutton, that I might dine."
19	*tšmᶜ . mṯt . ḥry /*	Lady Huraya listens;
20–21	*tṭbḫ . imr . w<y>lḥm*[161] *mgṯ . wyṯrm .*	Prepares a lamb he might eat, Mutton, that he might dine.
21–22	*hn ym / wṯn .* *yṯb . krt . lᶜdh /*	It's only a day, and a second— And Kirta returns to his prime.
23–24	*yṯb . lksi . mlk /* *lnḫt . lkḥṯ . drkt /*	He sits on the throne of his kingship, Ensconced in the seat of his rule.
25–26	*ap . yṣb . yṯb . bhkl /* *wysrnn . ggnh*[162]	Yassib, too, sits in the palace; And his spirit[163] instructs him this way:
27–29	*lk . labk . yṣb .* *lk / l[a]bk . wrgm .* *ṯny / lk[rt . a]d[nk .]*[164]	"Go to your father, O Yassib, Go to your father and say, Declare to Ki[rta, your sire]:
29–30	*ištm[ᶜ] / wtqǵ [. udn .]*	'Hearken, alert [your ear]!
30–31	*[kǵz . ǵzm] / tdbr .* *w[ǵ]rm [.] tṯwy*[165] */*	[In time of attack] you take flight, And lie low in the [moun]tains.[166]

32	*šqlt . bǵlt . ydk /*	You've let your hand fall to vice.
33–34	*ltdn . dn. almnt /* *ltṯpṭ . ṯpṭ . qṣr . npš /*	You don't pursue the widow's case,[167] You don't take up the wretched's claim.
35–36	*km . aḫt . ʿrš . mdw /* *anšt . ʿrš . zbln /*	Your sickbed is your consort,[168] Your infirmity,[169] your company.
37–38	*rd . lmlk . amlk /* *ldrktk aṯb an /*	Step down—and I'll be the king! From your rule—I'll sit on the throne!'"
39–40	*ytbʿ . yṣb ǵlm .* *ʿl / abh . yʿrb .*	Yassib the Young departs, He enters his father's presence.
40–41	*yšu . gh / wyṣḥ .*	He raises his voice and proclaims:
41–42 42	*šmʿ mʿ . lkrt / ṯʿ .* *ištmʿ . wtqǵ . udn /*	"Hear now, O Noble Kirta! Hearken, alert your ear!
43–44	*kǵz . ǵzm . tdbr /* *wǵrm . ṯṯwy .*	In time of attack you take flight, And lie low in the mountains.[170]
44–45	*šqlt / bǵlt . ydk .*	You've let your hand fall to vice.
45–47	*ltdn / dn . almnt .* *ltṯpṭ / ṯpṭ qṣr . npš.*	You don't pursue the widow's case, You don't take up the wretched's claim.
47–48	*ltdy / ṯšm*[171] *ʿl . dl .*	You don't expel the poor's oppressor.
48–50	*lpnk / ltšlḥm . ytm .* *bʿd / kslk . almnt .*	You don't feed the orphan who faces you, Nor the widow who stands at your back.
50–52	*km / aḫt . ʿrš . mdw .*	Your sickbed is your consort,

	anšt / ʿrš . zbln .	Your infirmity, your company.
52–54	*rd . lmlk / amlk .* *ldrktk . aṯb / an.*	Step down—and I'll be the king! From your rule—I'll sit on the throne!"
54	*wyʿny . krt ṯʿ .*	Noble Kirta answers:
54–57	*yṯbr / ḥrn . ybn .* *yṯbr . ḥrn / rišk .* *ʿṯtrt . šm . bʿl / qdqdk!*[173]	"May Horon[172] crack, my son, May Horon crack your head, Astarte-named-with-Baal, your skull!
57–58	*tqln . bgbl / šntk .* *bḥpnk . wtʿn /*	May you fall at the peak of your years, Be subdued while you still make a fist (?)!"
left edge:	*spr . ilmlk . ṯʿy*	Colophon: Written by[174] Ilimilku;[175] donated (by Niqmadd)[176]

Notes

1. Scribal identification of the tablet, indicating that it belongs to the series "Kirta," what we call the Epic of (King) Kirta.

2. The tablet reads *itdb,* a scribal metathesis; see line 24.

3. Of the offspring.

4. Winged god of pestilence, biblical Resheph.

5. An epithet of Rashap or of another god subordinate to the sea god Yamm.

6. The fractions from one-third through one-seventh actually add up to just a little more than one.

7. Not coins but pieces of precious metal, sliced from an ingot, measured by weight and used in commerce.

8. *CAT* reads *tlun*, interpreting the last sign as a long *n*.

9. An epithet of El.

10. *CAT* emends to *m<h> at,* which is the sense we too understand; cf., e.g., *lm . ank* in III 33 below; *UT* emends to *mn,* "Why?"

11. *CTA* reads *[. ṯ]r,* and *CAT* claims to see traces of *ṯ*. The new photograph reveals that the putative *r* is *k* and that there is no trace of a letter preceding it.

12. The god El.

13. Restored with Ginsberg on the basis of VI 22–24.

14. *CAT* reads *]šrm,* but traces of *ṯa* appear on the photograph.

15. The photograph and Pitard's collation support the reading, proposed by Ginsberg.

16. Line 20 is omitted from the present transcription and translation; it is apparently a defective writing of line 21 in which the scribe noticed that he omitted the initial *w* and recopied the line. Line 20 reads: *ʿl . lẓr . [mg]dl.*

17. The name of the town.

18. The sole surviving son of a family; cf. Genesis 22:2; Zechariah 12:10. This class of persons, and the rest that follow, are ordinarily excluded or exempted from military service; cf. Deuteronomy 24:5.

19. Two parallel lines at the bottom of column II indicate the bottom of the tablet's obverse side.

20. Written *m;* see IV 47. The several errors in the succeeding lines suggest that the scribe was nodding in copying this section.

21. The sign is clearly *h,* written over an erased *t.* The form is a masculine plural with possessive suffix, referring to Udum.

22. Literally, "its," viz., Udum's.

23. The *p,* which begins like *k,* was omitted by haplography.

24, Written *bbqr,* but see V 1–2.

25. The *ḫ* was erroneously copied dittographically as *y.*

26. The final *t* is written dittographically as *a.*

27. It is unclear if the reference is to the same two, or two different, messengers.

28. The final *t* does not appear in the word's occurrences below; it is probably a scribal error.

29. Feminine counterpart of "the Pleasant," an epithet of Kirta.

30. *CTA* reads *[?]dm[?];* the photograph seems to show *adm/t.*

31. In view of the extraordinary length of this line, the parallel passage in the command sequence (II 13–15), and the fact that the repeated portions of the performance sequence deviate minimally from the command sequence, it seems probable that a three-line verse needs to be reconstructed here. The scribe apparently jumped his eye from *imr* in the present line to *imr* in the next, copied *dbḥ* by mistake, and then neglected to copy the second line altogether. Our scribe tends to leave erroneously copied letters, words, and even lines in place, and then write them again; see, e.g., II 20, VI 33.

32. *CAT* sees traces of *a;* the photograph seems to show *u;* but see II 33.

33. The scribe wrote the last two letters as *bl,* which are almost identical to *ṣu,* with the bottom horizontal interchanged. If the text were to have a different verb (viz., *ybl*) here instead of the one used in the command passage (viz., *yṣu;* II 47–48), it would be the only instance in which an entirely different word was used in the performance sequence in place of the parallel in the command sequence. That the scribe tended first to make the verticals and then add the horizontals is clear from errors such as the one at text 3, I 12 (*ṣ* for *b*).

34. Cf. II 48–50.

35. Kirta.

36. The *k* is written long, as *w.*

37. Kirta vows a statue of Huraya, two-thirds overlaid with silver, a third with gold, to stand in adoration in the goddess's shrine. Compare the vow of a life-size statue of the Hittite king Hattusilis III by his wife Pudahepa (*ANET,* p. 394) whose

body would be overlaid with silver, the head, hands, and feet with gold. Or the king vows "twice her (weight) in silver, three of her in gold."

38. The second marching formula adds four days to the preceding three, totalling the conventional sequence of seven. "Sunrise on the fourth" should not be seen in contradiction to the immediately preceding count of four days. Poetic convention divides the days into pairs, mandating a count of one-two, three-four.

39. *CAT* reads the last sign as *a;* but the heads of the two horizontal wedges are not as deep as those of the usual *a.* The word has been written over a poorly erased *sʿt.*

40. Cf. III 7–8.

41. *CAT* reads *m* but emends to *grnt.* The new photograph shows either that *m* is written—in which case one should emend with *CTA*—or that *t* has been written over an erased *m.*

42. There follows an erased word, perhaps *ṯlṯ.*

43. There follows an erased word.

44. Read *l[qr .]* by *CTA* and *CAT.*

45. The *q* is written over a g, as noted by *CAT.*

46. The last two letters, unread by *CTA* and *CAT*, are legible on the photographs.

47. *CTA*: *laṯṯ/[h . k]y[ṣḥ .]; CAT*: *laṯṯ/[h . k]yṣ[ḥ .].* Our reading is based on an enlarged photograph.

48. *CAT* reads: *[ln]ʿmt [.].* Our reading, based on enlarged color as well as black and white photographs, sees part of what seems to be *l* and the possible impression of *y.* I am indebted to Prof. Bruce Zuckerman for his assistance in reading this line.

49. *CTA:]t . (?)r; CAT*: *k]rt . tk.* Our reading is based on new and enlarged photographs.

50. A possible reconstruction of lines 19–23, based on an enlarged and a new photograph and restored on the basis of III 12–14, is as follows: *[…]h . lʿdb / […a]bn . ydh / [mšdpt] . bl . išlḥ / [ḥẓm . qr]th . gm / [l…k]yṣḥ.*

51. Written *w,* as in *KTU.*

52. Cf. III 20ff.

53. Cf. lines 35–37 below.

54. The scribe mistakenly wrote *k* for *t,* then left the *k* and wrote *t* on the next line.

55. *CAT* reads partially *[x]ʿbdn.*

56. *CTA* and *CAT* read a final *h,* but there is no trace of it on the photograph.

57. At the bottom of col. I are two parallel horizontal lines, indicating the bottom of the tablet's obverse side; cf. at text 1, II 50 above.

58. The new photograph shows *aṯr* at the end of line 2.

59. A goddess, elsewhere paired with Asherah.

60. See note 4 above.

61. *CTA* reads *ʿ[ ]r* and *CAT* reads *ʿšr.* Traces on the photograph are consistent with *ǵ.*

62. Understood as a gesture of hospitality, not constraint; cf. Esther 1:8.

63. As *CTA* has observed, *ẓ* was miswritten *q; CAT* reads *ẓ.*

64. *CTA* and *CAT* see a *t* between *ṯ* and *m;* but the sign seems too high to be *t.*

65. Namely, "He who erects (his father's mortuary stela after his death)"; see text 4.

66. The reading is confirmed by an enlargement. *CTA* and *CAT*: *a[ṯ]rt.*

67. The restoration follows Ginsberg. The column ends with two parallel horizontal lines, as at the bottom of col. I.

68. For the restorations, see lines 13–15 below.

69. Ditana, a deified royal hero, a leader among the shades of the dead, invoked in a ritual text (*CAT* 1.124) to provide an oracle for a newborn child. In view of the fact that the final occurrence of this stanza seems to interrupt El's remarks about the soon-to-be-born daughters, the stanza may well have been declaimed not by El himself but by a chorus, like the type that is well known from the classical Greek theater. Directions for the performance of the Ugaritic epics are rare but attested.

70. Miswritten by metathesis, the word-divider preceding the *t.*

71. Namely, Kirta's wife Huraya.

72. For the restoration, see text 3, I 28–29.

73. Meaning, the Eighth, "Octavia."

74. El exercises a quasi-parental right to declare that the last-born daughter will have the legal prerogatives of the firstborn.

75. Kirta's.

76. Traces of the *l* on the photograph support Ginsberg's restoration.

77. More literally, "See now, is it even so. . . ."

78. I am indebted to Prof. Dennis Pardee for advising me on the interpretation of this line.

79. The letters *dt,* read partially by *CAT* after the *i,* can be otherwise deciphered.

80. So restored by Ginsberg, according to the formula in text 10, IV 29; text 12, III 15; and text 4, II 11.

81. Literally, "bulls."

82. Literally, "wild deer."

83. Although the reading of these lines is diverse and uncertain, line 10 may read: *wtbu . ẓbym,* "the chiefs enter."

84. Kirta.

85. *KTU* reads: *m/b?a?tk.* A reading such as *lm . mṯb[h]m . atw,* "to their seats they go," seems possible.

86. Huraya.

87. For the restoration, see below, VI 5.

88. The term ordinarily refers to a sacrifice or ritual meal, and probably does so here.

89. Huraya.

90. The restoration follows IV 15–16.

91. Written *br;* the restoration, if correct, presupposes a metathesis.

92. The restoration follows IV 17–18, but makes the uncertain assumption that the reference is to (another group of ?) Kirta's nobles (*ṯrm* and *ẓbym*); cf. *CAT.*

93. A plausible reading is: *aḫr [. bt kr]t [. tbu]n / lmṯb[hm .] t[ity .].* In contrast to *CTA* and *CAT*, which make out little or nothing of the beginning of line 7, the word *tqdm* is quite clear on the photograph; surely a phrase like that in IV 23 (*lḥm mr. tqdm*) must be restored.

94. Traces on the photographs support this restoration.

95. So *CTA* and cf. VI 6; but a reading such as *tk?b?d?n,* "they do homage," is also possible.

96. A figure for the end of life (cf., e.g., Psalm 90:6; Job 4:20) or, as in Egyptian thought, a portal to the netherworld.

97. Kirta's older son.

98. Collation by Pitard yields: *wy[ ]ry,* but the new photograph seems to show *n* not *r.* The sense is difficult in context.

99. The reading of all but the last letter is uncertain.

100. The reading of all but the last two letters is uncertain.

101. Impressions on the photograph are consistent with *lḥ;* cf. *CAT*. The restored *t* may be concealed within a bulge on the tablet.

102. Or: "your sire."

103. *CTA* and *CAT* read *u* where we read *k* on an enlarged photograph.

104. The reading is uncertain. *CTA* reads: *bḏrt.*

105. The traces resemble *dbḥ.*

106. See note 1 above.

107. Literally, "house"; cf. Job 3:15 and this sense of Akkadian *bītu.*

108. Mount Casius.

109. Written *any,* but see II 46 below and cf. Bordreuil 1989.

110. Mount Anti-Casius.

111. The two broad peaks, when observed at a side-by-side angle, resemble a gliding bird's wings.

112. Written *ṣ*; the scribe forgot his horizontals.

113. Ilha'u.

114. Written *a.*

115. Written *t.*

116. More literally, "moan," but there is a wordplay on "tears."

117. *CAT* and others emend to *y;* but *mḫ* is the source, not the substance, of the tears.

118. *CAT* reads: *dnn;* but the photograph shows a definite *a.*

119. Cf. lines 46 and 58 below. *CAT* reads *aḫr* partially.

120. Or: "I."

121. Apparently a figure for the moon, which is ordinarily represented in Ugaritic by the male deity Yarikhu.

122. *CAT* reads *a* for *t,* but an enlarged photograph shows a clear *t.*

123. Read from an enlarged photograph; *CAT*: *[b]r?l?tk.*

124. The reading on an enlarged photograph is clear. *CTA* and *CAT*: *adnk.*

125. The restoration is consistent with vague traces on the photograph. *CAT* reads *kdh* partially.

126. Part of a formula describing physical collapse out of fear or dismay; literally, "Her tendons to the ground break."

127. Convention suggests "neck" or "face."

128. Traces on the photograph support Ginsberg's restoration.

129. The couplet is so restored with Ginsberg; Herdner (1974).

130. The restored epithet is confirmed by a clear *l* on the photograph.

131. Restore perhaps *špš;* see text 2, V 18–20.

132. Cf. text 2, V 18–20.

133. See line 34 below; cf. *CAT*.

134. Baring the breast is a common female gesture of grief in the ancient Near East.

135. The restoration of *wt,* first proposed by Virolleaud, is consistent with traces on the photograph, where the ʿ is also legible.

136. Literally, if correctly interpreted, "ointment, oils."

137. Literally, "brother-in-law."

138. So restored by Ginsberg.

139. Virolleaud restored lines 55–56: *ǵr . y[šu . ʿl .] ydm . [ḫlb. lẓr . rḥtm],* "The mountain is borne on the hands,/ The summit on palms"; cf. text 10, VIII 5–6. Although there does not seem to be enough space for the full restoration of the second line, the first letters of the restoration on each line, *š* and *ḫ* respectively, are legible on the new photograph.

140. Compare the Story of Aqhat: text 6, column II.

141. Others read *h* where we favor *i.*

142. Baal, more commonly called the Son of Dagon.

143. *CTA* reads *[b]ʿ...* and *CAT* reads a fragmentary *b* followed by a space.

144. The *t* could be ʿ or a more complex sign.

145. Or: "Kirta's daughter. . . . "

146. Cf. text 12, VI 10.

147. Epithets of El.

148. See lines 6–8 and 10–12 below; cf. *CAT*.

149. *CTA* and *CAT* read the first sign as *b* and correct it to *d,* but we read *d* on the photograph.

150. A female is grammatically indicated.

151. Traces on the photograph support Ginsberg's restoration.

152. *CAT* reads *dt.*

153. Cf. text 2, II 18–20.

154. The name means, "the female who causes (the illness) to pass."

155. Restored with Ginsberg on the basis of VI 6–7 below.

156. *CTA* read the beginning of line 49: *mr[ṣ .* , but the present restoration follows VI 8 below.

157. The untying of the knot releases the disease in a typical procedure of ancient Near Eastern sympathetic magic.

158. Restoration of lines 48–52 based on VI 8–10 below.

159. Written *t;* cf. lines 13–14 below.

160. From the photograph it would seem that *ḫ* was written *z.*

161. Cf. *CTA* and *CAT*.

162. Probably to be emended to *g<n>gnh;* see text 10 VII 47–49.

163. Literally, perhaps, "windpipe," close in sense to "throat, seat of breath and appetite," which functions in many contexts like English "soul."

164. *CAT* reads: *lx[x]xr[xxxx].*

165. For the restoration of lines 29–31, see lines 42–44 below. The last word, unread by *CTA* and *CAT*, can be made out on the photograph.

166. Translation uncertain. An alternative is: "You speak [in gurgles], / Pronounce in a cro[ak]"; i.e., you are sickly.

167. As chief magistrate, the king would be approached for justice by people with prima facie claims. Thus an indigent widow, with no political clout, would depend on the decency of a magistrate to pursue her cause. Cf. Job 29:7–17.

168. Literally, "sister," or "kin." For the figurative use of "sister" to indicate a constant companion, see Proverbs 7:4 and compare Job 17:14.

169. Literally, "bed of disease."

170. See note 166 above.

171. *CAT* reads *qšm,* beginning with an erased *ṯ*.

172. A netherworld god.

173. Written long as *r.*

174. Literally, "document of."

175. A well-known scribe.

176. King of Ugarit in the mid-fourteenth century.

Aqhat

Translated by Simon B. Parker

The story of *Aqhat* is preserved on three tablets, discovered at Ras Shamra in 1930–1931 and first published in 1936 (Virolleaud 1936). The order of the three tablets and of the columns on the tablets is universally accepted. It is also clear that the story must have continued on a fourth tablet.[1] Of the three tablets we have, the first, six-column tablet and the second, four-column tablet each lack the two middle columns. The four columns of the third tablet are all preserved, though with damage to the first half of the first column and the second half of the second column.

As we have it, the story of Aqhat is as follows. It begins with an account of a ritual performed by the childless Daniel, to which Baal responds, calling on El to bless Daniel with a son. El does so. Daniel is informed of this fact and goes home rejoicing. After entertaining the Katharat, here functioning as goddesses of conception, he goes to bed with his wife and she becomes pregnant. Here the first big gap of two columns leaves us without the account of Aqhat's birth and the immediately following developments. When the text resumes in column V, Kothar and Khasis come bearing a bow. On Daniel's instruction, his wife plays hostess to the gods, as they confer the bow on Daniel. After their departure, Daniel passes the bow on to his son Aqhat with appropriate instructions.

After a short break, we find Aqhat in the presence of the goddess Anat, who offers him silver and gold, and then immortality, in exchange for the bow. Aqhat rebuffs her proposals. He tells her, first, that she can get a bow for herself from Kothar and Khasis, if she will just give them the component materials; and second, that death is the universal human destiny—adding the taunt that bows are not really for women anyway. With a parting threat, Anat leaves for El's residence, where she denounces Aqhat and threatens El. El recognizes Anat's essential character and authorizes her to have her way. She returns to Aqhat, but the declining condition of the text and the lack of the following two columns do not allow us to see the early development of her plot to dispose of him.

When the text resumes, Anat is negotiating with YTPN. She finally reveals to him her plan, which they immediately carry out. She carries YTPN like a bird of prey among a flock of such birds and releases him over Aqhat. He sweeps down on Aqhat and kills him. But apparently the bow is lost.

After the damaged, and largely incomprehensible beginning of the third tablet, the effect of the murder is seen in the withering of the vegetation. Daniel, accompanied by his daughter, Paghit, undertakes a series of ritual acts and pronouncements that address this crisis. Then two messengers approach, finally telling Daniel and his daughter that Anat has dispatched Aqhat. Daniel now directs his attention to the cause, not just the symptom, of the drought. He calls on Baal to bring down the various birds of prey, until he finds in the belly of one the remains of Aqhat, which he buries. After then cursing the three towns nearest the site of the murder, he returns home, where he is joined by mourners for seven years.

Dismissing the mourners, Daniel offers a sacrifice, at which Paghit asks him to bless her on a mission of vengeance against the killer of her brother. Daniel confers the requested blessing. Paghit then puts on a warrior's accoutrements beneath her female attire and sets out for YTPN's camp. She is received and they begin to drink, YTPN boasting of his prowess. Similar episodes in biblical narratives suggest that Paghit would eventually draw her sword and dispatch YTPN.[2] The avenging of Aqhat's death would release the land from its blight.

While different parts of the story have analogues in other ancient Near Eastern and biblical narratives, suggesting that the composers used traditional materials in their composition,[3] *Aqhat* is a unified, progressive narrative. Everything in the first two tablets leads up to the killing of Aqhat in column 4 of the second tablet, and everything in the third tablet devolves from that act of murder.

The Daniel of the story is a legendary, patriarchal figure. He appears briefly in the fragmentary Rapiuma texts (20–22 below). He is mentioned alongside Job and Noah in Ezek 14:12–20, verses which imply that all three were the subject of stories in which they save the lives of their children (unlike the Daniel of the biblical book of that name). He appears again as a model of wisdom or cleverness in Ezek 28:3. Later, in *Jub.* 4:20, he is mentioned among the antediluvian patriarchs.

The gods have a much more central role in this story than in *Kirta.* Kothar and Khasis confer upon Daniel the bow that leads to Aqhat's death. Anat tries to bargain with Aqhat for the bow, is enraged by his refusal and dismissal of her, and finally accomplishes his murder. Ritual too is much more prominent than in *Kirta.* In much of the third tablet, the action is constituted largely by Daniel's ritual acts and words, and ritual acts are woven into the account of Aqhat's origin in the first two columns of the first tablet. Finally, the story seems to be particularly concerned with social roles: that of the dutiful son in the refrain of the first two columns; of the host and hostess in column V; of men and hunters, as against gods and women, in the exchange between Aqhat and Anat in column VI; of the responsible elder/father and daughter/sister in the last tablet.

As far as possible, the transcription is based on new photographs made available by West Semitic Research. Because of the deterioration of the tablets, less of the text is visible now than earlier. Restorations in the transcription are based either on earlier readings of the tablets, or on parallel passages. I have not generally "restored" text for which there is no such support and have always inserted questions marks wherever an unsupported restoration has been suggested.

4. *CAT* 1.17		4. First Tablet
Column I		Column I
(Ca. ten lines missing.)		*(Ca. ten lines missing.)*
0–2	*[apnk/dnil.mt.rp]i.* *aph<n>.ǵz[r]/[mt.hrnmy.]*	[Now Daniel, man of Rapiu,] The hero, [man of the Harnemite,][4]
2–3	*uzr.ilm.ylḥm./* *[uzr.yšqy.]bn.qdš.*	Girded, gives food to the gods, [Girded, gives drink to] the deities,
3–5	*yd/[ṣth.yˁl.]wyškb.* *yd/[mizrth.]p yln!*[5]	Throws down [his garment] and lies, Throws down [his cloak] for the night.[6]
5–6	*hn.ym/[wṯn.*	One day passed, [and a second—]

6–8	*uzr.]ilm.dnil/* *[uzr.ilm].ylḥm.* *uzr/[yšqy.b]n.qdš*	[Girded,] Daniel gives food, [Girded,] gives food to [the gods], Girded, [gives drink to the] deities,
8	*ṯlṯ.rbᶜ ym/*	A third day passes, a fourth—
9–11	*[uzr.i]lm.dnil.* *uzr/[ilm.y]lḥm.* *uzr.yšqy.bn/[qdš.*	[Girded,] Daniel gives food, Girded, gives food [to the gods], Girded, gives drink to the [deities],
11	*ḫ]mš.ṯdṯ.ym.*	A fifth day passes, a sixth—
11–13	*uzr/[il]m.dnil.* *uzr.ilm.ylḥm./* *[uzr].yšqy.bn.qdš.*	Girded, Daniel gives food, Girded, gives food to the gods, [Girded,] gives drink to the deities,
13–15	*yd.ṣth/[dn]il.* *yd.ṣth.yᶜl.wyškb/* *[yd.]mizrth.pyln.*	Daniel throws down his garment, Throws down his garment and lies, [Throws down] his cloak for the night.
15–16	*mk.bšbᶜ.ymm/* *[w]yqrb.bᶜl.bḥnth.*	Then on the seventh day Baal draws near in compassion:[7]
16–18	*abynat/[d]nil.mt.rpi.* *anḫ.ġzr/mt.hrnmy.*	"The longing of Daniel, man of Rapiu! The moan of the hero, man of the Harnemite!
18–19	*din.bn.lh/km.aḫh.* *w.šrš.km.aryh/*	Who has no son like his siblings, No offspring like that of his fellows.
20–21	*bl.iṯ.bn.lh.k![8] m.aḫh.* *wšrš/km.aryh.*	Will he have no son like his siblings, No offspring like that of his fellows,
21–22	*uzrm.ilm.ylḥm/* *uzrm.yšqy.bn.qdš/*	Who, girded, gives food to the gods, Girded, gives drink to the deities?
23–23	*ltbrknn lṯr.il aby/* *tmrnn l bny.bnwt/*	Bless him, Bull, El my father, Prosper him, Creator of Creatures.

25–26	*wykn.bnh.bbt.* *šrš.bqrb/hklh.*	Let him have a son in his house, Offspring within his palace,
26–27	*nṣb.skn.ilibh.* *bqdš/ztr.ʿmh.*	To set up his Ancestor's stela, The sign of his Sib in the sanctuary;[9]
27–28	*larṣ.mšṣu.qṭrh/* *lʿpr.ḏmr.aṯrh.*	To rescue his smoke from the Underworld, To protect his steps from the Dust;
28–29	*ṭbq.lḥt/niṣh.* *grš.d.ʿšy.lnh/*	To stop his abusers' spite, To drive his troublers away;
30–31	*aḫd.ydh.bškrn.* *mʿmsh/[k]šbʿ yn.*	To grasp his arm when he's drunk, To support him when sated with wine;
31–32	*spu.ksmh.bt.bʿl/* *[w]mnth.bt.il.*	To eat his portion in Baal's house, His share in the house of El;
32–33	*ṭḫ.ggh.bym/[ṯi]ṭ.* *rḥṣ.npṣh.bym.rṯ/*	To daub his roof when there's [mu]d, To wash his stuff when there's dirt."
34	*[ks] yiḫd.il.!bdh*[10]	El takes [a cup] in his hand.
34–36	*ybrk/[dni]l.mt.rpi.* *ymr.ǵzr/[mt.h]rnmy.*	He blesses [Dani]el, man of Rapiu, Prospers the hero, [man of the] Harnemite:
36–37	*npš.yḥ.dnil/[mt.rp]i.* *brlt.ǵzr.mt hrnmy/*	"By my life, let Daniel, [man of] Rapiu, thrive, By my soul, the hero, man of the Harnemite!
38	*[ ].hw.mḫ.*	[. . .] flourish
38–39	*lʿršh.yʿl/[ ].*	Let him mount his couch [. . .]

39–40	*bm.nšq.aṯth/[ ].* *bḥbqh.ḥmḥmt/*	In kissing his wife, [conception]! In embracing her, pregnancy!
41–42	*[ ]kn ylt.* *ḥmḥmt/[mt.r]pi.*	[. . .]birth Pregnancy [. . . man] of Rapiu
42–43	*wykn.bnh/[bbt.* *šrš].bqrb hklh/*	And a son he will have [in his house, Offspring] within his palace,
44–45	*[nṣb.skn.i]libh.* *bqdš/[ztr.ʿmh.*	[To set up] his Ancestor's [stela, The sign of his Sib] in the sanctuary;
45–46	*la]rṣ.mšṣu/[qṭrh.* *lʿpr.ḏ]mr.aṯr[h]/*	To rescue [his smoke from the] Underworld, To protect his steps [from the Dust];
47–48	*[ṭbq.lḥt.niṣh.* *gr]š.d.ʿšy/[lnh.*	[To stop his abusers' spite, To drive his] troublers away;
	[aḫd.ydh.bškrn *mʿmsh kšbʿ yn*	[To grasp his arm when he's drunk, To support him when sated with wine;
	spu ksmh bt bʿl *wmnth bt il*	To eat his portion in Baal's house, His share in the house of El;
	ṭḥ ggh bym ṯiṭ *rḥṣ npṣh bym rṯ]*	To daub his roof when there's mud, To wash his stuff when there's dirt."]

(Ca. twenty lines are missing, the first of which would have contained the remainder of the list of filial duties as above, and the last of which would have contained the birth announcement and first part of the same list, but

(Baal goes, or El sends another deity, to announce to Daniel the good news of El's blessing.)

with second person suffixes, as follows.)

Column II		Column II
	[yld bn lk km aḫk *wšrš km aryk*	[Like your siblings, a son's to be born you, An offspring like that of your fellows,
0–1	*nṣb skn ilibk* *bqdš]/z[tr.ʿmk.*	To set up your Ancestor's stela, The sign of your Sib in the sanctuary;
1–2	*larṣ.mšṣu.qṭrk]/* *l.ʿpr.[ḏmr.aṯrk./*	To rescue your smoke from the Underworld], [To protect your steps] from the Dust;
2–3	*ṭbq]/lḥt.niṣk.* *gr[š.d ʿšy.lnk]/*	[To stop] your abusers' spite, To drive [your troublers away];
4–5	*spu.ksmk.bt.[bʿl.* *wmntk]/ bt il.*	To eat your portion in [Baal's] house, [Your share] in the house of El;
5–6	*aḫd.ydk[.]b[škrn]/* *mʿmsk.kšbʿt.yn.*	To grasp your arm when [you're drunk], To support you when sated with wine;
6–8	*ṭ[ḫ]/ggk.bym.ṭiṭ.* *rḥṣ/npṣk.bym.rṯ.*	To daub your roof when there's mud, To wash your stuff when there's dirt."
8–9	*bd!*[11]*ni[l]/pnm.tšmḫ.* *wʿl.yṣhl pi[t]/*	Daniel's face beams, His brow above lights up;
10–12	*yprq.lṣb.wyṣḥq/* *pʿn.lhdm.ytpd.* *yšu/gh.wyṣḥ.*	He breaks out into laughter, Sets his foot on the footstool, Raises his voice and cries:

12–14 *aṯbn.ank/wanḫn.*
wtnḫ.birty/npš.

“Now I'll sit down and rest,
In my breast my heart will rest.

14–15 *kyld.bn.ly.km/aḫy.*
wšrš.km.aryy/

Like my siblings, a son's to be born me,
An offspring like that of my fellows,

16–17 *nṣb.skn.iliby.*
bqd[š]/ztr.ʿmy.

To set up my Ancestor's stela,
The sign of my Sib in the sanctuary;

17 *<larṣ.mšṣu.qṭry>*
lʿpr[.]ḏmr.aṯr[y]/

<To rescue my breath from the Underworld,>
To protect [my] steps from the Dust;

18–19 *ṭbq.lḥt.niṣy.*
grš/dʿšy.ln.

To stop my abusers' spite,
To drive my troublers away;

19–20 *aḫd.ydy.bš/krn.*
mʿmsy.kšbʿt y[n]/

To grasp my arm when I'm drunk,
To support me when sated with wine;

21–22 *spu.ksmy.bt.bʿl.*
[wmnt]/y.bt.il.

To eat my portion in Baal's house,
My [share] in the house of El;

22–23 *ṭḫ.ggy.bym.ṯiṭ/*
rḥṣ.npṣy.bym.rṯ/

To daub my roof when there's mud,
To wash my stuff when there's dirt.”

24–25 *dn[.]il. bth.ymǵyn/*
yšṭql.dnil.lhklh/

Daniel comes to his house,
Daniel arrives at his palace.

26–27 *ʿrb.bbth.kṯrt.*
bnt/hll.snnt.

The Katharat enter his house,
The moon's radiant daughters.

27–29 *apnk.dnil/mt.rpi.*
ap[.]hn.ǵzr.mt/hrnmy.

Now Daniel, man of Rapiu,
The hero, man of the Harnemite,

29–31	*alp.yṯbḫ.lkṯ/rt.* *yšlḥm.kṯrt.* *wy/ššq.bnt.h[ll].snnt/*	Slaughters an ox for the Katharat, Dines the Katharat, And wines the moon's radiant daughters.
32	*hn.ym.wṯn.*	One day, and a second,
32–34	*yšlḥm/kṯrt.* *wyš[š]q.bnt.hll/snnt.*	He dines the Katharat, And wines the moon's radiant daughters.
34	*ṯlṯ.[r]bʿym.*	A third, a fourth day,
34–36	*yšl/ḥm kṯrt.* *wyššq/bnt.hll.snnt.*	He dines the Katharat, And wines the moon's radiant daughters.
36–37	*ḫmš/ṯdṯ.ym.*	A fifth, a sixth day,
37–38	*yšlḥm.kṯrt/* *wyššq.bnt.hll.s[nnt]/*	He dines the Katharat, And wines the moon's radiant daughters.
39	*mk.bš[bʿ].ymm.*	Then on the seventh day,
39–40	*tbʿ.bbth/kṯrt.* *bnt.hll.snnt/*	The Katharat leave his house, The moon's radiant daughters.
41–42	*[ ]d[ ]t.nʿmy.ʿrš.[ ]/* *ysmsmt.ʿrš.ḥl[ ]/*	[ ] the joy of the bed [ ] The delights of the bed of childbirth [ ]
43–45	*yṯb.dnil.[ls]pr yrḫh/* *yrḫ.[ ]/* *ṯlṯ.rb[ʿ]/*	Daniel settles to count her months. A month, [ ] A third, a fourth [ ]
46	*yrḫm.ymǵ[y]/*	Months com[e]

(Ca. ten lines are missing from the bottom of the column. Columns III and IV are completely missing. There is a further gap of some eleven lines at the beginning of column V.)

(Aqhat is born to Daniel and his wife. Whatever else the missing columns III and IV recounted, the origins of the bow that appears in column V would have been included.)

Column V		Column V
2–3	*[ ]abl.qšt* *ṯmn/ašrbᶜ.qṣᶜt*	["] I will bring the bow, I will convey there many arrows."
3–4	*whn.šb[ᶜ]/bymm.*	Then, on the seventh day,
4–5	*apnk.dnil.mt/rpi.* *a<p>hn.ǵzr.mt/hrnm[y]*	Now Daniel, man of Rapiu, The hero, man of the Harnemite,
6–7	*ytšu.yṯb.bap.ṯǵr.* *tḥt/adrm.dbgrn.*	Gets up and sits by the gateway, Among the chiefs on the threshing floor;
7–8	*ydn/dn.almnt.* *yṯpṭ.ṯpṭ.y[tm]/*	Takes care of the case of the widow, Defends the need of the orphan.
9–10	*bnši.ᶜnh.wyphn.* *bal[p]/šd.rbt.kmn.*	Raising his eyes, he sees At one thousand rods, ten thousand furlongs,
10–11	*hlk.kṯr/kyᶜn.* *wyᶜn.tdrq.ḫss/*	Observes the coming of Kothar, Observes the march (?) of Khasis.
12–13	*hlk.qšt.ybln.* *hl.yš/rbᶜ.qṣᶜt.*	Here they bring the bow, Here he conveys many arrows.[12]
13–15	*apnk.dnil/mt.rpi.* *aphn.ǵzr.mt/hrnm[y].*	Now Daniel, man of Rapiu, The hero, man of the Harnemite,
15–16	*gm.laṯth.kyṣḥ/* *šmᶜ.mṯt.dnty.*	Calls out aloud to his wife: "Attend, Danatiya the Lady:
16–19	*ᶜd[b]/imr.bpḫd.* *lnpš.kṯr/wḫss* *lbrlt.hyn d/ḥrš yd.*	Prepare a lamb from the flock For the relish of Kothar and Khasis, For the hunger (?) of clever Hayyan.
19–21	*šlḥm.ššqy/ilm* *sad.kbd.hmt.* *bᶜl/ḥkpt.il.klh.*	Dine and wine the gods, Uphold and honor them, The lords of Memphis, allotted by El(?)."

21–22	*tšmʿ/mṯt,dnty.*	Danatiya the Lady attends.
22–25	*tʿdb.imr/bpẖd.* *lnpš.kṯr.wẖss/* *lbrlt.hyn.dẖrš/ydm.*	She prepares a lamb from the flock For the relish of Kothar and Khasis, For the hunger (?) of clever Hayyan.
25–26	*aẖr.ymǵy.kṯr/wẖss.*	After Kothar and Khasis arrive,
26–28	*bd.dnil.ytnn/qšt.* *lbrkh.yʿdb/qṣʿt.*	They hand Daniel the bow, On his lap they lay the arrows.
28	*apnk.mṯt.dnty/*	Now Danatiya the Lady
29–31	*tšlḥm.tššqy ilm/* *tsad.tkbd.hmt.* *bʿl/ḥkpt il.klh.*	Dines and wines the gods, Upholds and honors them The lords of Memphis, allotted by El(?).
31–33	*tbʿ.kṯr/lahlh.* *hyn.tbʿ.lmš/knth.*	Kothar left for his tent, Hayyan left for his dwelling.
33–35	*apnk.dnil.m[t]/rpi.* *aphn.ǵzr.m[t]/hrnmy.*	Now Daniel, man of Rapiu, The hero, man of the Harnemite,
35–36	*qšt.yqb [gm(?) yd(?)]/rk.* *ʿl.aqht.kyq[rb(?)]/*	Strings(?) [and bends(?)] the bow, [Draws(?)] near to Aqhat:
37–39	*prʿm.ṣdk.yb[n]* *[ ]/prʿm.ṣdk.* *hn[ ]/ṣd.bhk[lh]*	"The best of your bag, my son, [ ] the best of your bag, Look, [ ] the bag in [his/her] temple

(Approximately twenty lines are missing between the last preserved part of column V and the first preserved part of column VI.)

(With appropriate counsel, the bow is bestowed upon Aqhat, a development that apparently comes to the attention of the goddess Anat.)

Column VI		Column VI
1	. . .	. . .
2	*[ ]ḥm[ ]*	
3–4	*[ ].ay.š[ ]/[ ]*	

4–5	*[bḫ]rb.mlḥ[t qṣ]/[mri*	[ ] with salt[ed kn]ife [a cutlet of fatling.]
5–6	*tšty krpnm].yn.* *bks.ḫr[ṣ]/[dm ʿṣm*	She drinks the wine by flagons, The vines' blood from goblets of gold,
6	*]n.krpn.ʿl.krpn/*	
7	*]qym.wtʿl.trṯ/*	
8	*[ ].yn.ʿšy.lḥbš/*	…
9	*[ ]ḥtn.qn.yṣbt*	
10	*[ ].bnši ʿnh wtphn/*	Raising her eyes she sees,
11	*[ ]l.kslh.kbrq/*	
		…
12	*[ ]y(?)ǵ[ ].thmt.brq/*	
13	*[ ].tṣb.qšt.bnt [?]/*	[ ] she longs for the bow
14	*[ʿ]nh.km.bṯn.yqr/*	[ ] her eye(s) like a snake …
15–16	*[ ]larṣ.* *ksh.tšpkm/[lʿpr.*	On the earth [she empties her flagon(?)], Her goblet she pours [on the ground].
15	*tšu gh] wtṣḥ.*	[She raises her voice] and cries:
16	*šmʿ.mʿ/[laqht ǵzr*	"Attend, now, [Aqhat the Hero],
17–18	*i]rš.ksp.watnk/* *[ḫrṣ wašl]ḥk.*	Ask me for silver—I'll give it, [For gold and I'll end]ow you:
18–19	*wtn.qštk.ʿm/[btlt ʿ]n[t]* *qṣʿtk.ybmt.limm/*	Give [Anat the Girl] your bow, The sister of LIMM your arrows."
20	*wyʿn.aqht.ǵzr.*	Aqhat the Hero answers:
20–23	*adr.ṯqbm/blbnn.* *adr.gdm.brumm/*	"From the Lebanon the strongest trees,

	adr.qrnt.byᶜlm. *<adr>(?) mtnm/bᶜqbt.t̲r.* *adr.qnm!*[14] *bǵl il/*	From the buffalo the strongest sinews, From the ibex the strongest horns, From the bull's heels <the strongest>(?) tendons, From the great brake the strongest canes
24	*tn.lkt̲r.wḫss*	Give to Kothar and Khasis:
24–25	*ybᶜl.qšt.lᶜnt/* *qṣᶜt.lybmt.limm.*	Let them make a bow for Anat, Arrows for the Sister of LIMM."
25–26	*wtᶜn.btlt/ᶜnt.*	Anat the Girl answers:
26–28	*irš.ḥym.laqht.ǵzr/* *irš.ḥym.watnk.* *blmt/wašlḥk.*	"Ask for life, Aqhat the Hero, Ask for life, and I'll give it, Deathlessness—I'll endow you.
28–29	*ašsprk.ᶜm.bᶜl/šnt.* *ᶜm.bn il.tspr.yrḫm/*	I'll let you count years with Baal, Count months with the offspring of El.
30–31	*kbᶜl.kyḥwy.yᶜšr.* *ḥwy.yᶜš/r.wy[š]qynh.*	As Baal revives, then invites, Invites the revived to drink,
31–32	*ybd.wyšr.ᶜlh/* *nᶜmn [wt]ᶜnynn.*	Trills and sings over him, With pleasant tune they respond;
32–33	*ap ank.aḥwy/aqh[t ǵz]r.*	So *I'll* revive Aqhat the Hero."
33	*w.yᶜn.aqht.ǵzr/*	Then Aqhat the Hero answers:
34–35	*al.tš[r]gn.ybtltm.* *dm.lǵzr/šrgk.ḫḫm.*	"Maid, don't beguile me: To a hero your guile is slime.
35–36	*mt!*[15]*.uḫryt.mh.yqḥ/* *mh.yqḥ.mt.at̲ryt.*	In the end a man gets what? A man gets what as his fate?
36–37	*spsg.ysk/[l]riš.* *ḥrṣ.lẓr.qdqdy/*	Glaze is poured on the head, Lye all over the skull.
38	*[ ] mt.kl.amt.*	[ ] the death of all I shall die,

	wan.mtm.amt/	I too shall die and be dead.
39	*[ap m]ṯn.rgmm.argm.*	And another thing I will say:
39–41	*qštm/[ ]mhrm.* *ht.tṣdn.tinṯt/[bh*	Bows are [weapons of(?)] warriors Will womankind now be hunting?"
41–42	*g]m.tṣḥq.ʿnt.* *wblb.tqny/[ ]*	Anat laughed out loud, But inwardly she plotted [ ]:
42–43	*ṯb.ly.laqht.ǵzr.* *ṯb ly wlk/[ ]*	"Come back, Aqhat the Hero, Come back to me, [I will warn(?)] you:
43–44	*hm.laqryk.bntb.pšʿ/* *[ ].bntb.gan.*	If I meet you in the paths of rebellion, [Find you(?)] in the paths of pride,
44–45	*ašqlk.tḥt/[pʿny a]n![16]k* *nʿmn.ʿmq.nšm/*	I will fell you under [my feet], Finest, cleverest of fellows!"
46	*[tdʿṣ pʿ]nm.wtr.arṣ.*	[She takes to her hee]ls and the earth shakes.
46–48	*idk/[lttn p]nm.* *ʿm.il.mbk![17].nhrm/* *[qrb ap]q.thmtm*	Then [she sets her fa]ce Toward El at the springs of the rivers, [Among the strea]ms of the deeps.
48–49	*tgly.ḏd il/* *[wtbu q]rš.mlk.ab šnm/*	She proceeds to the precinct of El, [Comes to the c]amp of the King, the Father of Years.
50–51	*[lpʿn il t]hbr.wtql.* *tšth/[wy wtkbd]nh.*	[At the feet of El she] bends and bows, Prostrates her[self and pays] him [respect].
51–52	*tlšn.aqht.ǵzr/* *[kdd dn]il.mt.rpi*	She denounces Aqhat the Hero, [Maligns(?) the child] of Daniel, man of Rapiu.
52–53	*wtʿn/[btlt ʿnt* *tšu] gh.wtṣḥ.*	Then [Anat the Girl] speaks up, [She raises] her voice and cries:

53–54	*hwt/[ ]*	
54	*aqht.yš[ ]*	…
55	*[ ]n.ṣ(?)[ ]*	

(About twenty lines are missing at the end of the column. On the left edge of the tablet: *[spr ilmlk šbn lmd atn p]rln.*)

(Anat's first speech maligning Aqhat and El's first response would have followed in the gap. On the left edge of the tablet is the remains of a colophon: [Scribe: Ilimalku, Shubbanite, student of Attenu,] diviner.)

5. *CAT* 1.18 — 5. Second Tablet

Column I — Column I

1–3	…	
4	*[ ] .aṯ [ ]*	…
5–6	*[ ] h.ap. [/]*	
6	*.wtʿn.[btlt ʿnt]/*	And [Anat the Girl] replies:
7–8	*[ ]k.yil[m* *[ ]* *al.tš[mh]*	["In] your [ ], El, [In your do not rejoice,] Do not rej[oice in your].
9	*[ ]ahdhm.[ ]*	
10	*[b]gdlt.ar[kty]*	…
11	*[qdq]dk.*	[ ] your head [ ]
11–12	*ašhlk[šbtk dmm]/* *[šbt dq]nk.mmʿm.*	I'll make [your head] run [with blood], Your old gre[y bea]rd with gore.
12–14	*w[ ]/aqht.wypltk.* *bn [dnil]/wyʿḏrk.* *byd.btlt.[ʿnt]/*	Then [cry to(?)] Aqhat to rescue you, To [Daniel's] son to save you From the hand of [Anat] the Girl!"
15	*wyʿn ltpn. il dp[id]/*	Then the Kind One, El the Compassionate, replies:
16–17	*ydʿtk.bt kanšt.* *wi[n bilht]/qlṣk.*	"I know you, daughter, as desperate, [Among goddesses no]thing resists you.

17	*tbʿ.bt.ḫnp.lb*	Go off, daughter, haughty of heart,
17–19	*ti]/ḫd.diṯ.bkbdk.* *tšt.b[ ]/irtk.*	[Lay] hold of what's in your liver,[18] Set up the[in] your breast.
19	*dṯ.ydṯ.mʿqbk*	To resist you is to be beaten."
19–20	*[tbʿt/btl]t.ʿnt.*	Anat the Girl [departs(?)].
20–22	*idk.lttn.[pnm]/* *[ʿm]aqht.ǵzr.* *balp.š[d/rbt]kmn.*	Now she sets [her face], [Towards A]qhat the Hero, At one thousand ro[ds, ten thousand] furlongs.
22–23	*wṣḥq.btlt.[ʿnt]/* *[tšu]gh.wtṣḥ.*	Then [Anat] the Girl laughs loud, [She raises] her voice and cries:
23–24	*šmʿ.m[ʿ]k*	"Attend, [Aqhat the H]ero,
24	*at.aḫ.wan.[ ]*	Come, brother, and I [ ][19]
25	*[ ].šbʿ.ṯirk. [ ]*	...
26	*[ ] by.ndt.ank[ ]*	
27	*[ ] t.lk.tlk.bṣd[ ]*	... you go on a hunt...
28	*[ ]mt.išryt[ ]*	
29	*[ ]r.almdk. [ ]*	... I will instruct you ...
30–31	*[ ]qrt.ablm.* *a[blm/qrt zbl y]rḫ.*	] the town of Abiluma, A[biluma, town of Prince] Yarikh,
31	*dmgdl.š[ ]*	Where a tower ...
32	*[ ]mn.ʿrp[ ]*	
33	*[ ]it[ ]*	... "
34	*[ ]ʿ[ ]*	

(Approximately twenty lines are missing from the bottom of column I, and the entirety of columns II and III is lost.)

(Anat's preliminary preparations for revenge on Aqhat must have occupied the following gap, which extends over the remaining lines of this column and two completely missing columns.)

Column IV		Column IV
1	*[ ]ps[ ]*	
2	*[ ].yṯbr[ ]*	[he breaks [ ]
3	*[ ].uṭm.ḏr[qm]*	. . .
4	*[btl]t.ʿnt.lkl.[ ]*	[ ] Anat the [Gi]rl to all [ ]
5–6	*[tt]bʿ.btlt.ʿnt* *[idk lttn pnm]/* *[ʿ]m.yṭpn.mhr.š[t*	Anat the Girl now [lea]ves, [Now she sets her face] Toward YTPN,[20] the Sut[ean] warrior.
6–7	*[tšu gh]/wtṣḥ.*	[She raises her voice] and cries:
7–8	*yṯb.yṭp.[* *]/qrt.ablm.* *ablm.[qrt zbl yrḫ]/*	"Let YTPN turn [ ] the town of Abiluma, Abiluma, [town of Prince Yarikh.]
9–11	*ik.al.yḥdṯ.yrḫ.* *b [ ]/bqrn.ymnh.* *banšt[ ]/qdqdh.*	How will Yarikh[21] not be renewed? In [ ] in his right horn, In the waning [ ] his head."
11	*wyʿn.yṭpn.[mhr št]/*	YTPN[, the Sutean warrior,] replies:
12	*šmʿ.lbtlt.ʿnt.*	"Attend, Anat the Girl,
12–13	*at.ʿ[l qšth]/tmḫṣh.* *qṣʿth.hwt.lt[ḥwy]/*	[For his bow] you strike him down, For his arrows take his life.
14–15	*nʿmn.ǵzr.št.ṯrm.* *w[ ]/ištir.bḏdm* *wnʿrs[ ]/*	The fine hero has laid a meal, . . . "
16	*wtʿn.btlt.ʿnt.*	Anat the Girl replies:
16–17	*ṯb.yṭp.w[ ]/lk.*	"Turn here, YTPN,[22] and [I'll teach(?)] you,
17–18	*aštk.km.nšr.bḫb[šy]/* *km.diy.btʿrty.*	Put you like a bird in my be[lt], Like a hawk into my sheath.
18–19	*aqht.[km.yṯb]/llḥm.* *wbn.dnil.lṯrm*	[When] Aqhat [sits down] to sup, The son of Daniel to dine,

19–21	*[ʿlh]/nšrm.trḫpn.* *ybṣr.[ḫbl d]/iym.*	The birds will circle [above him], [The flock of h]awks will hover(?).
21–22	*bn.nšrm.arḫp.an[k* *ʿ]l/aqht.ʿdbk.*	Among the birds I will circle, Over Aqhat I will aim you,
22–23	*hlmn.ṯnm.qdqd/* *ṯlṯid.ʿl.udn.*	To strike him twice on the head, Three times over the ear,
23–24	*špk.km.šiy/dm.* *km.šḫṭ.lbrkh.*	Spilling his blood like a butcher, Down to his knees, like a killer,
24–26	*tṣi.km/rḥ.npšh.* *km.iṯl.brlth.* *km/qṭr.baph.*	Let his life go off like a breath, His soul like a sneeze(?), From his nose like smoke,
26–27	*uap.mprh.ank/laḥwy.*	... I shall take his life."
27–29	*tqḥ.yṭpn.mhr.št/* *tštn.knšr.bḫbšh.* *km.diy/btʿrth.*	She takes YTPN, the Sutean warrior, Puts him like a bird in her belt, Like a hawk into her sheath,
29–30	*aqht.km.yṯb.llḥ[m]/* *bn.dnil.lṯrm.*	When Aqhat sits down to sup, The son of Daniel to dine,
30–31	*ʿlh.nšr[m]/trḫpn.* *ybṣr.ḫbl.diy[m.*	The birds circle [above him], The flock of hawks hovers(?)
31–33	*bn]/nšrm.trḫp.ʿnt.* *ʿl [aqht]/tʿdbnh.*	[Among] them Anat circles, Over [Aqhat] she aims him,
33–34	*hlmn.ṯnm [qdqd]/* *ṯlṯid.ʿl.udn*	To strike him twice [on the head], Three times over the ear,
34–35	*š[pk km]/šiy.dmh.* *km.šḫ[ṭ lbrkh]/*	Spi[lling] his blood [like] a butcher, [Down to his knees], like a killer.
36–37	*yṣat.km.rḥ.np[šh* *km iṯl]/brlth.* *km.qṭr.b[aph*	[His] life went off like a breath, His soul [like a sneeze](?), From [his nose] like smoke.
37–39	*uap.mprh]/ʿnt.bṣmt.* *mhrh.[ ]* *]/aqht.wtbk.*	[ ] Anat in the slaying, Her warrior [ ] [ ] Aqhat, and she wept.

39	*y [ ]/*	" ...
40	*abn.ank.*	
40–41	*wᶜl.q[štk mḫṣtk]* *[ᶜl]/qṣᶜtk.at.l[ḥwtk]/*	"And for your b[ow I struck you down] [For] your arrows I took your li[fe]."
41–42	*[ ]/wḫlq.ᶜpt.t[* [23]*]*	...

	6. *CAT* 1.19	6. Third Tablet
	Column I	Column I
		(The first line is a colophon. The second line continues the narrative from the end of column IV of the second tablet.)
1	*[l]aq[h]t*	[Belonging to] *Aqhat*
2–3	*[t]krb.[ ].lqrb mym/* *tql.[ ]lb.*	... [ ] into the waters, It falls [ ] ...
4–5	*tṯ[b]r/qšt.[* *]r.yṯbr [ ]mn*	The bow is broken ... [As?] is broken.
5	*[ ] btlt.[ᶜ]nt/*	Anat the Girl [–s]
6	*tṯb.[ ].ša*	...
7–8	*tlm.km[ ]ydh* *kš[r]/knr.uṣbᶜ<t>h*	Her hand strikes like [a bard?], Like a singer her fingers the lyre.
8	*kḫrṣ.a[b]n/*	
9	*ph.tiḫd.šnth.wakl.b[q]mm/*	
10	*tšt ḥrṣ.klb ilnm/*	
11	*wṯn.gprm.mn.gprh š[r]/*	...[24]
12	*aqht.yᶜn.kmr.kmrm/*	
13	*kapᶜ.il.bgdrt.kl*	
13–16	*[ᶜ]l/ḫth.imḫṣh.* *kd.ᶜl.qšth/imḫṣh.* *ᶜl.qṣᶜth.hwt/l.aḥw.*	For his staff I struck him down—[25] As I struck him for his bow, For his arrows took his life.
16–17	*ap.qšth.lttn/ly*	Now give me his bow

17	*wbmt[ ]mṣṣ[ ]/*	…
18–19	*[p]rʿ.qẓ.[ ]* *šblt/[b]ǵlph.*	The firstfruits of summer are … The ear [in] its husk.
19–21	*apnk.dn[i]l/[m]t.rpi.* *ap[h]n.ǵ[z]r/[mt hrnm]y.*	Now Daniel, [ma]n of Rapiu, The hero, [man of the Harnem]ite,
21–23	*yt[š]u/[yṯb bap ṯ]ǵ[r]* *[t]ḥt/[adrm dbgrn]*	Gets up [and sits by the gate]way, Among [the chiefs on the threshing floor],
23–25	*ydn/[dn almnt* *y]ṯpṭ/[ṯpṭ ytm*	Takes care of [the case of the widow], Defends [the need of the orphan].
25	*]h*	
26	*[ ]n*	
27	*[ ]*	…
28	*hlk.[ ]*	
	…	
28–29	*[bn]ši/ʿnh.wtphn*	Raising his eyes, he sees
29–31	*[ ]/bgrn.yḫrb* *[ ]/yǵly.* *yḫsp.ib[ ]/*	[ ] on the threshing floor dries, [ ] droops, The verdure [ ] is removed.
32–33	*ʿl.bt.abh.nšrm.trḫpn./* *ybṣr.ḥbl.diym/*	The birds circle over her father's house, The flock of hawks soars(?).
34–35	*tbky.pǵt.bm.lb/* *tdmʿ.bm.kbd/*	Paghit weeps in her liver, Sheds tears in her heart,[26]
36–37	*tmzʿ.kst.dnil.mt/rpi.* *al<l>.ǵzr.mt hrnmy./*	Torn is the mantle of Daniel, man of Rapiu, The robe of the hero, man of the Harnemite.
38–39	*apnk.dnil.mt/rpi.*	Now Daniel, man of Rapiu,
39–40	*yṣly.ʿrpt.b/ḥm.un.*	Adjures the clouds in the awful heat,

40–42	*yr.ʿrpt/tmṭr.bqẓ.* *ṭl.yṭll/lǵnbm.*	"Let the clouds make rain in the summer, the dew lay dew on the grapes."
42–44	*šbʿ.šnt/yṣrk.bʿl.* *ṯmn.rkb/ʿrpt.*	Seven years Baal is absent, Eight, the Rider of Clouds:
44–46	*bl.ṭl.bl rbb/* *bl.šrʿ.tḫmtm.* *bl/ṭbn.ql.bʿl.*	No dew, no downpour, No swirling of the deeps, No welcome voice of Baal.
46–48	*ktmzʿ/kst.dnil.mt.rpi/* *all.ǵzr.mt.ḫr[nmy]/*	Torn indeed is the mantle of Daniel, man of Rapiu, The robe of the hero, man of the Har[nemite].
49	*gm.lb[tḫ dnil kyṣḥ]*	[Daniel calls] to [his] daugh[ter]:
Column II		Column II
1–3	*šmʿ.pǵt.ṯkmt my/* *ḥspt.lšʿr.ṭl.* *ydʿ[t]/ḫlk.kbkbm.*	"Listen, Paghit, bearer of water, Collecter of dew from the fleece (?), Who knows the course of the stars:
3–5	*mdl.ʿr/ṣmd.pḥl.* *št.gpny dt ksp/* *dt.yrq.nqbny.*	Lead the donkey, rope up the ass, Lay on my silver harness(?), my golden bridle(?)."
5–7	*tš[mʿ]/pǵt.ṯkmt.my.* *ḥspt.[lšʿ]r.ṭl/* *ydʿt.ḫlk.kbkbm/*	Paghit att[ends], the bearer of water, Collecter of dew from the [flee]ce (?), Who knows the course of the stars.
8–9	*bkm.tmdln.ʿr/* *bkm.tṣmd.pḥl.*	Weeping, she leads the donkey, Weeping, ropes up the ass,
9–10	*bk[m]/tšu.abh.*	Weeping, she lifts up her father,
10–11	*tštnn.l[b]mt ʿr/* *lysmsm.bmt.pḥl/*	Onto the back of the donkey, The shapely back of the ass.
12	*ydnil.ysb.palth/*	Daniel[27] goes round the brush,
13–14	*bṣql.ypḫ.bpalt.*	Sees the stalks in the brush,

	bṣ[ql]/ypḫ.byǵlm.	Sees the stalks in the thicket,
14–15	*bṣql.yḥbq/wynšq.*	Embraces and kisses the stalks:
15	*aḥl.an.bṣ[ql]/*	"Let me console the sta[lks],
16–17	*ynpʿ.bpalt.bṣql.* *ypʿ.byǵlm/ur.*	Let the stalks shoot up in the brush, The wild plants sprout in the thicket,
17–18	*tispk.yd.aqht/ǵzr.* *tštk.bqrbm.asm/*	The hand of Aqhat the Hero collect you, Place you inside the storehouse."
19	*ydni!*[28]*<l>.ysb.aklth.*	Daniel[29] goes round his cracked earth,
19–20	*ypḫ/šblt.bak<l>t.* *šblt.ypḫ!/bḥmdrt.*	Sees the ears in the cracked earth, Sees the ears in the dried land,
21–22	*šblt.yḥ[bq]/wynšq.*	Embra[ces] and kisses the ears,
22	*aḥl.an.š[blt]/*	"Let me console the e[ars],
23–24	*tpʿ.baklt.šblt.* *tpʿ [bḥ]mdrt/ur.*	Let the ears shoot up in the cracked earth, The wild plants sprout [in the dr]ied land.
24–25	*tispk.yd.aqht.ǵ[zr]/* *tštk.bm.qrbm asm/*	The hand of Aqhat the Hero collect you, Place you inside the storehouse."
26	*bph.rgm.lyṣa.* *bšpt[h hwth]/*	The words have not left his mouth, Nor his speech his lips,
27	*bnši ʿnh.wtphn*	When, raising her eyes, she sees
27–28	*in.š[ ]/[ ]hlk.ǵlmm.*	No pe[ace(?) in] the messengers' gait.
28–29	*bddy.yṣ[ ]/* *[ ]yṣa.wl.yṣa.*	They mo[ve away(?] from each other, One over here, one there,
29–30	*hlm.ṯ[nm]/[q]dqd.*	Striking t[wice] on the head,

	ṯlṯid.ʿl.ud[n]/	Three times over the ear.
31	*[ ]sr.pdm.rišh[ ]*	[ ] their brows [ ]
32	*ʿl.pd.asr.ḫ[ ]l[ ]l[ ]*	On the brow [ ]
32–34	*[ ]/mḫlpt.wl.ytk.* *dmʿt km/rbʿt.ṯqlm.*	[ ] their tresses and flows, Tears like quarter shekels.
34	*mp(?)*[30]*[ ]bm*	
35	*yd.ṣpnhm.tliym[ ]pnhm[ ]*	…
36	*nṣḫy.šrr.mʿ[ ]ay*	
37	*abšrkm.dni[l]m.bh[ ]*	I will tell you both: Dani[el,]
38	*riš.rq[ ]ʿ[ ] hwt.*	…
38–39	*[š]ṣat krḫ.npšhm/* *kiṯl.brlt* *km [qṭr baph]/*	She expelled his life like a breath, His soul like a sneeze(?), From his nose like smoke."
40	*tmǵyn.tša.ghm.[wtṣḥn]/*	They come, raise [their] voices, [and cry]:
41	*šmʿ.ldnil.mt.[rpi]/*	"Attend, Daniel, man of [Rapiu]:
42	*mt.aqht.ǵzr.*	Aqhat the Hero is dead!
42–44	*[šṣat]/btlt.ʿnt.* *k[rḫ npšh]/* *kiṯl.brlth.*	Anat the Girl [has expelled] [His life] like [a breath], His soul like a sneeze(?)."
44–47	*[bh pʿnm]/tṭṭ.* *ʿl[n pnh tdʿ* *bʿdn]/ksl.yṯ[br* *ygṣ pnt kslh]/* *anš.[dt ẓrh*	[Below, his feet] tremble, Above, [his face perspires], [Around], his loins cr[ack], [The joints of his loins shake], [Those of his back] give way.
47–48	*yšu gh]/wyṣ[ḥ*	[He raises his voice] and cri[es]:

49	*mḫṣ[ ]*	
(Six lines missing.) Lower Edge		*(Daniel's initial response to the news of Aqhat's murder would have been included in the several missing lines here.)*
56–57	*bnši [ʿnh wyphn* *yḥd]/bʿrpt [nšrm*	Raising [his eyes, he sees], [Notes the birds] in the clouds.
57– Column III 1	*[yšu/gh]wyṣḥ*	Column III [He raises his voice] and cries:
1–3	*[knp nšrm]/bʿl.yṯb<r>.* *bʿl.yṯbr [diy hmt]/* *tqln.th<t> pʿny.*	"Let Baal break [their wings], Break [the birds' pinions], So they fall beneath my feet.
3–4	*ibq[ʿ kbdthm w]/aḥd.*	I'll spli[t their bellies and] look.
4–5	*hm.iṯ.šmt.* *hm.i[ṯ]/ʿẓm.*	If there's fat, If there's bone,
5–6	*abk![31]y.w.aqbrnh/* *ašt.bḫrt.ilm.arṣ![32]/*	I'll weep and bury him, Place him in the earth-gods' caves."
7	*bph.rgm.lyṣa.* *bšpth.hwt[h]/*	The words have not left his mouth, Nor his speech his lips,
8–10	*knp nšrm.bʿl.yṯbr/* *bʿl.ṯbr diyhmt.* *tq![33]ln/tḥt.pʿnh.*	When Baal breaks their wings, Breaks the birds' pinions, So they fall beneath his feet.
10	*ybqʿ.kbdthm.[wyḥd]/*	He splits their bellies [and looks].
11	*in.šmt.* *in.ʿẓm.*	There's no fat! There's no bone!
11–12	*yšu.gh/wyṣḥ.*	He raises his voice and cries:
12–13	*knp nšrm.<bʿl> ybn/* *bʿl.ybn.diy.hmt.*	"Let <Baal> mend their wings, Mend the birds' pinions.
13–14	*nšrm/tpr.wdu.*	Birds, take wing and fly!"

14–15	*bnši ʿnh.wyp<h>n/* *yḥd hrgb.ab.nšrm/*	Raising his eyes, he sees, Notes Hargub, Father of Birds.
16	*yšu.gh.wyṣḥ.*	He raises his voice and cries:
16–18	*knp.hr[g]b/bʿl.yṯb<r>.* *bʿl.yṯbr.diy hwt/* *wyql.tḥt.pʿny.*	"Let Baal b[rea]k Hargub's wings, Let Baal break his pinions, So he falls beneath my feet.
18–19	*ibqʿ.kbd[h]/waḥd.*	I'll split his belly and look.
19	*hm.iṯ.šmt.* *hm.iṯ [ʿẓm]/*	If there's fat, If there's [bone],
20–21	*abky waqbrn.* *ašt.bḫrt/ilm [arṣ*	I'll weep and bury him, Place him in the [earth-]gods' caves."
21–22	*bph rgm lyṣa* *bšp]/th.hwth.*	[The words have not left his mouth], Nor his speech his [lip]s,
22–24	*knp.hrgb.bʿl.ṯbr/* *bʿl.ṯbr.diy.hwt.* *wyql/tḥt.pʿnh.*	When Baal breaks Hargub's wings, Baal breaks his pinions, So he falls beneath his feet.
24	*ybqʿ.kbdh.wyḥd/*	He splits his belly and looks:
25	*in.šmt.* *in.ʿẓm.*	There's no fat! There's no bone!
25–26	*yšu.gh/wyṣḥ.*	He raises his voice and cries:
26–27	*knp.hrgb.bʿl.ybn/* *bʿl.ybn.diy.hwt.*	"Let Baal mend Hargub's wings, Let Baal mend his pinions.
27–28	*hrgb/tpr.wdu.*	Hargub, take wing and fly!"
28–29	*bnši.ʿnh./wyphn.* *yḥd.ṣml.um.nšrm/*	Raising his eyes, he sees, Notes Samal, Mother of Birds.
30	*yšu.gh.wyṣḥ.*	He raises his voice and cries:
30–32	*knp.ṣml./bʿl.yṯbr.*	"Let Baal break Samal's wings,

	bᶜl.yṯbr.diy/hyt. *tql.tḥt.pᶜny.*	Let Baal break her pinions, So she falls beneath my feet.
32–33	*ibqᶜ/kbdh.waḥd.*	I'll split her belly and look:
33–34	*hm.iṯ.š[m]t.* *<hm> iṯ/ᶜẓm.*	If there's fat, <If> there's bone,
34–35	*abky. waqbrnh.* *aštn/bḫrt.ilm.arṣ.*	I'll weep and bury him, Place him in the earth-gods' caves."
35–36	*bph.rgm.ly[ṣ]a/* *bšpth.hwth.*	The words have not left his mouth, Nor his speech his [lip]s,
36–38	*knp.ṣml.bᶜ[l]<(y)ṯbr>/* *bᶜl.ṯbr.diy.hyt.* *tql.tḥt/pᶜnh.*	When Baal breaks Samal's wings, Baal breaks her pinions, So she falls beneath his feet.
38	*ybqᶜ.kbdh.wyḥd./*	He splits her belly and looks:
39	*iṯ.šmt.* *iṯ.ᶜẓm.*	There *is* fat! There *is* bone!
39–40	*wyqḥ.bhm/aqht.* *yb.llqẓ.*	From them he takes Aqhat— He does not wake; he wails.[34]
40–41	*ybky.wyqbr/* *yqbr.nn.bmdgt.bknrt/*	He weeps and buries him Buries him in MDGT, in KNRT.
42	*wyšu.gh.wyṣḥ*	He raises his voice and cries:
42–44	*knp.nšrm/bᶜl.yṯbr.* *bᶜl.yṯbr.diy/hmt.*	"Let Baal break the birds' wings, Let Baal break their pinions,
44–45	*hm.tᶜpn.ᶜl.qbr.bny/* *tšḫṭann.bšnth.*	If they fly over the grave, To deprive my son of his sleep."
45–46	*qr.m[y]/m lk.yṣm.*	He curses QR-MYM …
46–47	*ylkm.qr.mym.* *dᶜlk/mḫṣ.aqht.ġzr.*	"Woe to you, QR-MYM, Near which Aqhat was slain:
47	*amd.grbt il/*	May El clothe you in leprosy(?)[35]

48	*ʿnt.brḫ.pʿlm.h.* *ʿnt.pdr.dr/*	Now, and fleet time for ever, Now and all generations."
49	*ʿdb.uḫry.mṭ.ydh/*	He gestures with Fate, his staff.
50	*ymǵ.lmrrt.tǵll.bnr/*	He comes to MRRT TGHLL BNR,
51	*yšu.gh.wyṣḥ*	He raises his voice and cries:
51–53	*ylk.mrrt/tǵll.bnr.* *dʿlk.mḫṣ.aqht/ǵzr.*	"Woe to you, MRRT TGHLL BNR, Near which Aqhat was slain:
53–54	*šršk.barṣ.al/ypʿ.* *riš.ǵly.bd.nsʿk/*	May your root not sprout in the earth, Your head droop as you're plucked.
55–56	*ʿnt.brḫ.pʿlmh./* *ʿnt.pdr.dr.*	Now, and fleet time for ever, Now and all generations."
56	*ʿdb.uḫry.mṭ ydh/*	He gestures with Fate, his staff.

Column IV		Column IV
1–2	*ymǵ.lqrt.ablm.* *ablm/qrt.zbl.yrḫ*	He comes to the town of Abiluma, Abiluma, town of Prince Yarikh.
2–3	*yšu.gh/wyṣḥ.*	He raises his voice and cries:
3–4	*ylk.qrt.ablm/* *dʿlk.mḫṣ aqht.ǵzr/*	"Woe to you, town of Abiluma, Near which Aqhat was slain:
5	*ʿwrt.yštk.bʿl.*	May Baal strike you blind
5–6	*lht/wʿlmh* *lʿnt.pdr.dr/*	From henceforth and for ever, From now and through all generations."
7	*ʿdb.uḫry.mṭ.ydh/*	He gestures with Fate, his staff.
8–9	*dnil.bth.ym[.]ǵyn.* *yšt/ql.dnil.lhklh.*	Daniel comes to his house, Daniel arrives at his palace.
9–11	*ʿrb.b/<bth b>kyt.*	The weepers come <into his house>,

	bhklh.mšspdt. *bḥẓrh/pẓǵm.ǵr.*	The mourners into his palace, Those breaking their skin to his court.
11–13	*ybk.laqht/ǵzr.* *ydmʿ.lkdd.dnil/mt.rpi.*	He weeps for Aqhat the hero, Sheds tears for the child of Daniel, man of Rapiu.
13–15	*lymm.lyrḫm/* *lyrḫm.lšnt.* *ʿd/šbʿ.šnt.*	From days to months, From months to years, To seven years,
15–17	*ybk.laq/ht.ǵzr.* *yd[mʿ] lkdd/dnil.mt.r[pi*	He weeps for Aqhat the hero, Sheds tears for the child of Daniel, man of Rapiu.
17–18	*mk].bšbʿ/šnt.*	Then, in the seventh year,
18–20	*wyʿn [dnil mt] rpi/* *yṯb.ǵzr.m[t hrnmy* *y]šu/gh.wyṣḥ.*	Daniel, man of Rapiu, speaks, The hero comes back, the man of the Harnemite, He raises his voice and cries:
20–22	*t[bʿ bbty]/bkyt.* *bhk[l]y.mšspdt/* *bḥẓry pẓǵm.ǵr.*	"G[o from my house], you weepers, Hence from my palace, you mourners, You, breaking your skin, from my court."
22–25	*wyq[ry]/dbḥ.ilm.* *yšʿly.dǵṯ[h]m(?)/bšmym.* *dǵṯ.hrnmy.[bk]/bkbm.*	He pres[ents] a meal for the gods, Into the heavens sends incense, [To the] stars the Harnemite's incense .
25–27	*[ ]/[ ]lh.yd.ʿd.[ ]* *[mṣ]/ltm.mrqdm.dšn[ ]l[ ]*	... [Cym]bals, castanets of ivory ...
28	*wtʿn.pǵt.ṯkmt.mym/*	Then Paghit, bearer of water, answers:
29–31	*qrym.ab.dbḥ.lilm/* *šʿly.dǵṯ[h(?)].bšmym/* *dǵṯ.hrnmy.[bk]bkbm/*	"My father's presented a meal for the gods, Into the heavens sent incense, [To the] stars the Harnemite's incense .

Lines	Text	Translation
32–33	*ltbrkn.alk brktm(?)/* *tmrn.alk.nmrrt/*	Bless me—I would go blessed! Empower me—I'd go empowered!
34–35	*imḫṣ.mḫṣ.aḫy.* *akl [m]/kl[y ᶜ]l.umty.*	I would slay the slayer of my sibling, finish [who] finished my brother."[36]
35–36	*wyᶜn [dn]/il mt rpi.*	Then [Dan]iel, man of Rapiu, answered:
36–38	*npš.tḥ pǵ[t]/ṯkmt.mym.* *ḥspt.lšᶜr/ṭl.* *ydᶜt hlk.kbkbm /*	"By my life, let [Paghit], bearer of water, live, Collecter of dew from the fleece (?), Who knows the course of the stars.
39	*a[37][ ]ḥ.hy.mḫ.*	... flourish!
39–40	*tmḫṣ.mḫṣ [aḫh]/* *tkl.mkly. ᶜl.umt[h*	May she slay the slayer of [her sibling], finish who finished [her] brother."[38]
40–41	*]/d.t[ ][39] l.bym.*	[ ] in the sea
41–43	*trtḥ[ṣ]/ w[ ]dm.* *tid![40]m.bǵlp ym/* *d[alp].šd.ẓuh.bym.*	She washes [ ] and [ ], Rouges herself with shellfish, Whose source is far in the sea.
43–46	*t[ ]/tlbš.npṣ.ǵzr.* *tšt.ḫl[pn b]/nšgh.* *ḥrb.tšt.btᶜr[th]/* *wᶜl.tlbš.npṣ.aṯt.*	She puts on a hero's outfit [below?], Places a knife(?) in her belt(?), In her [scabbard] places a sword, A woman's outfit on top.
46–50	*[l?]/ṣbi.nrt.ilm.špš.* *[ᶜ]r[bt]/pǵt.minš.šdm.* *lmᶜr[b]/nrt.ilm.špš.* *mǵy[t]/pǵt.lahlm.*	As Shapshu, the gods' lamp, departs, Paghit [approached] the encampment, As Shapshu, the gods' lamp, sets, Paghit arrived at the tents.
50–51	*rgm.lyṯ[pn y]/bl.*	Word was brought to YTPN:
51–52	*agrtn.bat.bḏdk.* *[pǵt]/bat.b<a>hlm.*	"The woman we hired[41] is come to your camp, [ ] is come to the tents."

52–53	*wyʿn.yṭpn.m[hr]/št.*	Then YTPN, Sutean [warrior] replies:
53–54	*qḥn.wtšqyn.yn.* *t[qḥ]/ks.bdy.* *qbʿt.bymny.*	"Take and drink the wine,[42] Ta[ke] the cup from my hand, The goblet from my fingers."
54–56	*[t]q/ḥ.pǵt.wtšqynh.* *tq!*[44]*[ḥ ks b]dh/* *qbʿt.bymnh.*	Paghit takes and drinks it,[43] Tak[es the cup from] his hand, The goblet from his fingers.[45]
56–57	*wyʿn.yṭ[pn mh]r/št*	YTPN, Sutean warrior, replies:
57–58	*byn.yšt.ila.il š[ ]* *il/dyqny.ḏdm.*	"By the wine that is drunk I'll defeat the god … The god who is master of camps.
58–59	*yd.mḫṣt.a[qh]t.ǵ/zr.* *tmḫṣ.alpm.ib.*	The hand that slew Aqhat the Hero Slay foes by the thousand!
59–60	*št[ ]št/ḥršm.lahlm.*	… enchanters to the tents."
60–61	*p[ ]km/ybl.lbh.* *km.bṯn.y[ ]ṣ(or l)ah.*	His heart … like a ram, His feces … like a snake.
61	*ṯnm.tšqy msk.* *hwt.tšqy*	Twice she gives the mixed wine, Gives to him the drink… .[46]

On the (left) edge of column IV, beginning opposite line 23:

On the side of the tablet where the plot resumes after the interruption caused by Daniel's rituals following Aqhat's death:

whndt.yṯb.lmspr

And here one returns to the story.

Notes

1. Some have argued that the Rapiuma texts (20–22 below) represent that continuation, but there is little evidence to support such a claim.
2. Cf. Judg 3:15-30; Jdt 8-13.
3. See Parker 1995: 2403-4 and, in more detail, 1989a.
4. Rapiu is the eponymous head of the Rapiuma, for which see the introduction to texts 20–22 below. The Harnemite is an epithet apparently formed from a place-name, Harnem.

5. The tablet reads *ynl.*

6. These are evidently ritual actions designed to draw the attention of the gods to Daniel's plight. "Lies"—literally, "goes up and lies down," perhaps on some naturally or artificially elevated place regarded as appropriate for catching the gods' attention.

7. In light of the preceding it would seem that Baal approaches Daniel, but from the following it is clear that he approaches El. In an earlier version there may have been an encounter between Baal and Daniel at this point.

8. The tablet reads *w.*

9. "Ancestor" and "Sib" probably refer to the deified ancestor or ancestral spirit.

10. The tablet apparently has a ᶜ instead of a word divider. However, the edges of the sign are much more irregular than the normal ᶜ, so this may just be damage to the tablet.

11. The tablet has *u.*

12. Watson suggests that this verse may be a monologue by Daniel—*UF* 24 (1992) 365.

13. Or: "in flour."

14. This word is actually written at the end of the line in the original. Some see such separation of the elements of a construct chain as a deliberate poetic device.

15. The tablet appears to read *mm.*

16. The tablet reads *t.*

17. The tablet reads *r.*

18. The liver is the seat of the emotions.

19. Or: "You are my brother and I am your si[ster].

20. The final "N" of the name is omitted here.

21. Evidently the physical moon here.

22. Again the final "N" is dropped from the name in the Ugaritic text.

23. *CAT* reads: *ᶜpt m[ḫṣk.*

24. The Ugaritic, though largely readable, remains obscure. No study to date has elucidated it sufficiently to justify a continuous translation.

25. Someone is now clearly speaking—presumably Anat—but it is not clear where the speech begins.

26. The liver is the seat of the emotions. "In one's heart" is often the equivalent of "to oneself."

27. The verb which constitutes the first half of the name is here in a different form with a prefixed "Ya-".

28. The tablet reads *h.*

29. Here the name is even more disfigured: "Ya" is prefixed and the final "l" is dropped.

30. *CAT* reads *tg* instead of *m* and only traces following.

31. The tablet reads *p.*

32. The tablet reads *t.*

33. The tablet has *ǵ.*

34. Daniel wails at Aqhat's unwaking state.

35. The specific curse has not been satisfactorily explained.

36. Literally, "my mother's child."

37. Or *n*.

38. Literally, "her mother's child."

39. There appear to be several horizontal wedges here, but it is not clear how they should be read.

40. The tablet reads *u*.

41. Or possibly: "who hired us." There is no other reference in the story to any hiring of or by YTPN's people.

42. Or (addressed to those bringing news of Paghit's arrival): "Take her and give her wine to drink."

43. Or, following the interpretation in the preceding note: "They take Paghit and give it to her to drink."

44. The tablet reads *p*.

45. The Ugaritic word behind "fingers" refers to the right hand, but unlike "right hand," it is completely unrelated to the word for "hand." The words "right hand" here would make for a very weak verse.

46. Or: "Twice she drinks the mixed wine, drinks it. . . ."

View of Mount Saphon from Ugarit.
Courtesy of Wayne Pitard.

The Baal Cycle

Translated by Mark S. Smith

The six tablets and various fragments (7–12 = *CAT* 1.1–1.6), variously called the Baal text, the Baal Cycle, or the Epic of Baal, were excavated between 1930 and 1933 from what has been called the "library of the High Priest," or scribal school situated between two temples on the acropolis, traditionally thought to belong to Baal and Dagan (Petersen 1994; Smith 1994b: 1). The original length of the cycle is unknown. The physical remains of the attested tablets total about 1,830 lines, but estimates for the original text go as high as 5,000 lines. The date of the Baal Cycle has been fixed to about 1400–1350 B.C.E. based on textual and archaeological evidence. The colophon at the end of the text's sixth and final tablet (12 VI 54–58) mentions the name of king *nqmd,* supposedly Niqmaddu II, who reigned ca. 1380–1346 B.C.E. While this reign provides a date for the final form of the extant text, the cycle shows signs of multiple stages, which may suggest a long period of development.

There is some question whether the six tablets represent a single text or a group of separate narratives about Baal (Clifford 1984; Margalit 1980: 9–11; Smith 1994b: 1–28). The second through the sixth tablets (8–12) clearly involve stories about Baal. The first tablet (7) refers to Baal and can be read in conjunction with the other stories about him, but there is no clear proof that the two pieces were part of a single "Baal Cycle." Indeed, due to the numerous gaps in the cycle, the degree of narrative continuity from tablet to tablet is unknown, except in the case of the last two, which are continuous. Circumstantial evidence may favor continuity between the third, fourth, and fifth tablets, but the narrative continuity between the first three tablets is less certain. The first three tablets could be parts of either a loosely or directly connected group of stories, or parts of different copies of the same text, or even, in the case of some pieces, parts of a different text(s). Given its fragmentary character, the first tablet's relationship to the other five tablets is especially acute. The six tablets and their fragments were not all found in a single spot, which would suggest that at least they were not parts of a single copy of the Baal Cycle.[1]

The order of the columns within each tablet is mostly clear, although some problems persist with respect to the first, second, and sixth tablets. The order of the columns in 7 was originally interpreted in the order II–III–IV–V, but thematic considerations suggest the opposite order (the summoning of the craftsman-god, Kothar wa-Hasis, to build the palace follows El's initiative in naming Yamm as the royal heir). For this reason the transliteration and translation of the columns are presented in the order V–IV–III–II. The second tablet, 8, contains two large fragments. The smaller one has been traditionally regarded as the third column, but many scholars prefer to place this fragment as a column before (or even separate from) those of the larger fragment; this approach is followed here. This smaller fragment may not be part of the same text as the larger fragment of 8, but part of another copy of the text, since it overlaps in content with 7 III. The two pieces of the sixth tablet, 12, have been accepted as a single text, but some doubts have been expressed recently.[2] Readers should also be aware of the fact that individual lines of Ugaritic poetry present a host of problems, and therefore many different interpretations have been proposed sometimes for a line or even a single word.[3] In the main, an attempt is made in the translation here to avoid idiosyncratic interpretations. Despite the preceding difficulties, the outline of the narrative is clear.

The text presents Baal's struggles to establish his kingship over the universe. The first two tablets (7–8) describe the conflict between Baal, the storm god, whose name means "Lord," and his enemy, Yamm, whose name means "Sea." The next two tablets (9–10) detail the process leading to Baal's acquisition of a palace, the crowning mark of his kingship. The last two tablets (11–12) relate Baal's confrontations with Mot ("Death"). The god Athtar (the meaning of whose name is disputed) is mentioned twice (8 III and 12 I) as a possible rival to Baal. These four warrior gods rule different realms of the universe: Baal is the god of the storm and lord of the sky; Yamm, the god of the sea; Mot, Death incarnate, the god of the underworld; and Athtar, an astral god who is perhaps a natural irrigator (Caquot 1958).

Other deities appear in the Baal Cycle. El's name means "God," perhaps in the sense of "the God" (i.e., the preeminent god, or the embodiment of divinity in some sense), or more literally, "the Strong One." As the older king and patriarch of the pantheon, El rules in conjunction with his wife and mother of the pantheon, Athirat (whose name remains a matter of debate).[4] Together El and Athirat oversee the divine family (Schloen 1993: 219–20), represented in specific terms as "the seventy sons of Athirat," or in more general terms as the divine assembly. This older couple are the parents of the pantheon, and they mediate their rival sons' claims to the divine throne. The other characters in the Baal Cycle manifest various aspects of nature and society. Kothar wa-Hasis, literally "Crafty and Wise," is a specialist who serves other deities with his craftsmanship, which includes spells. Shapsh ("Sun") is the divine messenger who communicates El's will to the rival claimants and travels between the realms of life and death. Athtart (Greek Astarte) and Anat (the meaning of whose names are debated) are Baal's warrior allies. The names of two of Baal's three women (*aṯtm*) and "brides" (*klt*), Tallay ("Dewy") and Pidray ("Flashy"?), evidence their meteorological kinship with Baal, while the name of the third, Arsay ("Earthy" or "Netherworldly"), may reflect a chthonic nature comparable to his. The unnamed messengers of Yamm, as well as Baal's messengers Gapn wa-Ugar ("Vine" and "Field"), and Athirat's messenger, Qudsh wa-Amrar ("Holy and Strong"), occupy the lowest level of the divine assembly.

The main theme of the cycle is the kingship of Baal. The cycle contains meteorological and ritualistic elements (de Moor 1971), but the text is not to be read against a putative ritualistic setting such as a New Year's festival (Marcus 1973) or interpreted according to a single annual cycle (Grabbe 1976). Although meteorological elements have been noted in each of the three major sections, 7–8, 9–10, and 11–12, the cycle need not be set against the background of a seasonal pattern, annual or otherwise. Rather, each of the three major parts draws on the weather of the fall, especially the arrival of the rains, to serve its larger political vision (Smith 1990: 60). In the first section of the cycle, the meteorological imagery thought to lie behind Baal's weapons in 8 IV presages the arrival of the autumn rains. In the second section of the cycle, Athirat rejoices at the prospect of the building of Baal's palace so that he can produce the rains, evidently lacking up to this point (10 V 6–9). After the palace is completed, Baal finally utters "his holy voice," that is, his thunder, through a rift in the clouds (10 VII 25–31). The third section of the cycle alludes to the absence of Baal's rains. El's dream-vision in 12 III indicates to him that the earth will flow with fertility now that Baal is alive again (12 III). The struggle between Baal and Mot in 12 VI may evoke on the cosmic level the interchange in the fall season between the rains coming off the Mediterranean Sea and the hot, dry winds coming from the eastern desert. The one season that fits the situations described in all three parts of the cycle is the autumn when the rains finally overtake the heat of late summer. In this way the Baal Cycle uses elements known from the natural sphere to advance the theme of Baal's kingship.

While kingship is the cycle's central theme, Baal does not represent an omnipotent figure like Marduk in Enuma Elish or Yahweh in the Hebrew Bible, to whom Baal is often compared (Clifford 1984). The Baal Cycle does not render the West Semitic storm god in the exalted terms reserved for Marduk or Yahweh. Nor does the Baal Cycle construe Baal as a champion who vanquishes his enemies for all time. Rather, Baal acquires a limited kingship, not primarily through his own exploits, but thanks largely to the aid of other deities. Baal's foes loom large not in a single combat, but in repeated engagements, and without definitive outcomes. The threat of their return is never overcome entirely, at least in the case of Mot, and perhaps their return was as expected as the return of Baal's rains. Baal's kingship is indeed finite, won despite his own limitations and perhaps the limitations of the great deities as well. The cosmos of Baal's kingship is a universe nurturing life wondrously, but precariously. This universe is frequently, if not usually, overshadowed by chaos, the transient character of life and finally death (Gibson 1984; Kapelrud 1979).

The cosmic battle described in the first section of the Baal Cycle was known in political texts outside of Ugarit. The most dramatic instance derives from Mari. In a letter to Zimri-Lim (Durand 1993; Bordreuil and Pardee 1993), the king is addressed by the West Semitic storm god, in this text called Adad, cognate with Baal's title, Haddu (apparently meaning "thunderer"). The king is told that when he ascended the throne of his father, Adad gave him the weapons with which the god slew Tiamat (meaning "Sea"). This proclamation alludes to the story of the divine conflict known from the first part of the Baal Cycle, in order to express divine support for the monarchy at Mari. Given such political use of the West Semitic conflict myth at Mari, it is plausible to suggest a political use for the Baal Cycle and its transmission at Ugarit, lying as it does in the heartland of devotion to Baal. Indeed, the Ugaritic dynasty considered Baal-Haddu as its divine patron, and the transmission and final production of the Baal Cycle at Ugarit may have resulted in part from the political values that it expressed on behalf of the Ugaritic dynasty.[5] If so, the Baal Cycle's presentation of a relatively weak Baal aided by other deities against the threatening cosmic powers of Yamm and Mot may have reflected the status of Ugarit and its ruling dynasty in a world dominated by the great Egyptian and Hittite empires of the Late Bronze Age (Stolz 1982; Smith 1994b: 96–110).

Baal's rule operates on three levels of reality: the cosmic, the human, and the natural (Gibson 1984; Kinet 1978; Smith 1994b: xxv, 96–110). First, the Baal Cycle concentrates on the interaction of the deities on the cosmic level. Ritual texts and other mythological works involve deities, but no other text focuses so strongly on the Ugaritic deities and the cosmos as the Baal Cycle. Second, the political events in the Baal Cycle reflect a concern for human society. The implications of Baal's fortunes for humanity are occasionally expressed in the text, and the divine struggles are a matter of life and death for Ugarit's society. The struggles of Baal mirror the struggles of humanity against the vicissitudes of a dangerous world, but the victories of Baal also herald the divine victory, which reinvigorates not only the world of the divine pantheon but also human society. Third, the Baal Cycle uses natural phenomena, especially lightning, thunder, and rain to underscore the political power of Baal, the storm god. In sum, the Baal Cycle interrelates humanity, nature, and divinity in its political vision of Baal's struggles and victories, and thereby yields an integrated political vision of chaos, life, and death. The dangers and defeats, the victories and the glories described in the cycle provide a religio-political interpretation of the experience of ancient Ugaritic society.

Many motifs in the Baal Cycle enjoyed a long history after the demise of ancient Ugarit (Cassuto 1975; Cooper 1981; Cross 1973; Rummel 1981; Smith 1990). Numerous type-scenes and literary formulas in the Baal Cycle are found in the Bible. For example, the scene of a divine council headed by El attested in 8 I, reappears with Yahweh enthroned in the divine council in prophetic and apocalyptic visions (1 Kings 22; Isaiah 6; Zechariah 3; Daniel 7); the divine council also becomes a more general literary topos (Job 1–2; cf. Psalm 82).

The Baal Cycle also furnishes information pertinent to the religious environment of ancient Israel. Deities known from Ugaritic literature generally and the Baal Cycle specifically are attested in ancient Israel as well. Baal and Athirat (biblical Asherah), for example, were worshiped and condemned in ancient Israel according to 1 Kings 18 and other biblical passages (Smith 1990). The relationship between West Semitic religion as represented by the Baal Cycle and Israelite religion may well run deeper. It is arguable that the original god of Israel was El, as the name of Israel contains this divine name. The depictions of Yahweh as enthroned king in Isaiah 6 and Daniel 7 reflect the assimilation of Yahweh and El (Mosca 1986). Not only do general literary motifs associated with Baal, Yamm, and Mot appear in biblical texts, but also the names, titles, and homes of these gods are reshaped in descriptions of the biblical cosmos and Yahweh, Israel's main deity. For example, in Psalm 29 Yahweh is presented as a warrior-god of the storm like Baal; in Ps 68:5 one of Baal's epithets is attributed (with modifications) to Yahweh; and in Ps 48:3 the name of Baal's traditional home, Sapan (Zaphon), is identified with Yahweh's dwelling on Mount Zion (J. Day 1985; Kloos 1986). These examples suggest that material traditionally associated with Baal was eventually applied to Yahweh. Similarly, the political function of the West Semitic conflict story was inherited by ancient Israel's monarchy. Just as the battle between the West Semitic storm god and the cosmic Sea served to support the dynasty at Mari and quite possibly at Ugarit, so too ancient Israel used this imagery to affirm Yahweh's support of the monarch (Psalm 18 = 2 Samuel 22). Psalm 89:26 makes this support explicit: Yahweh promises that he will set the hand of the king on Sea and his right hand on River (Cross 1973: 258; Smith 1994a: 313–14).

Several renderings of deities and literary features of the West Semitic milieu reflected in the Baal Cycle passed into ancient Israelite culture and then into later Jewish and Christian tradition (Jacobs 1977). The message of peace on Christmas night, the heavenly banquet, the depiction of God as father, the beast of Revelation, and many other features familiar from the New Testament and rabbinic literature stem from a long history that includes the Baal Cycle. The closing chapters of Revelation provide a glimpse of the future that recalls the three major themes of the Baal Cycle: Baal's defeat of Yamm, the building of Baal's heavenly palace, and his conflict with Mot. Revelation 21 mentions the death of Sea, the descent of the heavenly city (akin to Baal's palace), and the final destruction of Death (Smith 1994a: xxvii). In sum, the early forms of many formative religious concepts of Western civilization may be found in the Baal Cycle.

7. *CAT* 1.1 — 7. First Tablet

(Columns I and VI not preserved)

Column II (*CAT* col. V) — Column II (*CAT* col. V)

(This fragmentary column details El and Yamm's plans to attack Baal. The number of lines missing from the beginning and end of this column is unknown.)

El Speaks to Yamm (?)

Line	Text	Translation
1	*[ ]b*	...
2–3	*[wym.ym]m[.yʿtqn]*	["... and a day,] two [days] [will pass] ...
3	*[ymǵy.]npš*	[... he will arrive] with his game ...
4	*[h]d.tngṯnh*	[... Ha]ddu (?), you will meet him ...
5	*[ ].bṣpn*	... at Sapan[6] ...
6	*[ ]nšb.bʿn*	... a cut ... when he sees ..."

Yamm (?) Speaks to El

Line	Text	Translation
7	*[ ]bkmyʿn*	... he speaks: "...
8	*[ydʿl]ydʿt*	... truly] I know
9	*[ ]asrn*	... will bind him (?) [O Bull El]
10	*[ ]trks*	... you (?) will bind ...
11	*[ ]bnm.uqpt*	... stones (?) ... I (?) am constrained (?)
12	*[ ]l[ ]ǵrmtny*	... and he (?) will attack (me) in my loins
13	*[ḏ(?)]rq.gb*	[... red st]uff (?), back ...

El Responds to Yamm (?)

Line	Text	Translation
14	*[ ]kl.tgr.mtnh*	... you shall attack (?) (him) in his loins ...
15–16	*[ ]h.wymymm[.yʿtqn]*	... a day, two days [will pass ...]
16	*[ ].ymǵy.npš*	... he will arrive with a life
17	*[ ]t.hd.tngṯnh*	... Haddu ... you will meet him
18	*[ ]ḥmkbṣpn*	... your (?) [... f]ood (?) on Sapan ...
19	*[ ]išqb.aylt*	... a doe

		Yamm (?) Responds to El
20	[ ]gmbkm.yʿn	... then he speaks: "...
21	[ ].ydʿ.lydʿt	... truly I know ...
22	[ ]tasrn.ṯril	... you (?) will bind him (?), O Bull El ...
23	[ ]rks.bn.abnm	... will bind ... stones ...
24	[ ]upqt.ʿrb	... I am (?) constrained (?) ... enter ...
25	[ ]r.mtnyatzd	... attack (me) in my loins ... I will be provisioned ...
26	[ ]tʿrb.bši	... you will enter when he lifts [his head/eyes?]
27	[ ] zd.ltptq	... with provisions you will be fed ...
28	[ ].g[ ]larṣ	... to the earth ... ...

Column III (*CAT* col. IV) — Column III (*CAT* col. IV)

(*The number of lines missing from the beginning and end of this column is unknown.*)

1	[ ].ṣ[ ]	...
		Invitation to El's Feast
2–4	gm.ṣḥ.lqb[ṣ.ilm (?)]	Aloud they summon the ass[embly of the gods (?),]
	[ṣḥ (?)]/lrḥqm.	[... They summon (?)] the distant ones,
	lp[ḫr.il.(?)]/ṣḥ.	The as[sembly of El (?)] they summon:
4–5	il.yṯb.bm[rzḥh?]	"El sits in [his] ma[rzeah (?)] ...
	bṯt.ʿllmn.[ ]	The shame (?) of the Eternal One (?) ...
6–8	ilm.bt.bʿlk[ ]	O Gods, to the house of your lord (?) ...
	dl.ylkn.ḥš.ba[rṣ (?)]	Who travels quickly through the l[and (?),]

	bᶜpr.ḫblṭtm[ ]	[Who goes (?)] in the dust of (?) destruction …"
9–10	*šqy.rṯa.tnmy.* *ytn[.ks.bydh]/* *krpn.bklatyd.*	He drinks curdled milk overflowing, He takes [a cup in his hand,] A flagon in both his hands.
10–11	*[ ]/kmll.* *kḥṣ.tusp[ ]*	… like pulp (?) … Like … is gathered …
12	*tgr.il.bnh.* *ṯr[ ]*	El appoints his son … The Bull …
		El's and Asherah's Proclamation Concerning Yamm
13	*wyᶜn.lṭ<p>n.ild[pid]*	And Beneficent El the Beni[gn] speaks: …
14	*šm.bny.yw.ilt[ ]*	"The name of my son (is?) Yw, O Elat …"
15	*wpᶜr.šm.ym[ ]*	And he pronounces the name Yamm …
15–16	*[ ]/tᶜnyn.* *lzntn[ ]*	… they answer … … for sustenance (?) …
17	*at.adn.tpᶜr[ ]*	"You, O Lord, you proclaim [his name (?)] …"
18	*ankl ṭpn.il[ ]*	"I, Beneficent El …
19	*ᶜl.ydm.pᶜrt[ ]*	Upon the hands … I pronounce …
20	*šmk.mdd.i[l]*	Your name … Beloved of E[l …
21	*btkspy.dt[ ]*	My house of silver which (?) …
22	*bdaliynb[ᶜl]*	In the hand of Mightiest B[aal] …
23	*kdynaṣn[ ]*	Thus he reviles me (?) …
24–25	*gršnn.lk[si.mlkh.]/* *[lnḫt.lkḥṯ]drkth.*	Drive him from [his royal] thr[one,] [From the resting place, the throne] of his dominion,
	š[ ] *[ ]*	… [7]

26–27	*whm.ap.l[tgršh.lksih (?)]/*	But if then [you] do not [drive him from his throne (?),]
	ymḫṣk.k[ ]	He will beat you like … ,
	[ ]	…"[8]

El's Feast

28	*ildbḥ.[ ]*	El sacrifices …
29	*pʿr.b[ ]*	He proclaims …
30–32	*ṭbḫ.alp[m.ap.ṣin]/*	He slaughters large st[ock as well as small:]
	[šql]ṯrm.w[mri.ilm.]	[He fells] bulls and [fatling rams,]
	[ʿglm.dt.šnt]/	[Year-old calves,]
	imr[.q]m[ṣ.llim]	Sheep by the fl[ock, and kids.]

Column IV (*CAT* col. III) — Column IV (*CAT* col. III)

(The number of lines missing from the beginning and end of this column is unknown.)

El's Two Messengers Journey to Kothar

	[idk.al.ttn.pnm.]	[Then they head out]
	[tk.ḥqkpt.il.klh]	[For great and wide Memphis]
1	*[kptr].ks[u.ṯbth.]*	[—Kaphtor], the thr[one where he sits,]
	[ḥkpt.arṣ.nḥlth]	[Memphis, the land of his heritage—
2–3	*balp.šd.r[bt.kmn.]*	From a thousand acres, ten thou[sand hectares,]
	[lpʿn.kṯr]/hbr.wql.	[At the feet of Kothar] they bow down and fall,
	t[šthḥwy.wkbd.hwt]	They [prostrate themselves and honor him.]

The Messengers Deliver El's Message

4–5	*w.rgmlk[ṯr.whss.]*	And they speak to Ko[thar wa-Hasis,]

	[ṯny.lḥyn]/dḥrš.y[dm.]	[Recite to the Skilled Arti]san[9]:
5–6	*[tḥm.ṯr.il.abk]/*	["Decree of Bull El, your Father,]
	hwt.lṭpn[.ḥtkk]	Word of the Beneficent One, [your Begetter:]
6	[ ]	'...
7	*yh.kṯr.b[ ]*	... Kothar ...
8	*št.lskt.n[ ]*	... prepare to pour (?) ...
9	*ʿdb.bġrt.[ ]*	... prepare in the mountains (?) ...
10	*ḥšk.ʿṣk.ʿ[bṣk.]*	You hasten! You hurry! You r[ush!]
10–12	*[ʿmy.pʿnk.tlsmn]/*	[To me let your feet run,]
	ʿmytwtḥ.i[šdk.]	To me let [your] l[egs] race,
	[tk.ḫršn]/ġr.ks.	[To the mountain,] Mount KS.
12–13	*dm.r[gm.iṯ.ly.wargmk]/*	For a me[ssage I have, and I will tell you,]
	hwt.waṯnyk[.]	A word, and I will recite to you:
13–14	*[rgm.ʿṣ.wlḥšt.abn]/*	[The word of tree and the whisper of stone,]
	tunt.šmm.ʿm[.arṣ.]	The converse of Heaven [to Hell,[10]]
	[thmt.ʿmn.kbkbm]	[Of Deeps to Stars;]
15	*rgm.ltdʿ.nš[m.]*	The word peop[le] do not know,
	[wltbn.hmlt.arṣ]	[Earth's masses not understand.]
16	*at.w.ank.ibġ[yh]*	Come and I will [reveal it]
	[ ]	...[11]'"
17	*wyʿn.kṯr.wḫss[.]*	And Kothar wa-Hasis answers:
17–18	*[lk.lk.ʿnn.ilm]/*	["Go, Go, Divine Servants!]
	atm.bštm.wan[.šnt.]	You, you delay, but I, I [depart.]
18–19	*[kptr]/lrḥq.ilm.*	[Kaphtor] is very far, O Gods,
	ḥkp[t.lrḥq.ilnym]	Memphi[s is very far, O Deities—]

20–21	*ṯn.mṯpdm.tḥt.[ʿnt.arṣ.]*	Two lengths beneath [Earth's springs,]
	[ṯlṯ.mtḥ]/ǵyrm.	[Three, the expanse] of caves."
		Kothar's Journey to El's Abode
21–22	*idk.lyt[n.pnm.]* *[ʿm.lṭpn]/ildpid.* *tkḫrš[n.ǵr.ks]*	Then he h[eads out] [To Beneficent] El the Benign, To the mounta[in, Mount KS.]
23–24	*yglyḏd.i[l.wybu.]*	He enters E[l]'s mountain [and comes]
	[qrš.mlk]/ab.šnm.	[To the tent of the King,] the Father of Years.
24–25	*l[pʿn.il.yhbr.wql]/* *yštḥwy[.wykbdnh]*	A[t El's feet he bows down and falls,] Prostrates himself [and honors him.]
		El's Speech to Kothar
25–26	*[ ]/ṯr.il[.abh]* *[ ]*	Bull El, [his Father, speaks(?)] [… :]
27–28	*ḥšb[htm.tbnn.]* *[ḥš.trmn.hklm]/* *btk.[ ]*	"Hurry, [let a ho]use [be built,] [Hurry, let a palace be erected] In the midst of …
28	*[ ]*	…
29	*bn.[ ]*	Build/son (?) …
30	*a[ ]*	I (?) …

Column V (*CAT* col. II) — Column V (*CAT* col. II)

(The number of lines missing from the beginning and end of this column is unknown.)

		El Gives His Messengers a Message for Anat
	[idk.al.ttn.pnm.] *[tk.inbb]*	"[Then you shall head out] [To INBB].

	[balp.ḫẓr.rbt.bt]	[Across a thousand courts, ten thousand houses (?),]
	[lpʿn.ʿnt.hbr.wql.]	[At the feet of Anat bow down and fall,]
	[tštḥwy.kbd.hyt]	[Prostrate yourselves and honor her.]
	[wrgm.lbtlt.ʿnt]	[And say to Adolescent[12] Anat,]
	[ṯny.lybmt.limm]	[Recite to the In-law of the Peoples:]
	[tḥm.ṯr.il.abk]	['Message of Bull El, your Father,]
	[hwt.lṭpn.ḥtkk]	[Word of the Beneficent One, your Begetter:]
	[qryy.barṣ.mlḥmt]	["Place in the earth war,]
	[št.bʿprm.ddym]	[Set in the dust love;]
	[sk.šlm.lkbd.arṣ]	[Pour peace amid the earth,]
	[arbdd.lkbd.šdm]	[Tranquillity amid the fields.]
1	*[ḥšk.ʿṣk.ʿbṣk.]*	[You hurry! You hasten! You rush!]
1–3	*[ʿ]my.pʿnk/[tlsmn.]*	[T]o me let your feet [run,]
	[ʿmy.twt]ḥ.išdk/	[To me let] your legs [haste]n
	[tk.ḫršn]	[To the mountain ...]"'"
3	*r[ ]ḫmk.wšt*	*(Lines 3–13 are very damaged lines. They may describe the impending construction of a palace for Yamm and perhaps the planned destruction of Baal.)*
4	*[ ]ẓ[ ]rdyk*	
5	*[i]qnim*	
6	*[ ]šu.bqrb*	
7	*[ ].asr*	
8	*[ ]m.ymtm*	
9	*[ ]kiṯl*	
10	*[ ]m[ ]ʿdb.larṣ*	
11	*[ ].špm.ʿdb*	
12	*[ ].tʿtqn*	
13	*[ ]šb.*	

		El's Messengers Go and Speak with Anat
13–14	*id(!)k*[13]*/[lytn.pnm.]* *[tk.]in.bb.*	Then [they head out] [To] INBB.
14–17	*balpḥẓr/[rbt.bt]* *[lpᶜ]n.ᶜnt/[yhbr.wql.]* *[yšt]ḥwyn.wy/[kbdnh.]*	Across a thousand courts, [ten thousand houses ?,] [At the fe]et of Anat [they bow down and fall,] [They prostr]ate themselves and honor her.
17	*[yšu.gh.wy]ṣḥ.*	[And they raise their voices and de]clare:
17–18	*tḥm/[ṯr.il.abk.]* *[hwt.l]ṭpn.ḥtkk*	"Message [of Bull El, your Father,] [Word of the Bene]ficent One, your Begetter:
19–20	*[qryy.barṣ.mlḥ]mt.* *štbᶜp/[rm.ddym.]*	['Place in the earth wa]r, [Set in the du]st love;
20–21	*[sk.šlm].lkbd.arṣ/* *[arbdd.lkbd.š]dm.*	[Pour peace] amid the earth, [Tranquillity amid the fie]lds.
21–22	*ḥšk/[ᶜṣk.ᶜbṣk.]*	You hurry! [You hasten! You rush!]
22–24	*[ᶜmy.pᶜ]nk.tlsmn/* *[ᶜmy.twtḥ.išd]k* *tk.ḫršn/[ ]*	[To me] let your [fe]et run, [To me let] your [legs hurry] To the mountain ...'"
24	*[ ]bdk.spr*	*(Lines 24–25 are untranslatable.)*
25	*[ ]nk*	

8. *CAT* 1.2 — 8. Second Tablet

Column I (*CAT* col. III) — Column I (*CAT* col. III)

(The number of lines missing from the beginning and end of this column is unknown.)

		Kothar's Response to El's Messengers Continued
1	*[ ]n[ ]*	"…
2–3	*[kpt]r.lr[ḥ]q[.ilm]* *[ḥkpt.lrḥq]/[ilnym.]*	[Kapht]or is very f[a]r, [O Gods,] [Memphis so far, O Deities.]
3	*[ṯn.mṯ]pdm.t[ḥt.ʿnt.arṣ.]* *[ṯlṯ.mtḥ.ǵyrm]*	Two lengths beneath Earth's springs, Three, the expanse of caves."
		Kothar Travels and Speaks with El
4	*[idk.]lytn[.]pnm.* *ʿm[.i]l.mbk[.nhrm.]* *[qrb.apq.thmtm]*	[Then] he heads out Towards [E]l at the springs of the [Rivers,] [Amid the streams of the Deeps.]
5	*[ygly.]ḏd(!)*[14]*i[l].wybu* *[.q]rš.mlk[.ab.šnm.]*	[He comes to] the mountain of E[l] and enters The [te]nt of the King, [the Father of Years.][15]
5–6	*[lpʿn.il]/[yhbr.]wyql[.]* *[y]šthḥw[y.]wykb[dnh]*	[At El's feet he bows down] and falls, [He] prostrates himself and honor[s him.]
		El's Messengers (?) Address Kothar
6–7	*[ ]y[ ]/[ ]*	…[16]
7	*kṯr.wḫ[ss.]tbʿ.*	"[Ko]thar wa-Ha[sis], depart!
7–8	*bn[.]bht.ym[.]* *[rm]m.hkl.ṯpṭ.[nhr]/* *[ ]rt.[ ]*	Bui[ld] the house of Yamm, [Erec]t the palace of Judge Rive[r,] [In the hea]rt of (?) …
8	*tbʿ(?).kṯr[wḫss.]*	Depart (?), Kothar [wa-Hasis!]
8–9	*[t(?)]bn.bht[z]blym/* *[t(?)r]mm.hk[l.ṯpṭ].nhr.*	[May you] build the house of [Pr]ince Yamm, [May you er]ect the pala[ce of Judge] River,

	bt.k[ ]p[...]	Amid ...
10	*[ḫš.bh]th.tbn[n.]* *[ḫ]š.trm[mn.hklm.]*	[Hurry, let his ho]use be bui[lt,] [Hur]ry, let a palace be er]ected.
10–11	*[alp.šd.aḫd.]bt/* *[rbt.]kmn.hk[l]*	[A thousand acres may] the house [cover,] [A thousand] hectares the pala[ce."]
11	*[ ]šbš[ ]lm[ ]lšdt [ ]mm*	*(Lines 11–14 are too broken to translate.)*
12	*[ ]bym.ym.y[ ]t.yʿ [ ].ʿṯtr.d[ ]*	
13	*[ ]ḥrḥrtm.w[ ]n. [ ]iš[ ]h[ ]išt*	
14	*[ ]y.yblmm.u[ ]k. yrd[ ]i[ ]n.bn*	

Shapshu and Athtar Converse

15	*[tʿ(?)]nnrt[.]ilm[.]špš.* *tšu.gh.w[tṣḥ.]*	The Divine Lamp, Shapsh, [spea(?)]ks, She raises her voice and [declares:]
15–16	*[šm]ʿ.mʿ[ʿṯ]/[tr.]* *[yṯ]ir.ṯr.il.abk* *l.pn.zbl.ym.* *lpn.[ṯ]pṭ[.nh]r*	"[Hea]r now, [O Athtar:] Bull El, your Father, will take vengeance (?) Before Prince Yamm, Before Judge River.
17	*[ik.a]l.yšmʿk.* *ṯr.[i]l.abk.*	How will he hear you, Bull El, your Father?
17–18	*lysʿ[.a]l[t]ṯ[btk.]* *[lyh]p[k]/[ksa.]mlkk.* *lyṯbr.ḫṭ[.]mṯpṭk.*[17]	Surely he will remove the support of your throne, Surely he will overturn the seat of your kingship, Surely he will break the scepter of your rule."
18	*wyʿn[.ʿṯtr].d[ml(?)]k[ ]*	And Athtar [the kin]g (?) answers:
19	*[ ]ḥ.by.ṯr.il.ab[y].*	"... me, Bull El, my Father,

19–20	*ank.in.bt[.l]y[.km.i]lm*	As for me, I have no house like the gods,
	[.w]ḥẓr[.kbn]/[qd]š	Nor a court like the holy ones;
	lbum.ard.bn[p]šny.	Like a lion I will descend with my desire.
20–21	*trḥṣn.kṯrm[ ]*	Kothar shall wash me
	bb[ht]/[zbl.]ym.	In the h[ouse of Prince] Yamm,
	bhkl.ṯpṭ.nh[r].	In the palace of Judge River.
21–22	*yṯir.ṯr.ilabh*	May Bull El his Father take vengeance (?)
	lpn[z]bly[m]/	Befo[re Pr]ince Ya[mm,]
	[lpn.ṯp]ṭ[.nhr.]	[Before Judge River.]
22	*mlkt.[ ]m.lmlkt.*	Am I king ... or not king (?)?
	wn[.]in.aṯt[.l]k.km	But [y]ou have no wife li[ke the gods ..."]
23	*[ ]zbl.ym.*	... (?) Prince Yamm ...
	y[ ]ṯpṭ.nhr	Judge River ... (?)
24	*[ ]yšlḥn.*	"... he will send me (?) ..."
24	*wyʿnʿṯtr*	Athtar answers: ...
		"..."

Column II (*CAT* col. I) — Column II (*CAT* col. I)

Baal's Messengers Deliver Their Message to Yamm (?)

1	*[...]*	...
2	*[...]*	...
3	*at.ypʿtb[...]*	"You, you rose against ...
4	*aliynbʿl[...]*	Mightiest Baal ...
5	*drk.tk.mšl[...]*	Your dominion (?) ...
6–7	*brišk.aymr[zbl.ym.]*	On your head be Ayyamarri, [Prince Yamm,]

	[bn.ydk]/ṯpṭ.nhr.	[Between your arms (?)], Judge River.
7–8	*yṯb[r.ḥrn.yymm]* *[yṯbr.ḥrn]/rišk.* *ʿṯtrt.[šm.bʿl.qdqdk.*	May [Horon] bre[ak, O Yamm,] [May Horon break] your head, Astarte, the Na[me of Baal, your crown.]
8–9	*[…]/[ ]t.mṭ.* *tpln.bg[bl.šntk …]*	… staff … May you fall at the he[ight of your years.]
10	*[ab.]šnmaṯtm.t[…]* *[…]*	[Father of] Years (?) … two women … …"

Yamm Instructs His Messengers

11	*[m]lakm.ylak.ym.* *[tʿdt.ṯpṭ.nhr]*	Yamm sends messengers, [Judge River, a legation.]
12–13	*[b]ʿlṣʿlṣm* *npr.š[18][mḫ.lbhm?]/* *[ ]ṭ.ṯbr.aphm.*	They rejoice exceedingly, [Their heart] re[joices?,] Their nose breaks (?).
13–14	*tbʿ.ǵlm[m.al.ṯṯb.]* *[idk.pnm]/[a]lttn.* *ʿm.pḫr.mʿd.* *t[k.ǵr.ll.]*	"Go, you boy[s; do not sit still;] [Now] head out For the Assembled Council, T[o Mount LL.]
14–15	*[lpʿn.il]/al.tpl.* *al.tšṭḥwy.pḫr[mʿd.]*	Do not bow down [at El's feet,] Do not prostrate yourselves before the [Assembled] Council.
15–16	*[qmm.amr.am]/r* *ṯny.dʿtkm.*	[Standing, make your spee]ch, Recite your instructions.
16–17	*wrgm.lṯr.a[by.]* *[ṯny.lpḫr]/mʿd.*	So tell Bull [(?) my] Father, [Recite to the] Assembled [Council:]
17	*tḥm.ym.bʿlkm.* *adnkm.ṯp[ṭ.nhr]*	'Decree of Yamm, your Master, Your Lord, Ju[dge River:]

18	*tn.ilm.dtqḥ.* *dtqyn.hmlt.*	"Give up, O Gods, the one you obey, The one you obey, O Multitude;
18–19	*tn.bˁl[.wˁnnh]/* *bn.dgn.arṯm.pḏh.*	Give up Baal [that I may humble him,[19]] The Son of Dagan that I may seize his gold."'"

The Assembly Reacts to the Sight of Yamm's Messengers

19–20	*tbˁ.ġlmm.lyṯb.* *[idk.pnm]/lytn.* *tk.ġr.ll.* *ˁm.pḫ(!)r*[20]*.mˁd.*	The boys depart, they do not sit still; I[mmediately they he]ad To Mount LL. To the Assembled Council
20–21	*ap.ilm.lḥ[m]*[21]*/yṯb.* *bn.qdš.lṯrm.* *bˁl.qm.ˁl.il.*	Meanwhile the gods sit down to fea[st,] The holy ones to dine, Baal waits on El.
21–22	*hlm/ilm.tphhm.* *tphn.mlak.ym.* *tˁdt.ṯpṭ[.nhr]*	There! the gods perceive them, They perceive Yamm's messengers, The legation of Judge [River.]
23–24	*tġly*[22]*.i(!)lm*[23] *rišthm.* *lẓr.brkthm.* *wlkḥṯ[.]/zblhm.*	They lower their heads, On top of their knees, Onto their royal thrones.
24	*bhm.ygˁr bˁl.*	Baal rebukes them:
24–25	*lm.ġltm.ilm.rišt/km* *lẓrbrktkm.* *wln.kḥṯ.zblkm.*	"Why do you lower, O Gods, your heads On top of your knees, Onto your royal thrones?
25–26	*aḥd/ilm.tˁny* *lḥt.mlak.ym.* *tˁdt.ṯpṭ.nh<r>*	Together will the gods answer The tablet of Yamm's messengers, Of the legation of Judge Riv<er>?

27–28	*šu[.]ilm.raštkm.* *lẓr.brktkm.* *lnkḥṯ/zblkm.*	Raise, O Gods, your heads From the tops of your knees, From your royal thrones.
28	*wank.ʿny.mlak.ym.*	And I myself will answer Yamm's messengers,
	tʿdt.ṯpṭ.nhr	The legation of Judge Riv<er>."
29	*tšuilm.rašthm.* *lẓr.brkthm.* *lnkḥṯ[.]zblhm*	The gods raise their heads From the tops of their knees, From their royal thrones.
		The Messengers Deliver Yamm's Message
30	*aḫr.tmġyn.mlak.ym[.]* *tʿdt.ṯpṭ.nhr.*	Then Yamm's messengers arrive, The legation of Judge River.
30–31	*lpʿn.il/[lt]pl.* *ltštḥwy.pḫr.mʿd.*	At El's feet they [do not] bow down, They do not prostrate themselves before the Assembled Council.
31–32	*qmm.a[mr].amr/* *[ṯn]y.dʿthm.*	Standing, they speak a speech, [Reci]te their instructions.
32–33	*išt.ištm.yitmr.* *ḥrb.lṭšt[lš]nhm*[24]	A flame, two flames they appear, Their [ton]gue a sharp sword.
33	*rgm.lṯr.abh.il.*	They tell Bull El, his Father:
33–34	*thm.ym.bʿlkm/* *[adn]km.ṯpṭ.nhr.*	"Word of Yamm, your Lord, Your [Master], Judge River:
34–35	*tn.ilm.dtqh.*	'Give up, O Gods, the One you obey,
	dtqynh/[hml]t.	The One you obey, O Multitude;
35	*tn.bʿl.wʿnnh.*	Give up Baal that I may humble him,[19]
	bn.dgn.arṯm.pḏh	The Son of Dagan, that I may possess his gold.'"

		El and Baal Respond
36	*[ ].ṯr.abh.il[.]*	[And] Bull El, his Father, [answers?[25]:]
36–37	*ʿbdk.bʿl.yymm.* *ʿbdk.bʿl/[nhr]m.* *bn.dgn.a[s]rkm.*	"Your slave is Baal, O Yamm, Your slave is Baal, [O River,] The Son of Dagan, your captive.
37–38	*hw.ybl.argmnk.* *kilm/[ṯʿyk]ybl.* *wbn.qdš.mnḥyk*	He will bring tribute to you, Like the Gods, bring [a gift to you,] Like the Holy Ones, offerings to you."
38–39	*ap.anš.zbl.bʿ[l]/* *[yuḫ]d.byd.mšḫṭ.* *bm.ymn.mḫṣ.* *ǵlmm.yš[ḫṭ(?)]*	Then Prince Baal is shaken: [He seize]s with his hand a striker, In his right hand a slayer, The lads he st[rikes (?).]
40	*[ymnh.ʿn]t.tuḫd.* *šmalh.tuḫd.ʿṯtrt.*	[His right hand A]nat seizes, His left hand Athtart seizes.
40–41	*ik.m[ḫṣt.mlak]/[.ym.]* *[tʿ]dt.ṯpṭ.nhr.]*	"Why did [you st]rike [Yamm's messengers,] [The lega]tion of Judge River?"
41	*[mlak.]mṭḫr.yhb[...]*	The messenger(s?) ... he ...
42	*[ ]mlak.bn.ktpm.* *rgm.bʿlh.w.y[...]*	... the messengers ... Between the shoulders ... his lord's word (?) and ...
43	*[ ].*	
43	*ap.anš.zbl.bʿl.* *šdmt.bg[...]*	Then Prince Baal is shaken. The terraces in ...
44	*[ ]dm.mlak.ym.* *tʿdt.ṯpṭ.nh[r...]*	... Yamm's messengers, The legation of Judge Riv[er.]
45	*[ ].*	...[26]
45–46	*an.rgmt.lym.bʿlkm.* *ad[nkm.ṯpṭ]/[nhr]*	"I myself say to Yamm, your lord, [Your] mast[er, Judge] River,

46	*[ ]hwt.gmr.hd.lw[ ]y[...]*	'[Hear?] the word of the Annihilator Haddu ...
47	*[ ]iyrh[.]thbr[...]*	... you (?) bow down ...
48	*[...]*	...'"

Column III	Column III
(The few remaining wedges preserve only a handful of words.)	*(Based on the few surviving words, it would seem that originally this column may have described a declaration of battle by either Yamm or Baal [or both?] sent via messengers, perhaps as a prelude to their conflict in the following column.)*

	Column IV	Column IV
		The First Conflict between Yamm and Baal (?)
1	*[...]y[ ]ḫtt.mtt[ ]*	... drive out (?) ... die (?) ...
2	*[ ]ḥy[ ]*	... live (?) ...
2–3	*lašṣi.hm.*	... "I will send them out ...
	ap.amr[...]/[...].	If then I dri[ve ...] (?) ...
3–4	*wbym.mnḫlabd.*	And in Yamm will be the sieve of destruction,
	bym.irtm.m[ ]/	And in Yamm will be the breast of de[ath] (?),
	[ṯpṭ].nhr.tlʿm.	[... Judge] River will be ... (?).
4–5	*ṯmḥrbm.its.*	There the sword I will destroy (?).
	anšq/[b]htm.	I will burn the [ho]use (?).
5	*larṣ.ypl.ulny.*	To the earth the noble will fall,
	wl.ʿpr.ʿẓmny/	And to the dust the mighty."
		Astarte (?) Proclaims Baal's Demise
6	*[b]ph.rgm.lyṣa.*	The word has not left his mouth,
	bšpth.hwth.	Nor his speech his lips,

6–7	*wttn.gh.* *yǵr/tḥt.ksi.zbl.ym.*	When she raises her voice: "May he sink beneath Prince Yamm's throne."
		Kothar Speaks to Baal
7	*wʿn.kṯr.wḫss.*	And Kothar wa-Hasis speaks:
7–8	*lrgmt/lk.lzbl.bʿl.* *ṯnt.lrkb.ʿrpt.*	"Indeed, I tell you, Prince Baal, I reiterate, O Cloudrider[27]:
8–9	*ht.ibk/bʿlm.* *ht.ibk.tmḫṣ.* *ht.tṣmtṣrtk*	Now your enemy, Baal, Now smash your enemy, Now vanquish your foe.[28]
10	*tqḥ.mlk.ʿlmk.* *drktdtdrdrk.*	So assume your eternal kingship, Your everlasting dominion."
		Kothar Prepares Two Weapons for Battle Against Yamm
11	*kṯrṣmdm.ynḥt.* *wypʿr.šmthm.*	Kothar fashions the weapons, And he proclaims their names[29]:
11–13	*šmkat/ygrš.* *ygrš.gršym* *gršym.lksih/* *[n]hrlkḥṯdrkth.*	"Your name, yours, is Yagarrish[30]: Yagarrish, drive Yamm, Drive Yamm from his throne, [Na]har from the seat of his dominion.
13–14	*trtqṣ.bdbʿl.* *kmnš/r.buṣbʿth.*	May you leap from Baal's hand, Like a raptor from his fingers.
14–15	*hlm.ktp.zbl.ym.* *bnydm/[ṯp]ṭnhr.*	Strike the torso of Prince Yamm, Between the arms of [Jud]ge River."
15–16	*yrtqṣ.ṣmd.bdbʿl.* *km.nšr/[bu]ṣbʿth.*	The weapon leaps from Baal's hand, Like a raptor from his [fin]gers.
16–17	*ylm.ktp.zblym.* *bn.ydm.ṯpṭ/[nh]r.*	It strikes the torso of Prince Yamm, Between the arms of Judge River.

17–18	*ʿz.ym.lymk.* *ltngṣn[.]pnth.* *lydlp/tmnh.*	Strong is Yamm, he does not sink. His joints do not shake, His form does not collapse.
18	*kṯr.ṣmdm.ynḥt.* *wpʿr.šmthm*	Kothar fashions the weapons, And he proclaims their names:
19–20	*šmk.at.aymr.* *aymr.mr.ym.* *mr.ym/lksih.* *nhrlkḥṯ.drkth.*	"Your name, yours, is Ayyamarri[31]: Ayyamarri, expel Yamm, Expel Yamm from his throne, Nahar from the seat of his dominion.
20–21	*trtqṣ/bdbʿl.* *km.nšrbuṣbʿth.*	Leap from Baal's hand, Like a raptor from his fingers.
21–23	*hlm.qdq/d.zblym.* *bn.ʿnm.ṯpṭ.nhr.* *yprsḥym/wyql.larṣ.*	Strike the head of Prince Yamm, Between the eyes of Judge River. May Yamm sink and fall to the earth."
23–24	*wyrtqṣ.ṣmdbdbʿl/* *[km]nšr.buṣbʿth*	The weapon leaps from Baal's hand, [Like] a raptor from his fingers,
24–25	*ylm.qdqd.zbl/[ym].* *bn.ʿnm.ṯpṭ.nhr.*	It strikes the head of Prince [Yamm,] Between the eyes of Judge River.
25–26	*yprsḥ.ym.yql/larṣ.* *tngṣn.pnth.* *wydlp.tmnh*	Yamm collapses and falls to the earth, His joints shake, And his form collapses.
27	*yqṯbʿl.wyšt.ym.* *ykly.ṯpṭ.nhr*	Baal drags and dismembers (?) Yamm, Destroys Judge River.
		Astarte Rebukes Baal
28	*bšm.tgʿrm.ʿṯtrt.*	By name Astarte rebukes (him):
28–29	*bṯlaliyn.b[ʿl]/* *bṯ.lrkb.ʿrpt.*	"Scatter, O Mighty Ba[al,] Scatter, O Cloudrider.

29–30	*kšbyn.zb[l.ym.]* *[k(?)]/šbyn.ṯpṭ.nhr.*	For our captive is Prin[ce Yamm,] [For (?)] our captive is Judge River."

Baal Acts

30–31	*wyṣa.b[ ]/* *ybṯ.nn.aliyn.bʿl.*	... and he goes out ... Mighty Baal scatters him ...

Two Deities Proclaim Baal's Kingship

31	*w[y/tʿn]*	...and [s/he speaks:]
32	*ym.lmt.* *bʿlm.yml[k]*	"So Yamm is dead! Baal rei[gns! (?)]
33	*ḥm.lšrr.w[ ]*	... so he rules!"
34	*yʿn.*	... he speaks:
34–35	*ym.lmt[ ]* *[bʿl.ymlk]/* *lšrr.*	"So Yamm is dead! [Baal reigns (?),] So he rules!"
35	*wt[ʿn]*	... and she spea[ks (?):]
36	*bʿlm.hmt.[ ]*	"May Baal [reign] ... ,
37	*lšrr.*	So he rules!"
37	*št[ ]*	...
38	*brišh.[ ]*	... on his head ...
39	*ibh.mš[ ]*	... his enemy ...
40	*[b]n.ʿnh[ ]*	... [bet]ween his eyes ...
41	*[ ]*	...

9. *CAT* 1.3 / 9. Third Tablet

Column I

(About 25 lines are missing.)

–2	*[ ]/al.tǵl* *[ ]/prdmn.*	"... do not ... ..."

Lines	Ugaritic	Translation
		Baal's Victory Feast
2–4	*ʿbd.ali[yn]/bʿl.* *sid.zbl.bʿl/arṣ.*	He serves Mightiest Baal, Waits on the Prince, Lord[32] of the Earth.
4–8	*qm.yṯʿr/w.yšlḥmnh/* *ybrd.ṯd.lpnwh*[33] *bḥrb.mlḥt/qṣ.mri.*	He rises, arranges, and offers him food, Slices a breast before him, With a salted knife, a cut of fatling.
8–11	*ndd/yʿšr.wyšqynh/* *ytn.ks.bdh/* *krpn.bklat.ydh*	He stands, serves, and offers him drink, Puts a cup in his hand, A goblet in his two hands:
12–13	*bkrb.ʿẓm.ri* *dn/mt.šmm.*	A large vessel great to behold,[34] A container for mighty men;
13–15	*ks.qdš/ltphnh.aṯt.* *krpn/ltʿn.aṯrt.*	A holy cup women may not see, A goblet Athirat[35] may not eye.
15–17	*alp/kd.yqḥ.bḫmr/* *rbt.ymsk.bmskh*	A thousand pitchers he draws from the wine, Mixes a myriad in his mixture.
18–19	*qm.ybd.wyšr/* *mṣltm.bd.nʿm*	He rises, chants, and sings, With cymbals in the singer's[36] hands.
20–22	*yšr.ǵzr.tb.ql/* *ʿl.bʿl.b.*[37]*ṣrrt/ṣpn.*	With a sweet voice the hero sings, Over[38] Baal on the summit of Sapan.
22–25	*ytmr.bʿl/bnth.* *yʿn.pdry/bt.ar.* *apn.ṭly/b[t.]rb.*	Baal sees his daughters, Eyes Pidray, Daughter of Light, Then Tallay, [Daughter] of Rain.
25–27	*pdr.ydʿ/[ ]t.* *hm.[klt.]/[kny]t.*	Pidru[39] knows[40] … Indeed, the [Nobl]e [Br]ides[41] …
27–28	*w[…]/[…]* *[…]t*	…

(About twelve to fourteen lines are missing.)

Column II		Column II
(About twenty-five lines are missing.)		
		Anat's Preparations for Battle
1	*[...]š[ ]*[42]	...
2–3	*kpr.šbʿ.bnt.* *rḥ.gdm/wanhbm.*	Henna of seven maids, Scent of coriander and murex.
		Anat's Battle
3–5	*klat.ṯǵrt/bht.ʿnt.* *wtqry.ǵlmm/bšt.ǵr*	The gates of Anat's house are closed, She meets youths at the foot of the mountain.[43]
5–7	*whln.ʿnt.tm/tḫṣ.bʿmq.* *tḫtṣb.bn/qrytm*	And look! Anat fights in the valley, Battles between the two towns.
7–8	*tmḫṣ.lim.ḫpy[m]*[44]*/* *tṣmt.adm.ṣat.š[p]š*	She fights the people of the se[a]-shore, Strikes the populace of the su[nr]ise.[45]
9–11	*tḥth.kkdrt.ri[š]/* *ʿlh.kirbym.kp.* *k.qṣm/ǵrmn.kp.mhr.*	Under her, like balls, are hea[ds,] Above her, like locusts, hands, Like locusts, heaps of warrior-hands.
11–13	*ʿtkt/rišt.lbmth.* *šnst/kpt.bḥbšh.*	She fixes heads to her back, Fastens hands to her belt.
13–15	*brkm.tǵl[l]*[46]*/bdm.ḏmr.* *ḫlqm.bmm[ʿ]/mhrm.*	Knee-deep she glea[n]s[47] in warrior-blood, Neck-deep in the gor[e] of soldiers.
15–16	*mṭm.tgrš/šbm.* *bksl.qšth.mdnt*[48]	With a club she drives away captives, With her bow-string, the foe.
		Anat's Cannibalistic Feast
17–18	*whln.ʿnt.lbth.tmǵyn/* *tštql.ilt.lhklh*	And look! Anat goes to her house, The goddess takes herself to her palace,

19–20	*wl.šbʿt.tmtḫṣh.bʿmq/* *tḫtṣb.bn.qrtm.*	Unsated with her fighting in the valley, With battling between the two towns.
20–22	*tṯʿr/ksat.lmhr.* *ṯʿr.ṯlḫnt/lṣbim.* *hdmm.lǵzrm*	She arranges chairs for the soldiery, Arranges tables for hosts, Footstools for heroes.[49]
23–24	*mid.tmtḫṣn.wtʿn/* *tḫtṣb.wthdy.ʿnt*	Hard she fights and looks about, Battling Anat surveys.
25–27	*tǵdd.kbdh.bṣḥq.* *ymlu/lbh.bšmḫt.* *kbd.ʿnt/tšyt.*	Her innards swell with laughter, Her heart fills with joy, Anat's innards with victory.
27–28	*brkm.tǵllbdm/ḏmr.* *ḫlqm.bmmʿ.mhrm*	Knee-deep she gleans in warrior-blood, Neck-deep in the gore of soldiers,
29–30	*ʿd.tšbʿ.tmtḫṣ.bbt/* *tḫtṣb.bn.ṯlḫnm.*	Until sated with fighting in the house, With battling between the tables.
		Anat Cleans Her Palace and Herself
30–32	*ymḫ/[b]bt.dm.ḏmr.* *yṣq.šmn/šlm.bṣʿ.*	Warrior-blood is wiped [from] the house, Oil of peace is poured in a bowl.
32–33	*trḥṣ.ydh.bt/[l]t.ʿnt.* *uṣbʿth.ybmt.limm.*	Adoles[ce]nt Anat washes her hands, The In-law of the Peoples, her fingers.
34–35	*[t]rḥṣ.ydh.bdm.ḏmr/* *[u]ṣbʿth.bmmʿ.mhrm*	[She] washes her hands in warrior-blood,[50] Her [fi]ngers in the gore of the soldiers.
36–37	*[ṯ]ʿr.ksat.lksat.* *ṯlḫnt/[l]ṯlḫn<t>*[51]*.* *hdmm.tṯʿr*[52]*.lhdmm*	She [ar]ranges chairs with chairs, Tables [with] table<s>; Footstools she arranges with footstools.

38–40	*[t]ḥspn.mh.wtrḥṣ/* *[ṭ]l.šmm.šmn.arṣ.* *rbb/[r]kb.ʿrpt.*	[She] draws water and washes [With D]ew of Heaven, Oil of Earth, Showers of the Cloud[r]ider,
40–41	*ṭl.šmm.tskh/* *[rbb.]nskh*[53]*.kbkbm*	Dew which the Heavens pour on her, [Show]ers the Stars pour on her.
Column III		Column III
		Anat's Application of Her Cosmetics (Continued) and Song for Baal
1–2	*ttpp.anhb[m.]* *[dalp.šd]/ẓuh.bym*	She beautifies herself with murex, [Which] comes [from a thousand acres] in the sea.
2–3	*[ ]/[ ]rn.l[ ]*	…
(About twenty lines are missing.)		
4–5	*[tiḫd.knr.bydh]*[54] *[t*[55]*]štrimt/lirth.*	[She takes her harp in hand,] [P]uts the lyre[56] to her breast.
5–6	*tšr*[57]*.l.dd.aliyn/bʿl.* *yd.pdry.bt.ar*	She sings the love of Mightiest Baal, The passion of Pidray, Daughter of Light,
7–8	*ahbt[.]ṭly.bt.rb.* *dd.arṣy/bt.yʿbdr.*	The desire of Tallay, Daughter of Showers, The love of Arsay, Daughter of the Wide World.[58]
		Baal Instructs His Messengers[59]
8–10	*kmġlmm/w.ʿrbn.* *lpʿn.ʿnt.hbr/wql.* *tštḥwy.kbdhyt*	"Like messengers then enter, At the feet of Anat bow down and fall, Prostrate yourselves and honor her.
11–12	*w.rgm.lbtlt.ʿnt/* *ṯny.lybmt*[60]*.limm*	And say to Adolescent Anat, Recite to the In-law of the Peoples:

13–14	*tḥm.aliyn.bʿl.* *hwt/aliy.qrdm.*	'Message of Mightiest Baal, Word of the Mightiest of Warriors:
14–15	*qryy.barṣ/mlḥmt* *št.bʿprm.ddym*	"Place in the earth war,[61] Set in the dust love;
16–17	*sk.*[62]*šlm.lkbd.arṣ/* *arbdd.lkbd.šdm*	Pour peace[63] amid the earth, Tranquillity amid the fields.
18	*ḥšk.ʿṣk.ʿbṣk*	You hasten! You hurry! You rush!
19–20	*ʿmy.pʿnk.tlsmn.* *ʿmy/twtḥ.išdk.*	To me let your feet run, To me let your legs race,
20–22	*dm.rgm/iṯ.ly.w.argmk/* *hwt.w.aṯnyk.*	For a message I have, and I will tell you, A word, and I will recount to you,
22–25	*rgm/ʿṣ.w.lḥšt.abn/* *tant.šmm.ʿm.arṣ/* *thmt.ʿmn.kbkbm*	The word of tree and the whisper of stone, The converse of Heaven with Hell, Of Deeps with Stars,
26–28	*abn.brq.dl.tdʿ.šmm/* *rgmltdʿ.nšm.* *wltbn/hmlt.arṣ.*	I understand the lightning which the Heavens do not know, The word people do not know, And earth's masses not understand.
28–31	*atm.wank/ibǵyh.* *btk.ǵry.il.ṣpn/* *bqdš.bǵr.nḥlty/* *bnʿm.bgbʿ.tliyt*	Come and I will reveal it In the midst of my mountain, Divine Sapan, In the holy mount of my heritage, In the beautiful hill of my might.'"[64]
	——————— ———————	(*Two horizontal lines mark the end of this column.*)

		Baal's Messengers Come to Anat
32–34	*hlm.ʿnt.tph.ilm.* *bh.pʿnm/tṭṭ.* *bʿdn.ksl.tṯbr/* *ʿln.pnh.tdʿ.*	There! Anat perceives the gods; On her, her feet shake, Around, her loins tremble, Above, her face sweats.
34–35	*tġṣ.pnt/kslh.* *anš.dt.ẓrh.*	The joints of her loins convulse, Weak are the ones of her back.[65]
35–36	*tšu/gh.wtṣḥ.*	She raises her voice and declares:
36–38	*ik.mġy.gpn.wugr/* *mn.ib.ypʿ.lbʿl.*[66] *ṣrt/lrkb.ʿrpt.*	"Why have Gapn and Ugar come? What enemy rises against Baal, What foe against the Cloudrider?
38–40	*lmḫšt.mdd/ilym.* *lklt.nhr.il.rbm/* *lištbm.tnn.ištm[ ]h*[68]	Surely I fought Yamm, the Beloved of El, Surely I finished off River, the Great God,[67] Surely I bound Tunnan and destroyed (?) him.
41–42	*mḫšt.btn.ʿqltn/* *šlyṭ.d.šbʿt.rašm*	I fought the Twisty Serpent,[69] The Potentate with Seven Heads.[70]
43–44	*mḫšt.mddil.ar[š]/* *ṣmt.ʿgl.il.ʿtk*	I fought Desi[re], the Beloved of El, I destroyed Rebel, the Calf[71] of El.
45–47	*mḫšt.klbt.ilm.išt/* *klt.bt.il.ḏbb.* *imtḫṣ.ksp/itrṯ.ḫrṣ.*	I fought Fire, the Dog of El, I annihilated Flame, the Daughter of El That I might fight for silver and inherit gold."

Column IV

(This column continues from the previous one.)

Column IV

(This column continues from the previous one.)

47– Column IV 2		**Anat's Response to Baal's Messengers (Continued)**
	ṭrd.bˁl/bmrym.ṣpn.	Has Baal banished from the summit of Sapan[72]
	mšṣṣ.k.ˁ[ ][73]/udnh.	The One who pecks his ear like a bir[d,]
2–3	*gršh.lksi.mlkh/*	Driven him from his royal throne,
	lnḫt.lkḥṯ.drkth	From the resting place, the throne of his dominion?
4	*mnm.ib.ypˁ.lbˁl.*	What enemy has risen against Baal,
	ṣrt.lrkb.ˁrpt	What foe against the Cloud-Rider?"
5	*[ ][74]ˁn.ǵlmm.yˁnyn.*	The youths speak up and answer:
5–6	*lib.ypˁ/lbˁl.*	"No enemy has risen against Baal,
	ṣrt.lrkb.ˁrpt	No foe against the Cloudrider.
7–8	*tḥm.aliyn.bˁl.*	Message of Mightiest Baal,
	hwt.aliy/qrdm.	Word of the Mightiest of Warriors:
8–9	*qryy.barṣ.mlḥmt/*	'Place in the earth war,
	št.bˁprm.ddym.	Set in the du[s]t love;
9–10	*sk.šlm/lkbd.arṣ.*	Pour peace amid the earth,
	arbdd.lkbdšdm	Tranquillity amid the fields.
11	*[ḥ]šk.ˁṣk.ˁbṣk.*	You [ha]sten! You [hu]rry! You rush!
11–12	*ˁmy.pˁnk/[tls]mn*	To me let your feet [ru]n,
	[ˁ]my.twtḥ.išdk	[T]o me let your legs race,
13–14	*[dm.rgm.iṯ.ly.]wargmk.*	[For a message I have,] and I will tell you,
	hwt/[waṯnyk.]	A word, [and I will recount to you,]
14–16	*[rgm.]ˁṣ.wlḫšt/[abn.]*	[The word] of tree and the whisper of [stone,]

	[rgm.ltd]ʿ.nš[m.]	[The word pe]ople [do not know,]
	[wlt]bn/[hmlt.a]rṣ.	[And] ear[th's masses not under]stand.
16–18	*[tant.šmm.ʿm.a]rṣ/*	[The converse of Heaven with He]ll,
	thmt.ʿ[mn.kbkbm.]	Of Deeps [with Stars,]
	[abn.brq]/dl.t[dʿ.š]mm[.]	[I understand the lightning which the Heavens] do not [know,]
18–20	*[atm.wank]/ib[ǵyh.]*	[Come and I] will reve[al it]
	[btk.ǵ]ry.[i]l.ṣpn/	[In the midst of] my moun[tain], Divine Sapan,
	bqd[š.b]ǵ[r.n]ḥlty	In the ho[ly mount of] my herit[age.'"]

Anat Responds

21–22	*wtʿn.btlt.[ʿ]nt.*	And Adolescent [A]nat an[wers,]
	tṯb/[ybmt.]limm.	[The In-law] of the Peoples responds:
22–24	*[a]n[75].aqry/[barṣ].mlḥmt[.]*	"I will place [in the earth] war,
	[aš]t.bʿprm/dd[ym.]	[Se]t in the dust love;
24–25	*ask.[šlm.]lkbd.arṣ/*	I will pour [peace] amid the earth,
	ar[bdd.].lkb[d.š]dm.	Tran[quillity] ami[d the fields.]
25–27	*yšt/[bšmm.[76]]bʿl.mdlh.*	May Baal set his bolts [in the Heavens,]
	ybʿr/[q[77]]rnh.	May [[78]] radiate his ['ho]rns.'[79]
27–29	*aqry/[[80]]barṣ.mlḥmt/*	I will place in the earth war,
	ašt[.b]ʿp[r]m.ddym	Set [in] the du[s]t love.
29–31	*ask/šlm.lkbd.ar(!)ṣ[81].*	I will pour peace amid the earth,
	arbdd/lkbd.š[d]m.	Tranquillity amid the fi[el]ds.
31–32	*ap.mṯn.rgmm/argmn.*	On a second subject I would speak:

32–33	*lk.lk.ʿnn.ilm/* *atm.bštm.wan.šnt*	Go, Go, Divine Servants! You, you delay, but I, I depart.
34–35	*uǵr.lrḫq.ilm.* *inbb/lrḫq.ilnym.*	UǴR is very far, O Gods, INBB is very far, O Deities—
35–36	*ṯn.mṯpdm/tḫt.ʿnt.arṣ.* *ṯlṯ.mtḫ.ǵyrm*	Two lengths beneath Earth's springs, Three, the expanse of caves."
37–38	*idk.lttnpnm.* *ʿm.bʿl/mrym.ṣpn.*	Then she heads out For Baal on the summit of Sapan.
38–40	*balp.šd.rbt.kmn/* *hlk.aḫth.bʿl.yʿn.* *tdrq/ybnt*[82]*.abh.*	From a thousand fields, a myriad of hectares The advance of his sister Baal eyes, The approach of the {In-law} Daughter of his Father.
40–42	*šrḫq.aṯt.lpnnh/* *št.alp.qdmh./* *mria.wtkpnh.*	He removes women from his presence; He places an ox before her,[83] A fatling right before her.
42–43	*tḫspn.mh.wtrḫṣ/* *ṭl.šmm.šmn.arṣ.*	She draws water and washes With Dew of Heaven, Oil of Earth,
43–44	*ṭl.šm[m.ts]kh/* *rbb.nskh.kbkbm.*	Dew the Heave[ns p]our on her, Showers the Stars pour on her.
45–46	*ttpp.anhbm.* *dalp.šd/ẓu[h.bym]*	She beautifies herself with murex, [Which comes from] a thousand acres [in the sea.]

(About fifteen lines are missing, including the following two bicola and the first two words of the bicolon in lines 47–48.)

(After cleaning herself, Anat confers with Baal. He expresses his wish that she ask El for permission for a palace for Baal, because, as the following lines indicate, Baal laments that he has no house.)

	[any.lyṣḥ.ṯr.il.abh]	[In lament he cries to Bull El his Father,]
	[il/mlk.dyknnh]	[To El the King who created him.[84]]
	[yṣḥ.aṯrt/wbnh.]	[He cries to Athirat and her sons,]
	[ilt.wṣbrt.aryh.]	[The goddess and the band of her brood:]
48	*[wn.in.]/bt[.]l[bʿl.km.ilm.]*	["For Baal has no] house [like the gods,]
	[wḥẓr]/kbn[aṯrt.]	[No court] like [Athirat's] sons.
48–49	*[mṯb.il.mẓll]/bnh.*	[The dwelling of El is the shelter of] his children,
	mṯ[b.rbt.aṯrt.ym]	The dw[elling of the Lady Athirat of the Sea,]
50–51	*mṯb.pdr[y.bt.ar.]*	The dwelling of Pidr[ay, Daughter of Light,]
	[mẓll]/ṭly.bt.r[b.]	[The shelter of] Tallay, Daughter of Sho[wers,]
51–53	*[mṯb.arṣy]/bt.yʿbdr[.]*	[The dwelling of Arsay,] Daughter of the Wide World,
	[mṯb.klt]/knyt.	[The dwelling of the] Noble [Brides."]
53	*wtʿn[.btlt.ʿnt]*	And [Adolescent Anat] answers:
54–55	*yṯb.ly.ṯr.il[.aby]/ ytb.ly.wlh.[ ]*	"May Bull E[l, my Father], heed me, May he heed me ... [ ]

Column V | Column V

Anat's Response to Baal (Continued)

1–3	*[i]mṣḥ.nn.kimr.larṣ/*	[... I will] drag him like a lamb to the ground;
	[ašhl]k.šbth.dmm.	[I will ma]ke his gray hair [run] with blood,

	šbt.dqnh/[mmʿm]	The gray hair of his beard [with gore,]
3–4	*[ ]d*[85]*.lytn.bt.lbʿl.kilm/*	Unless he gives Baal a house like the gods',
	[wḥẓ]r.kbn.at̲rt[.]	[And a cou]rt like that of Athirat's sons."
		Anat's Journey to and Audience with El
4–7	*[tdʿṣ.p]ʿn/[wtr.]arṣ.*	[She thrusts her fe]et, [and] the earth [shakes;][86]
	id[k.al.ttn.p]nm/	S[o she hea]ds out
	[ʿm.il].mbk.nhr[m.]	[For E]l at the springs of the River[s,]
	[qr]b.[ap]q/[thm]tm.	[Ami]d [the stream]s of the [Deeps.]
7–8	*tgl.d̲[d.]il[.]wtbu/*	[She comes to] the mountain of E[l] and enters
	[qr]š.m[l]k.ab[.šnm.]	[The te]nt of the Ki[n]g, the Father of [Years.]
8–9	*[ ]r[ ]/[t]bu.d̲dm.*	... [she] enters the mountain,
	[ ]n[ ]n[ ]l[ ][87]	...
10–12	*qlh.yšmʿ.t̲r[.i]l.abh.*	Her voice Bull [E]l, her Father, hears;
	y[ʿn[88]*.]/bšbʿt.ḥ[d]rm.*	E[l] an[sw]ers from the seven r[oo]ms,
	[bt̲]mn[t.ap]/sgrt[89]*.*	[From the] eigh[t en]closures.
12–16	*[...]/*	*(Lines 12-16 are too damaged to interpret.)*
	ʿ.t̲k[...]/	
	ʿln.t̲[...]/	
	lpʿn.ǵl[m]m[...]/	
	mid.a[ ]n[...]	
17–18	*nrt.ilm.špš[.]*	The Divine Lamp, Shapsh,
	[ṣḥr]rt/la.šmm[.]	[Bur]ns the orb[90] of Heaven
	by[d.bn.ilm.m]t[91]	By the po[wer of Divine[92] M]ot.
19	*wtʿn.btlt.ʿn[t.]*	And Adolescent Ana[t] answers:

19–21	*[bnt]bht/k.yilm*	"[In the building] of your house, O El,
	bnt[.]bh[tk].a[l.t]šmḫ/	In the building of your hou[se] do [not re]joice,
	al.tšmḫ.brm[.h]kl[k]	Do not rejoice in the construction of [your pa]lace.
22–23	*al.aḫdhm.by[mn]y[.]*	Or else I will seize it with my [right han]d,
	[ ]/bgdlt.arkty[.]	... by my mighty, long arm.
23–25	*am[ḫṣ]/qdqdk.*	I will sm[ash ...] your crown;
	ašhlk[93]*.šbtk[.dmm]/*	I will make your beard run with blood,
	šbt.dqnk.mmʿm[.]	The gray hair of your beard with gore."
25–27	*yʿny/il.bšbʿt.ḥdrm.*	El answers from the seven rooms,
	bṯmnt/ap.sgrt.	From the eight enclosures:
27–29	*ydʿ[tk.]bt.kan[št]/*	"[I] know [you], O daughter, that [you are fu]rious,
	kin.bilht.ql[ṣ]k.	Among goddesses no sc[or]n is like yours.
	mh.taršn/lbtlt.ʿnt.	What do you desire, O Adolescent Anat?"
29	*wt[ʿ]n.btlt.ʿn[t]*	And Adolescent Anat ans[we]rs:
30–31	*tḥmk.il.ḥkm[.]*	"Your decree, O El, is wisdom,
	ḥkmk/ʿm.ʿlm.	Your wisdom is eternal,
	ḥyt.ḥẓt.tḥmk	A victorious life[94] is your decree.
32–33	*mlkn.aliyn.bʿl.*	Our king is Mightiest Baal,
	ṯpṭn/in.dʿlnh.	Our ruler, with none above him.
33–34	*klnyy.qšh/nbln.*	All of us will bring him a gift,
	klnyy.nbl.ksh	All of us will bring him a cup.
35–36	*any.lyṣḥ.ṯr.il.abh.*	In lament he cries to Bull El, his Father,

il/mlk.dyknnh.	To El, the King who created him.
36–37 *yṣḥ.aṯrt/wbnh.* *ilt.wṣbrt.aryh*[95]	He cries to Athirat and her sons, The goddess and the band of her brood:
38–39 *wn.in.bt[.]lbʿl.km.ilm/* *wḥẓr.kb[n.a]ṯrt.*	'For Baal has no house like the gods, No court like Athirat's so[ns.]
39–41 *mṯb.il/mẓll.b[nh.]* *[m]ṯb.rbt.aṯrt/ym.*	The dwelling of El is the shelter of [his child]ren, [The dw]elling of Lady Athirat of the Sea,
41–42 *mṯb.[pdr]y.bt.ar/* *[mẓll.]ṭly[.bt.]rb*	The dwelling of [Pidr]ay, Daughter of Light, [The shelter of] Tallay, [Daughter of] Showers,
42–44 *mṯb/[arṣy.bt.yʿbdr.]* *mṯb/[klt.knyt...]*	The dwelling of [Arsay, Daughter of the Wide World,] The dwelling of [the Noble Brides.'"]
(About twenty-two lines are missing.)	
Column VI	Column VI
(About ten lines are missing.)	
	Baal Instructs His Messengers
1 *[ ]*	"...
2 *[r]išk* 3 *[ ]bnʿnkm*	... your [h]ead ... ... between your eyes ...
4 *[ ]alp* 5 *[ ]ym.rbt* 6 *[ ]bnhrm*	... a thousand ... ... sea ... a myriad ... in a river ...
7–9 *[ʿ]br.gbl.ʿbr/qʿl.*	[C]ross Byblos, Cross QʿL,[96]

	ʿbr.iḫt/npšmm	Cross to the islands of Heavenly Memphis.
9–11	*šmšr/ldgy.atrt/* *mǵ.lqdš.amrr*	Convey, O Fisher of Athirat, Proceed, O Qudsh wa-Amrar.
12–14	*idk.al.ttn/pnm.* *tk.ḥqkpt*[97]*/il.klh.*	Then you shall head For great and wide Memphis,
14–16	*kptr/ksu.ṯbth.*	To Kaphtor, the throne where he sits,
	ḥkpt/arṣ.nḥlth	Memphis, the land of his heritage.
17–20	*balp.šd.rbt/kmn.*	From across a thousand acres, a myriad of hectares,
	lpʿn.kṯ<r>/hbr.wql.	At the feet of Kothar bow down and fall,
	tštḥ/wy.wkbdhwt	Prostrate yourself and honor him.
21–23	*wrgm.lktr/wḫss.* *ṯny.lh/yn.dḥrš.ydm*	And say to Kothar wa-Hasis, Recite to the Skilled Craftsman:
24–25	*tḥm.al[iyn.bʿl]/* *h[wt.aliy.qrdm]*	'Decree of Migh[tiest Baal,] Wo[rd of the Mightiest of Warriors:]

(About twenty lines are missing.)

(The approximately twenty missing lines supply the rest of Baal's message to Kothar, including Baal's complaint that he has no palace and his request that Kothar produce gifts for Athirat, as well as the beginning of the messengers' speech to Kothar which is continued in the next column.)

10. *CAT* 1.4

10. Fourth Tablet

Column I

Column I

(About twenty lines are missing.)

		The Messengers Convey Baal's Message to Kothar
1	*[ ]*	"' …
2	*[ ]y*	…
3	*[ ]*	…
4–6	*[any.lyṣ]ḥ.ṯr/[il.abh.]*	[In lament he cr]ies to Bull [El, his Father,]
	[i]lmlk[98]/[dyknnh.]	[To E]l, the King [who created him.]
6–8	*[yṣ]ḥ.aṯ/[rt.wbnh.]*	[He cri]es to Athi[rat and her sons,]
	ilt/[wṣbrt.ary]h	The goddess [and the band of] her [brood:]
9–11	*[wn.in.bt.lbˁl/km.ilm.]*	["For Baal has no house like the gods,]
	[wḥẓr/kbn.aṯ]r[t]	[No court like Athirat's sons.]
12–14	*[mṯ]bil.mẓll/bnh.*	The dw[el]ling of El is the shelter of his children,
	mṯb.rbt/aṯrt.ym.	The dwelling of Lady Athirat of the Sea,
14–16	*mṯb/klt.knyt/*	The dwelling of the Noble Brides,
	mṯb.pdry.b<t.>ar	The dwelling of Pidray, Daughter of Light,
17–18	*mẓll.ṭly.btrb/*	The shelter of Tallay, Daughter of Showers,
	mṯb.arṣy.bt.yˁbdr	The dwelling of Arsay, Daughter of the Wide World."
19–20	*ap.mṯn.rgmm/argmk.*	On a second subject I would speak with you:
20–22	*šsknmˁ/mgn.rbt.aṯrtym/*	Produce, please, a gift for Lady Athirat of the Sea,

	mǵẓ.qnyt.ilm	A present for the Creatress of the Gods.'"
		Kothar's Response
23–24	*ḫyn.ˁly.lmpḫm/*	The Skilled One goes up to the bellows,
	bd.ḫss.mṣbṭm	With tongs in the hands of Hasis.
25–28	*yṣq.ksp.yšl/ḫ.ḫrṣ.* *yṣq.ksp/lalpm.* *ḫrṣ.yṣq/m.lrbbt*	He casts silver, he pours gold, He casts silver by the thousands, Gold he casts by the myriads.
29	*yṣq.ḫym.wtbṯḫ/*	He casts a canopy and couch:
30–32	*kt.il.dt.rbtm/* *kt.il.nbt.bksp/* *šmr[g]t.bdm.ḫrṣ/*	A grand dais two myriads-weight, A grand dais coated in silver, Covered with liquid gold.
33–35	*kḫṯ.il.nḫt/bẓr.* *hdm.il(!)*[99]*/dpršа.bbr/*	A grand throne with a seat in gold, A grand footstool overlaid in electrum.
36–37	*nˁl.il.d.qblbl/* *ˁln.yblhm.ḫrṣ*	Grand laced sandals, With gold poured on them.
38–40	*ṯlḫn.il.dmla/mnm.* *dbbm.d/msdt.arṣ*	A grand table filled with figures, Creatures of the Earth's foundations.
41–43	*ṣˁ.il.dqt.kamr/*	A grand bowl with flocks like Amurru's,
	sknt.kḫwt.yman/ *dbh.rumm.lrbbt*	Figured like the beasts of Yaman, With buffalo by the myriads.
	———— ————	*(Two horizontal lines mark the end of this column.)*

Column II		Column II
(About twenty lines are missing.)		
		Athirat at Domestic Chores
1	*[...]*	[ ]
2	*[ ]abn[...]*	... the stone [ ]
3–4	*aḫdt.plkh[.bydh]/* *plk.tʿlt*[100]*.ymnh*	She takes her spindle [in her hand,] A mighty spindle in her right hand.
6–7	*tmtʿ.mdh.bym.*	She conveys her garment in the sea,
	ṯn/npynh.bnhrm/	Her two robes in the rivers,
5	*npynh.mks.bšrh*[101]	Her robes, the covering of her skin.
8–9	*štt.ḫprt.lišt/* *ḫbrṯ.lẓr.pḥmm*	She sets a pot on the fire, A pot on top of the coals.
10–11	*tʿpp.ṯr.il.dpid/*	All the while she is servile before Bull El the Beneficent,
	tǵẓy.bny.bnwt	Deferential to the Creator of Creatures.[102]
		Athirat Receives Baal and Anat
12–14	*bnši.ʿnh.wtphn/* *hlk.bʿl.aṯ{t}rt*[103]*.ktʿn*	When she lifts her eyes, she looks, Athirat sees the advance of Baal,
14–16	*hlk.btlt/ʿnt[.]* *tdrq.ybmt/[limm].*	The advance of Adolescent Anat, The approach of the In-law [of the Peoples.]
16–18	*bh.pʿnm/[ṭṭṭ.]* *[bʿ]dn.ksl/[ṯṯbr.]* *[ʿln.p]nh*[104]*.td[ʿ]*	On her, her feet [shake,] [Aro]und, her loins [tremble,] [Above], her fa[ce sw]eats
19–20	*tǵṣ[.pnt.ks]lh/* *anš.dt.ẓr[h]*	[The joints of] her loi[ns] convulse, Weak are the ones of [her] back.
21	*tšu.gh.wtṣḥ[.]*	She raises her voice and declares:

21–24	*[i]k/mǵy.aliynb[ʿl]/* *ik.mǵyt.b[t]lt/ʿnt*	"Why has Mightiest Ba[al] come? Why has Ado[les]cent Anat come?
24–26	*mḫṣyhm[.m]ḫṣ/bny.* *hm[.mkly.ṣ]brt/aryy[.]*	Would you murder me or [mur]der my sons, Or [destroy the ban]d of my brood?"
26–28	*[ẓl].ksp.[a]ṯrt/ktʿn.* *ẓl.ksp.wn[r]t*[105]*/ḫrṣ.*	[The gleam of] silver [A]thirat eyes, The gleam of silver, [the glint (?) of] gold.
28–29	*šmḫ.rbt.aṯ[rt]/ym.* *gm.lǵlmh.k[tṣḥ]*	Lady Ath[irat] of the Sea rejoices, Aloud to her attendant [she declares:]
30–31	*ʿn.mkṯr.apt[ ]/* *dgy.rbt.aṯr[t.ym]*	"See the skilled work, also … , O Fisher[106] of Lady Athir[at of the Sea.]
32–33	*qḥ.rṯt.bdkt[ ]/* *rbt.ʿl.ydm[ ]*	Take a net in your hand … , A great one in your hands … .
34–36	*bmdd.il.y[m]/* *bymil.d[ ]/* *[n]/hr.il.y[ ]*	In the Beloved of El, Se[a,] In Divine Sea [,] [Ri]ver, the God.
37–38	*aliyn.[bʿl]* *btlt.[ʿnt]*	Mightiest [Baal ,] Adolescent [Anat] …"
39	*mh.k[ ]*	*(Lines 39-48 are too damaged to translate.)*
40	*wat[ ]*	
41	*aṯr[t]*	
42	*bim[ ]*	
43	*bl.l[ ]*	
44	*mlk[ ]*	
45	*[ ]*	
46	*bṭ[ ]*	
47	*gm[ ]*	
48	*y[ ]*	

Column III		Column III
(About twelve lines are missing.)		*(Lines 1-9 are too damaged to translate.)*
1	*[ ]*	
2	*[ ]dn*	
3	*[ ]dd*	
4	*[ ]n.kb*	
5	*[ ]al.yns*	
6	*[ ]ysdk.*	
7	[*]r.dr.dr*	
8	*[ ]yk.wrḫd*	
9	*[ ]yilm.dmlk*	
		Events in the Divine Council are Recounted
10–11	*y[ ]*[107]*.aliyn.bʿl/* *ytʿdd.rkb.ʿrpt*	"Mightiest Baal [answers (?),] The Cloudrider testifies:
12–14	*[ ].ydd.wqlṣn/* *yqm.wywptn* *btk/p[ḫ]r.bn.ilm.*	'... He stood and abased me, He arose and spat on me, Amid the ass[em]bly of the sons of El.[108]
14–16	*štt/p[ ]btlḫny.* *qlt/bks.ištynh*	Dis[grace] I drank from my table, Dishonor I drank from my cup.
17–18	*d(!)m*[109]*.ṯn.dbḥm.šna.bʿl.* *ṯlṯ/rkb.ʿrpt.*	For two feasts Baal hates, Three, the Cloudrider:
18–21	*dbḥ/bṯt.wdbḥ{.wdbḥ}/dnt.* *wdbḥ.tdmm*[110]*/amht.*	A feast of shame, a feast of degradation, And a feast of the lewdness of maidens.[111]
21–22	*kbh.bṯt.ltbṭ/* *kbh.tdmmt.amht*	For there shame is seen, And there is the lewdness of maidens.'"
		Baal and Anat Speak with Athirat
23–24	*aḫr.mǵy .aliyn.bʿl/* *mǵyt.btlt.ʿnt*	Just when Mightiest Baal arrives, Adolescent Anat arrives,

25–26	*tmgnn.rbt[.]aṯrtym/*	They entreat Lady [A]thirat of the Sea,
	tǵẓyn.qnytilm	Beseech the Creatress of the Gods.
27	*wtʿn.rbt.aṯrtym*	And Lady Athirat of the Sea answers:
28–30	*ik.tmgnn.rbt/atrt.ym.*	"Why do you entreat Lady Athirat of the Sea?
	tǵẓyn/qnyt.ilm.	Why do you beseech the Creatress of the Gods?
30–32	*mgntm/ṯr.il.dpid.*	Have you entreated Bull El the Beneficent,
	hm.ǵẓtm/bny.bnwt	Or beseeched the Creator of Creatures?"[112]
32–33	*wtʿn/btlt.ʿnt.*	And Adolescent Anat answers:
33–36	*nmgn/[ ]m[113].rbt.aṯrt.ym/*	"Let us entreat Lady Athirat of the Sea,
	[nǵ]ẓ.qnyt.ilm/	Let us beseech the Creatress of the Gods,
	[ ].nmgn.hwt	[ ] we will entreat him."
37	*[ ].aliyn.bʿl*	Mightiest Baal [… ,]
38	*[ ]rbt.aṯrt.ym*	Lady Athirat of the Sea [… ,]
39	*[ ]btlt.ʿnt*	Adolescent Anat [… .]
40–43	*[ʿdtl]ḥm.tšty/[ilm.]*	[As the gods ea]t, drink,
	[wtp]q.mrǵtm/[ṯd.]	A suckling of [breast is provided,]
	[bḥrb.ml]ḥt.qṣ/[mri.]	[With a sal]ted [knife], a cut of [fatling.]
43–44	*[tšty.]krpnmyn/*	[They drink wine from gob]lets,
	[wbks.ḫrṣ.d]m.ʿṣm	[And from cups of gold, the blood] of trees.
45	*[…]*	*(There is a gap of seven lines (lines 45-*
46	*[…]*	*51). The last two lines are barely pre-*
47	*[…]*	*served and are unintelligible. In these*

48	*[...]*	*nine lines, Athirat's feast provides the setting for Anat and Baal's pleading with the mother of the pantheon to intercede with El in favor of the Cloudrider's palace.)*
49	*[...]*	
50	*[...]*	
51	*[...]*	
52	*[ ]ˁln*	
53	*[ ]ln*	

Column IV		Column IV
(About twelve lines are missing.)		
		Athirat and Her Servant Travel to El
1	*ṯr.[il.ab...]*	...Bull [El ... Father.]
1–2	*[wtˁn.rbt]/aṯr[/t.ym]*	[And Lady] Athir[at of the Sea answers:]
2–4	*[šmˁ.lqdš]/wamr[r.]* *[ldgy.rbt]/aṯrt.ym[.]*	"[Hear, O Qudsh] wa-Amr[ar,] [O Fisher of Lady] Athirat of the Sea:
4–7	*[mdl.ˁr]/ṣmd.pḥl.* *š[t.gpnm.dt]/ksp.* *dt.yrq[.nqbnm]/* *ˁdb.gpn.atnt[y]*[114]	[Tie the donkey], bind the mule; Se[t ropes of] silver, [Bridles] of gold; Prepare the ropes of [my] ass."[115]
8	*yšmˁ.qd<š>.wamr[r]*	Qud<sh> wa-Amrar complies.
9–12	*mdl.ˁr.ṣmd.pḥl/* *št.gpnm.dt.ksp/* *dt.yrq.nqbnm/* *ˁdb.gpn.atnth*	He ties the donkey, binds the mule; He sets ropes of silver, Bridles of gold; He prepares her ass.
13–15	*wyḥbq.qdš.wamrr/* *yštn.aṯrt.lbmt.ˁr/* *lysmsmt.bmt.pḥl*	Qudsh wa-Amrar clasps, Sets Athirat on the back of a donkey, On the beautiful back of a mule,
16–17	*qdš.yuḫdm.šbˁr/* *amrr.kkbkb.*	Qudsh starts to burn,[116] Amrar, like a star.

17–19	*lpnm/aṯr.btlt.ʿnt/* *wbʿl.tbʿ.mrym.ṣpn*	Ahead Adolescent Anat goes, While Baal departs for the summit of Sapan.
20–22	*idk.lttn.pnm/* *ʿm.il.mbk.nhrm/* *qrb.apq.thmtm*	Now she[117] heads out For El at the springs of the Rivers, Amid the streams of the Deeps.
23–24	*tgly.ḏd.il.wtbu/* *qrš.mlk.ab.šnm*	She comes to the mountain of El and enters The tent of the King, the Father of Years.
25–26	*lpʿn.il.thbr.wtql/* *tštḥwy.wtkbdh*	At the feet of El she bows down and falls, Prostrates herself and honors him.
27–28	*hlm.il.kyphnh/* *yprq.lṣb.wyṣḥq/*	There El perceives her, He breaks into a smile and laughs.
29–30	*pʿnh.lhdm.yṯpd.* *wykrkr/uṣbʿth.*	His feet on the footstool he stamps, And twirls his fingers.
		El and Athirat Converse
30	*yšu.gh.wyṣ[ḥ]*	He raises his voices and declares:
31–32	*ik.mǵyt.rbt.aṯr[t.y]m/* *ik.atwt.qnyt.i[lm]*	"Why has Lady Athir[at] of the Sea arrived? Why has the Creatress of the G[ods] come?
33–34	*rǵb.rǵbt.wtǵt[ ]/* *hm.ǵmu.ǵmit.wʿs[ ]*	Are you very hungry, having travel[ed,] Or are you very thirsty, having jour[neyed?]
35–38	*lḥm.hm.štym* *lḥ[m]/bṯlḥnt.lḥm* *št/bkrpnm.yn.* *bk<s>[118].ḫrṣ/dm.ʿṣm.*	Eat or drink: E[at] food from the tables, Drink wine from goblets, From a golden c<up>, the blood of trees.[119]

38–39	*hm.yd.ilmlk/yḫssk.*	Or does the 'hand'[120] of El the King excite you,
	ahbt.ṯr.tʿrrk	The love of the Bull arouse you?"
40	*wtʿn.rbt.aṯrtym*	And Lady Athirat of the Sea answers:
41–43	*tḥmk.il.ḥkm.*	"Your decree, O El, is wise,
	ḥkmt/ʿmʿlm.	You are wise for eternity,
	ḥyt.ḥẓt/tḥmk.	A victorious life is your decree.
43–44	*mlkn.aliy[n.]bʿl/*	Our king is Mightie[st] Baal,
	ṯpṭn.in.dʿlnh	Our ruler, with none above him.
45–46	*klnyn.q[š]h[.]nb[ln]/*	All of us will br[ing] him a gi[ft,]
	klnyn[.nbl.]ksh	All of us [will b]ring him a cup.
47–48	*[an]y[.]lyṣḥ.ṯril.abh/*	[In lament] he cries to Bull El, his Father,
	[i]l.mlk.dyknnh.	To [E]l, the King who created him.
48–50	*yṣḥ/aṯrt.wbnh.*	He cries to Athirat and her sons,
	ilt.wṣbrt/aryh.	The goddess and the band of her brood:
50–51	*wn.in.bt.lbʿl/km.ilm.*	'For Baal has no house like the gods,
	wḥẓr.kbn.aṯrt	No court like Athirat's so[ns,]
52–53	*mṯbil.mẓll.bnh/*	The dwelling of El is the shelter of his children,
	mṯb[.]rbtaṯrt.ym	The dwelling of the Lady Athirat of the Sea,
54–55	*[mṯb.]klt[.]knyt/*	The dwelling of the Noble Brides,
	mṯb.pdry.bt.ar	The dwelling of Pidray, Daughter of Light,
56–57	*mẓll.ṭly[.]bt.rb/*	The shelter of Tallay, Daughter of Showers,

	mṯb.arṣ<y>.btyʿbdr	The dwelling of Arṣ<ay>, Daughter of the Wide World.'"
58	*wyʿnlṭpnildpid*	And Beneficent El the Benign replies:
59–62	*pʿbd.an.ʿnn.aṯrt/*	"So am I a slave, Athirat a slave-girl?
	pʿbd.ank.aḫd.ulṯ/	Am I a slave who handles tools,
	hm.amt.aṯrt.tlbn/lbnt	Or Athirat a servant who molds bricks?"
Column V		Column V
[This column continues from the previous one.]		
62–V 1		**El's Speech to Athirat (Continued)**
	ybn.bt.lbʿl/kmilm.	"Let a house be built for Baal like the gods,
	wḥẓr.kbn.aṯrt	A court, like Athirat's sons."
2	*wtʿn.rbt.aṯrtym*	And Lady Athirat of the Sea answers:
3–5	*rbt.ilm.lḥkmt/*	"You are great, O El, so very wise;
	šbt.dqnk.ltsrk/	The gray hair of your beard instructs you,
	rḫn[ ]t.d[ ].lirtk	[Your] soft b[eard] down to your chest.
6–7	*wnap.ʿdn.mṭrh/bʿl.*	So now may Baal enrich with his rain,
	yʿdn.ʿdn.ṯr(!)t[121].bglṯ	May he enrich with rich water in a downpour.
8–9	*wtn.qlh.bʿrpt/*	And may he give his voice[122] in the clouds,
	šrh.larṣ.brqm	May he flash[123] to the earth lightning.
10–11	*bt.arzm.ykllnh/*	Is it a house of cedar that he would complete,

	hm.bt.lbnt.yᶜmsnh	Or a house of bricks that he would construct?
12	*lyrgm.laliynbᶜl*	Let it be told to Mightiest Baal:
13–14	*ṣḥ.ḥrn.bbht(!)k*[124]/	'Call a caravan into your house,
	ᶜḏbt.bqrb.hklk	Wares amid your palace.
15–17	*tblk.ǵrm.mid.ksp/*	Let the mountains bring you abundant silver,
	gbᶜm.mḥmd.ḥrṣ/	The hills, the choicest gold;
	yblk.udr.ilqṣm	Let the best ore be brought to you.
18–19	*wbn.bht.ksp.wḥrṣ/*	And build the house with silver and gold,
	bht.ṯhrm.iqnim	The house with purest lapis lazuli.'"
		Anat's Delivery of the News To Baal
20–21	*šmḫ.btlt.ᶜnt*	Adolescent Anat rejoices;
	tdᶜṣ/pᶜnm.	She thrusts her feet,
	wtr.arṣ	And the earth shakes.
22–24	*idk.lttn.pnm/*	So she heads out
	ᶜm.bᶜl.mrym.ṣpn/	For Baal on the heights of Sapan,
	balp.šd.rbt.kmn	Across a thousand acres, a myriad of hectares.
25–26	*ṣḥq.btlt.ᶜnt.*	Adolescent Anat laughs,
	tšu/gh.wtṣḥ.	She raises her voice and declares:
26–27	*tbšrbᶜl/*	"Receive the news, O Baal,
	bsrtk.yblt.	Good news is brought to you:
27–29	*ytn/bt.lk.km.aḫk.*	'Let a house be given you like your brothers,
	wḥẓr/km.aryk.	A court, like your kin.
29–31	*ṣḥ.ḥrn/bbhtk.*	Call a caravan into your house,
	ᶜḏbt.bqrb/hklk.	Wares amid your palace.

31–33	*tblk.ǵrm/mid.ksp.* *gbʿm.mḥmd./ḫrṣ.*	Let the mountains bring you abundant silver, The hills, the choicest gold.
33–35	*wbn.bht.ksp/wḫrṣ.* *bht.ṭhrm/iqnim.*	And build the house with silver and gold, The house with purest lapis lazuli.'"

Baal's Preparations for the Building of His Palace

35–37	*šmḫ.aliyn/bʿl.* *ṣḥ.ḫrn.bbhth/* *ʿḏbt.bqrbhklh*	Mightiest Baal rejoices; He calls a caravan into his house, Wares amid his palace.
38–40	*yblnnǵrm.mid.ksp/* *gbʿmm(!)ḥmd*[125]*.ḫrṣ/* *yblnn.udr.ilqṣm*	The mountains bring him abundant silver, The hills, the choicest gold; The best ore is brought to him.
41	*y<l>ak.lkṯr.wḫss*	He <s>ends for Kothar wa-Hasis.
	—————— ——————	—————— ——————
42–43	*wṯblmspr. .* *ktlakn/ǵlmm*	And turn to the point in the text: "When the lads are sent."[126]
	——————	——————
44–46	*aḫr.mǵykṯr.wḫss/* *št.alp.qdmh.* *mra/wtk.pnh.*	Then Kothar wa-Hasis arrives; He[127] sets an ox before him, A fatling right before him.
46–48	*tʿdb.ksu/wyṯṯb.* *lymn.aliyn/bʿl.* *ʿd.lḥm.št[y.ilm]*	A throne is set up and he is seated, At the right hand of Mightiest Baal, As [the gods] eat, drin[k.]
49	*[w]yʿn.al[iyn.bʿl]*	[And] Mighti[est] Baal speaks:
50–52	*[ ]b[ ]/* *[ḥ]š.bhtm.[kṯr]/* *ḥš.rmm.hk[lm]/*	"...[128] Quickly, the house, O Kothar, Quickly erect the palace.
53–55	*ḥš.bhtm.tbn[n]/*	Quickly you must build the house,

	ḥš.trmmn.hk[lm]/ *btk.ṣrrt.ṣpn*	Quickly you must erect the palace, Amid the summit of Sapan.
56–57	*alp.šd.aḫd.bt/* *rbt.kmn.hkl*	A thousand fields may the house cover, A myriad hectares, the palace."
58	*wyᶜn.kṯr.wḫss*	And Kothar wa-Hasis responds:
59–60	*šmᶜ.laliynbᶜl/* *bn.lrkb.ᶜrpt*	"Hear, O Mightiest Baal, Understand, O Cloudrider:
61–62	*bl.ašt.urbt.bbh[tm]/* *ḥln.bqrb.hklm*	Shall I not install a window in the hou[se,] An aperture amid the palace?"
63	*wyᶜn.aliynbᶜl*	And Mightiest Baal answers:
64–65	*al.tšt.urbt.b[bhtm]/* *[ḥl]n.bqrb.hk[lm]*	"You shall not install a window in [the house,] [An aper]ture amid the pala[ce."]

(Perhaps three lines are missing.)

Column VI	Column VI

Kothar and Baal Debate Over Installing A Window

1	*wyᶜn.k[ṯr.wḫs]s*	And Ko[thar wa-Hasis] responds:
2	*ṯṯb.bᶜl.l[hwty]*	"You will return, O Baal, to [my word."]
3	*ṯn.rgm.k[ṯr.]wḫss*	Ko[thar wa-Hasis] speaks again:
4–6	*šmᶜ.mᶜ.lal[i]ynbᶜl/* *bl.ašt.ur[bt.]bbhtm/* *ḥln.bqr[b.hk]lm*[129]	"Hear please, O Migh[tie]st Baal: Shall I not install a win[dow] in the house, An aperture ami[d the pala]ce?"

7	*wʿn.ali[yn]bʿl*	And Migh[tiest] Baal answers:
8–9	*al.tšt.u[rb]t.bbhtm/* *ḫln.bq[rb.h]klm*	"You shall not install a wi[ndo]w in the house, An aperture a[mid the pala]ce.
10–11	*altd[pdr]y.btar/* *[ṭl]y.bt.rb/*	So that [Pidr]ay, Daughter of Light, does not … , [Tall]ay, Daughter of Showers …
12–13	*[m]dd.ilym/* *[ ]qlṣn.* *wpṯm/[ ]*	[The Be]loved of El, Yamm … , … abased, And spat …"[130]
14–15	*wyʿn.kṯr/[wḫss.]*	And Kothar [wa-Hasis] responds:
15	*ṯṯb.bʿl.lhwty*	"You will return, O Baal, to my word."
		The Creation of the Palace
16–17	*[ḥš.]bhth.tbnn/* *[ḥš.]trmm.hklh*	[Quickly] he builds his house, [Quickly] he erects his palace.
18–19	*y[tl]k.llbnn.wʿṣh/* *l[šr]yn.mḥmd.arzh*	He [se]nds to Lebanon for its wood, To [Sir]yon for its choicest cedar.
20–21	*h[n.l]bnn.wʿṣh/* *šryn.mḥmd.arzh*	In[deed (?) to Le]banon for its wood, To Siryon for its choicest cedar.
22–23	*tšt[.]išt.bbhtm/* *nb[l]at.bhklm*	A fire is set in the house, A f[l]ame in the palace.
24–26	*hn[.]ym.wṯn.* *tikl/išt[.]bhtm* *nblat/bhk[l]m.*	There! For a day and a second, A fire burns[131] in the house, A flame in the palace.
26–28	*ṯlṯ.r(!)bʿ[132]ym/* *tikl[.i]št.bhtm/* *nbla[t.]bhklm*	For a third and a fourth, [A f]ire burns in the house, A flame in the palace.
29–31	*ḫmš.ṯ[d]ṯ.ym.*	For a fifth and a si[x]th,

	tikl/išt.[b]bhtm.	A fire burns [in] the house,
	nblat/b[qrb.hk]lm.	A flame a[mid the pa]lace.
31–33	*mk/bšb[ᶜ.]y[mm].*	Then on the seventh d[ay,]
	td.išt/bbhtm.	The fire leaves the house,
	n[bl]at.bhklm	The f[lam]e, the palace.
34–35	*sb.ksp.lrqm.*	The silver had turned to plates,
	ḫrṣ/nsb.llbnt.	The gold had turned to bricks.
35–36	*šmḫ/aliyn.bᶜl.*	Mightiest Baal rejoices:
36–38	*<b>hty.bnt/dt.ksp.*	"My house I have built of silver,
	hkly[.]dtm/ḫrṣ.	My palace of gold."

Baal Prepares a Divine Banquet

38–40	*ᶜdbt.bht[h.bᶜ]l/yᶜdb.*	[Baa]l makes arrangements for [his] house,
	hd.ᶜdb[.ᶜd]bt/hklh.	Hadd makes [arrange]ments for his palace.[133]
40–43	*ṭbḫ.alpm[.ap]/ṣin.*	He slaughters large stock [as well as] small:
	šql.ṯrm[.w]m/ria.il[134].	He fells bulls [and] fatling rams,
	ᶜglm.d[t]/šnt.	Year-old calves,
	imr.qmṣ.l[l]im	Sheep by the flock, and k[i]ds.
44–46	*ṣḥ.aḫh.bbhth.*	He invites his brothers into his house,
	aryh/bqrbhklh.	His kinsmen amid his palace;
	ṣḥ/šbᶜm.bn.aṯrt	He invites the seventy sons of Athirat.[135]
47–48	*špqilm.krm*	He provides the gods with rams,
	y/špq.ilht.ḫprt/	Provides the goddesses with ewes.
49–50	*špq.ilm.alpm.*	He provides the gods with bulls,
	y/špq.ilht.arḫt/	Provides the goddesses with cows.
51–52	*špq.ilm.kḥṯm.*	He provides the gods with thrones,

	y[136]*/špq.ilht.ksat/*	Provides the goddesses with chairs.
53–54	*špq.ilm.rḥbtyn/*	He provides the gods with jars of wine,
	špq.ilht.dkrt[.yn][137]*/*	Provides the goddesses with cruets [of wine.]
55–58	*ʿd.lḥm.šty.ilm/* *wpqmrǵṯm.ṯd/* *bḥrb.mlḥt.qṣ[.mr]/i.*	As the gods eat, drink, A suckling of breast is provided, With a salted knife, a cut of [fat]ling.
58–59	*tšty.krp[nm.y]n/* *[bk]s.ḫrṣ.d[m.ʿṣm]/*	They drink [wi]ne from gob[lets,] [From] gold [cu]ps, the blo[od of trees.]
60	*[ ]n*	*(Lines 60-64 are unintelligible.)*
61	*[ ]t*	
62	*[ ]ṯ*	
63	*[ ]n*	
64	*[ ]*	

(About one line is missing.)

Column VII		Column VII
		(There may be a lacuna of one line. The import of lines 1-6 is unclear; perhaps Baal deals another defeat to Yamm.)
1	*[i]qni[m ...]*	... lapis la[zuli] ...
2	*[ ]aliyn.bʿl*	... Mightiest Baal ...
3–4	*[ ]k.mddil/y[m]*	... Beloved of El, Ya[mm] ...
4–5	*[ ]lṯr.qdqdh/il*	... Bull ... his crown ... El
5–6	*[ ]ḥqbǵr/km.y[*	... in the mountain ...
6	*[ ]ilm.bṣpn*	... gods on Sapan (?).

Baal's Victory Tour

7–8	*ʿb(!)r*[138]*.l[ʿr].ʿrm/* *ṯb.lpd[r.p]drm/*	He crosses from [city] to city, He tours from to[wn] to town.

9–10	*ṯṯ.lṯṯm.aḫd.ˁr/* *šbˁm.šbˁ.pdr/*	Sixty-six cities he seizes, Seventy-seven towns.
11–14	*ṯmnym.bˁl.[ ]/* *tšˁm.bˁl.mr[ ]/* *b[ ]b[139]bˁl.bqr[b]/bt.*	Eighty Baal ... Ninety Baal ... Baal is enthroned (?) amid the house.
		Baal Reverses His Decision
14–15	*wyˁn.aliyn/bˁl[.]*	And Mightiest Baal speaks:
15–16	*aštm.kṯrbn/ym.* *kṯr.bnm.ˁdt*	"I will install, O Kothar, Son of Sea, Kothar, Son of the Confluence:
17–19	*ypṯḥ.ḥln.bbhtm/* *urbt.bqrb.[h]kl/m*	Let an aperture be opened in the house, A window amid the palace.
19–20	*wy[p]th.bdqt.ˁrpt/* *ˁlh[wt].kṯr.wḫss*	So let a break in the clouds be [op]ened, According to the word of Kothar wa-Hasis."
21–22	*ṣḥq.kṯr.wḫss/* *yšu[.]gh[.]wyṣḥ*	Kothar wa-Hasis laughs, He raises his voice and declares:
23–25	*lrgmt.lk.lali/yn.bˁl.* *ṯṯbn.bˁl/lhwty[.]*	"I truly told you, O Mightiest Baal: 'You will return to my word.'"
		The Window Is Installed
25–27	*ypṯḥ.ḥ/ln.bbhtm.* *urbt/bqrb.hk[lm.]*	He opens an aperture in the house, A window amid the palace.[140]
27–29	*[yp]tḥ/bˁl.bdqt[.ˁrp]t/* *qlh.qdš[.]b[ˁl.y]tn*	Baal opens a break in the clouds, Baal gives vent to his holy voice.
30–31	*yṯny.bˁl.ṣ[at (?).š(?)]pth/* *qlh.q[dš (?).t(?)]r.arṣ*	Baal recites the is[sue of (?)] his [li(?)]ps, His ho[ly (?)] voice, the earth [sha(?)]kes,
32–33	*[...]*	...

	[...]/r[ ]q[...]	...
33–35	*[...]/qdmym* *bmt.a[rṣ]/tṭṭn.*	... The high places of the Ear[th] shake.
35–37	*ib.bʿl.tiḫd/yʿrm.* *šnu.hd.gpt/ǵr.*	The enemies of Baal take to the woods, The haters of Hadd to the mountain-sides.
37–38	*wyʿn.aliyn/bʿl.*	And Mightiest Baal speaks:
38–39	*ib.hd{t}.lm.tḫš/* *lm.tḫš.nṯq.dmrn*	"O Enemies of Hadd, why do you quake? Why quake, O Weapon-wielders of the Warrior[141]?"
40–41	*ʿn.bʿl.qdm* *ydh/ktǵḏ.* *arz.bymnh*	Baal eyes the East; His hand indeed shakes, With a cedar in his right hand.[142]
42	*bkm.yṯb.bʿl.lbhth*	So Baal is enthroned in his house:
43–44	*umlk.ublmlk/* *arṣ.drkt[143]yštkn*	"Will either king or commoner Establish a land of dominion?
45–47	*dll.al.ilak.lbn/ilm.mt.* *ʿddlydd/il.ǵzr.*	So I will send a legate to Divine Mot, An envoy to El's Beloved, the Hero,
47–49	*yqra.mt/bnpšh.* *ystrnydd/bgngnh*	That he may call Mot with his throat,[144] Instruct the Beloved with his insides.
49–52	*aḫdy.dym/lk.ʿl.ilm.* *l[145]ymru/ilm.wnšm.* *dyšb/[ʿ].hmlt.arṣ.*	I myself am the one who reigns over the gods, Indeed orders for[146] gods and men, Who satis[fies] the multitudes of the Earth."

52–53	*gm.lǵ/[l]mh.bʿl.kyṣḥ*[147].	Aloud to his l[a]ds Baal declares:
53–56	*ʿn/[gpn].wugr.* *b<n.>ǵlmt/[ʿmm.]ym.* *bn.ẓlmt.r/[mt.prʿ]t[.]*	"See, [Gapn] and Ugar, Sons of the Lass, Kinsmen of Sea (?), Sons of … , Exalted First-Born (?).[148]
56–57	*ibrmnt/[ṣḥrrm.]* *[ḥbl .]ʿrpt*	… …
58	*[tḥt.mʿṣrm.]ḥt*	*(Lines 56-60 are poorly preserved and their meaning is very unclear. The approximately seven lines missing from the end of this column presumably continue Baal's instructions to the messengers which they are to deliver to Mot. The exchange of messages between Baal and Mot continues in the following column.)*
59	*[ ]m*	
60	*[ ]h*	
(About seven lines are missing.)		

Column VIII

Column VIII

Baal Sends Messengers to Proclaim His Kingship to Mot

1–4	*idk.al.ttn.pnm/* *ʿm.ǵr.trǵzz/* *ʿm.ǵr.ṯrmg/* *ʿm.tlm.ǵṣr.arṣ*	"Then you shall head out To Mount TRGZZ, To Mount THRMG, The two hills at Earth's edge.
5–6	*ša.ǵr.ʿl.ydm/* *ḫlb.lẓr.rḥtm*	Lift the mountain on your hands, The hill on top of your palms.
7–9	*wrd.btḫpṯt/arṣ.* *tspr.by/rdm.arṣ*	And descend to Hell, the House of "Freedom,"[149] Be counted among the descendants to Hell.
10–12	*idk.al.ttn/pnm.* *<ʿm.bn.ilm.mt.>* *tk.qrth/hmry.*	Then you shall head out <For Divine Mot,> At his town, the Pit,
12–14	*mk.ksu/ṯbth.*	Low, the throne where he sits,

	ḫḫ.{.}arṣ/nḥlth.	Filth, the land of his heritage.
14–20	*wnǵr/ʿnn.ilm.* *al/tqrb.lbn.ilm/mt.* *al.yʿdbkm/kimr.bph/* *klli.bṯbrn/qnh.tḫtan*	But take care, divine servants: Do not get too close to Divine Mot, Do not let him take you like a lamb in his mouth, Like a kid crushed in the chasm of his throat.
21–24	*nrt.ilm.špš/* *ṣḥrrt.la/šmm.* *byd.md/d.ilm.mt.*	The Divine Lamp, Shapsh, Burns the orb of Heaven, By the power of Divine Mot.
24–29	*ba/lp.šd.rbt.k/mn.* *lpʿn.mt/hbr.wql/* *tštḥwy.wk/bdhwt.*	From across a thousand fields, a myriad of hectares, At the feet of Mot bow down and fall, Prostrate yourselves and honor him.
29–32	*wrgm/lbn.ilm.mt/* *ṯny.lydd/il.ǵzr.*	And say to Divine Mot, Recite to El's Beloved, the Hero:
32–35	*tḥm/aliyn.bʿl/* *[hw]t.aliy.q/[rdm.]*	'Decree of Mightiest Baal, [Wor]d of the Mightiest of Wa[rriors:]
35–37	*bhty.bnt/[dt.ksp.]* *[dtm]/[ḫrṣ.hk]ly*	My house I have built [of silver,] [Of gold, my pa]lace ... '"
38	*[ ]aḫy*	*(Lines 38-48 are too broken to translate, and another sixteen lines are missing. These twenty-seven lines presumably complete Baal's proclamation of his kingship to Mot and begin Mot's response to Baal's messengers, here reconstructed on the basis of the same speech delivered to the storm god in the next column.)*
39	*[ ]aḫy*	
40	*[ ]y*	
41	*[ ]h*	
42	*[ ].ṣḥt*	
43	*[ ]t*	
44	*[ ]ilm*	
45	*[ ]u.yd*	
46	*[ ]k*	
47	*[gpn.]wugr*	

____

__________[150]

48 *[ ]*

(About sixteen lines are missing.)

Mot's Invitation to Baal as His Guest and Main Course

[tḫm.bn.ilm.mt.]	["Message of Divine Mot,]
[hwt.ydd.il.ǵzr.]	[Word of El's Beloved, the Hero:]
[pnpš.npš.lbim.thw]	['Is my appetite[151] the appetite of the lion in the wild,]
[hm.brlt.anḫr.bym.]	[Or the desire of the dolphin in the sea?]
[hm.brky.tkšd.rumm.]	[Or does it go to a pool like a buffalo,[152]]
[ʿn.kd̲d.aylt.]	[Or travel to a spring like a hind,[153]]
[hm.imt.npš.blt.ḥmr.]	[Or, truly, does my appetite consume like an ass?]
[pimt.bklat.ydy.ilḥm.]	[So will I truly eat with both my hands,]
[hm.šbʿ.ydty.bṣʿ.]	[Or my portions amount to seven bowls' worth,]
[hm.ks.ymsk.nhr.]	[Or my cup contain a whole river?]
[kn.ṣḥn.bʿl.ʿm.aḫy.]	[So invite me, O Baal, with my brothers,]
[qran.hd.ʿm.aryy]	[Summon me, O Hadd, with my kinsmen,]
[wlḥmm.ʿm.aḫy.lḥm]	[To eat food with my brothers,]
[wštm.ʿm.aryy.yn]	[And drink wine with my kinsmen.]
[pnšt.bʿl.ṭʿn.iṭʿnk]	[So let us drink, O Baal, that I may pierce you,]

	[m k.]	[…]
	(The following colophon is written on the left-hand edge of the tablet:)	*(The edge of the tablet has the following colophon:)*
	[spr.ilmlk.ṯʿ]y.nqmd.mlk.ugrt[154]	[The scribe is Ilimalku, the Tha]ite[155] of Niqmaddu, King of Ugarit.

	11. *KTU* 1.5	11. Fifth Tablet
	Column I	Column I
		Mot's Message to His Messengers (Continued)
1–4	*ktmḫṣ.ltn.bṯn.brḥ/* *tkly.bṯn.ʿqltn.[ ]/* *šlyt.d.šbʿt.rašm/* *tṯkḥ.ttrp.šmm.*	"When you killed Litan, the Fleeing Serpent,[156] Annihilated the Twisty Serpent, The Potentate with Seven Heads, The heavens grew hot, they withered.
4–6	*krs/ipdk.ank./* *ispi.uṯm/ḏrqm.amtm.*	But let me tear you to pieces, Let me eat flanks, innards, forearms.
6–8	*lyrt/bnpš.bnilm.mt.* *bmh/mrt.ydd.il.ǵzr*	Surely you will descend into Divine Mot's throat, Into the gullet of El's Beloved, the Hero."[157]
		Mot's Invitation Delivered to Baal
9–11	*tbʿ.wl.yṯbilm.* *idk/lytn.pnm.* *ʿm.bʿl/mrym.ṣpn.*	The gods depart, they do not sit still; So they head out To Baal on the summit of Sapan.
11–12	*wyʿn/gpn.wugr.*	And Gapn and Ugar speak:
12–14	*tḥm.bnilm/mt.*	"Message of Divine Mot,

	hwt.ydd.{bn.}[158]*il/ǵzr*	Word of El's Beloved {son}, the Hero:
14–16	*pnp{.}š.npš.lbim/thw.*	'Is my appetite the appetite of the lion in the wild,
	hm.brlt.anḫr/bym.	Or the desire of the dolphin in the sea?
16–19	*hm.brky.tkšd/rumm.*	Or does it go to a pool like a buffalo,
	ᶜn.kḏd.aylt/	Or travel to a spring like a hind,
	hm.imt.{imt[159]*.}npš .blt/ḥmr.*	Or, truly, does my appetite consume like an ass?
19–22	*pimt.bkl<a>t/ydy.ilḥm.*	So will I truly eat with both my hands,
	hm.šbᶜ/ydty[.]bṣᶜ.	Or my portions amount to seven bowls' worth,
	hm.ks.ymsk/nhr[.]	Or my cup contain a whole river?
22–23	*k[n].ṣḥn[.]bᶜl.ᶜm/aḫy[.]*	S[o] invite me, O Baal, with my brothers,
	qran.hd.ᶜm.aryy	Summon me, O Hadd, with my kinsmen,
24–25	*wlḥmmᶜm.aḫy.lḥm/*	To eat food with my brothers,
	wštm.ᶜm.a[r]y<y.y>[160]*n*	And drink wine with my kins-[men.]
26–27	*pnšt.bᶜl.[t]ᶜn.iṭᶜnk/*	So let us drink, O Baal, that I may pierce you,
	[ ]k.	[… .]
27–31	*ktmḫṣ/[ltn.btn.br]ḥ.*	When you killed [Litan, the Fl]eeing [Serpent,]
	tkly/[btn.ᶜqltn.]	Annihilated [the Twisty Serpent,]
	šlyṭ/[d.šbᶜt.rašm].	The Potentate [with Seven Heads,]

	tṯkḥ/[ttrp.šmm.]	[The heavens] grew hot, [they withered.]
31–33	*[krs.ipd]k/[ank.]* *[ispi.uṭm/ḏrqm.amtm.]*	[So let me tear] you [to pieces,] [Let me eat flanks, innards, forearms.]
33–35	*[lyrt.bnpš/bn.ilm.mt.]* *[bmhmrt/ydd.il.ǵzr...]*	[Surely you will descend into Divine Mot's throat,] [Into the gullet of El's Beloved, the Hero.'"]

(About thirty lines are missing.)

Column II — Column II

(About twelve lines are missing.)

1	*[ ]*	...

Mot's Cosmic Appetite To Devour Baal

2–3	*[špt.la]rṣ.špt.lšmm/* *[l]šn.lkbkbm.*	[One lip to He]ll, one lip to Heaven, [a to]ngue to the Stars.[161]
3–6	*yʿrb/[b]ʿl.bkbdh.* *bphyrd/kḥrr.zt.* *ybl.arṣ.wpr/ʿṣm.*	[Ba]al will enter his innards, Into his mouth he will descend like a dried olive,[162] Produce of the earth, and fruit of the trees.

Baal Announces His Surrender

6–7	*yraun.aliyn.bʿl/* *ṯtʿ.nn.rkb.ʿrpt*	Mightiest Baal is afraid, The Cloudrider is scared:
8–9	*tbʿ.rgm.lbn.ilm.mt/* *ṯny.lydd.ilǵzr*	"Go, say to Divine Mot, Recite to El's Beloved, the Hero:
10–11	*tḥm.aliyn.bʿl.*	'Decree of Mightiest Baal,

	hwt.aliy/qrdm.	Word of the Mightiest of Warriors:
11–12	*bhṯ.lbn.ilmmt/* *ʿbdk.an.wdʿlmk*	Greetings, O Divine Mot: Your servant I am, and yours forever.'"
13–15	*tbʿ.wl.yṯb.ilm* *idk/lytn.pn<m>.* *ʿm.bn.ilm.mt/* *tk.qrth.hmry.*	The gods depart, they do not sit still; So they head out For Divine Mot, To his town, the Pit,
15–16	*mk.ksu/ṯbt<h>.* *ḫḫ.arṣ.nḥlth.*	Low, the throne where he sits, Filth, the land of his heritage.
16–17	*tša/ghm.wtṣḥ.*	They raise their voices and declare:
17–18	*tḥm.aliyn/{bn.}bʿl.* *hwt.aliy.qrdm*	"Decree of Mightiest {son of} Baal, Word of the Mightiest of Warriors:
19–20	*bhṯ.lbn.ilm.mt.* *ʿbdk.an/wdʿlmk.*	'Greetings, O Divine Mot: Your servant I am, and yours forever.'"
20–21	*šmḫ.bnilm.mt/* *[yšu]gh.wyṣḥ*[163].	Divine Mot rejoices, [He raises] his voice and declares:
21–23	*ik.y{.}ṣḥn/[bʿl.ʿm.aḫy].* *yqrun[.]hd/[ʿm.aryy.]*	"Why does [Baal] invite me [with my brothers,] Why does Hadd call me [with my kinsmen,]
23–24	*[lḥm.ʿm.aḫy.(?)a]p.mlḥmy/* *[wštm.ʿm.aryy.yny (?)]*	[To eat] my food [with my brothers (?)] as well, [And drink my wine with my kinsmen (?)?"]
	]lt.qẓb	
25	*[ ].šmḫy*	*(The very broken lines 24-27 may continue*
26	*[ ]tbʿ*	*Mot's speech.)*
27	*[ ]*	

(About twenty-five lines are missing.)

	Column III	Column III
	(About ten lines are missing.)	*(The extant part of the column is missing its right-hand side.)*
1	*[ ]m[…]*	[ ]
2	*[ ]bt.ṯbt.[…]*	[ ] … the dwelling …
3	*rbt.ṯbt.ḥš[…]*	Great … the dwelling …
4	*y.arṣ.ḥšn[…]*	… the earth …
5	*tʿtd.tkl.[…]*	…
6	*tkn.lbn[…]*	… will be to [ ] son …
7	*dt.lbnk[…]*	which … to your son (?) …
8	*dk.k.kbkb[…]*	… like the stars …
		Baal Offers Food to Mot (?)
9	*dm.mt.aṣḥ[…]*	"Then to Mot I will call[…]
10	*ydd.bqr[b…]*	The Beloved ami[d …]
11	*al.ašt.b[…]*	Truly I will set … […]
12	*ahpkk.l[…]*	I will replace you … […]
13	*ṯmm.wlk[…]*	There and go[…]
14	*wlk.ilm[…]*	And go, O Gods,[…]
15	*nʿm.ilm.[…]*	O gracious gods[…]
16	*šgr.mu[d…]*	SHGR[164] … mu[ch …]
17	*šgr.mud[…]*	SHGR … much[…]
18	*dm.mt.aṣ[ḥ…]*	Truly to Mot I will ca[ll … ,]
19	*yd<d>.bqrb[…]*	The Belov<ed> ami[d …]
20	*wlk.ilm.[…]*	And go, O Gods[…]
21	*wrgm.l[…]*	And say to [Mot … :]
22	*bmud.ṣin[…]*	With much sheep[…]
23	*mud.ṣink[…]*	Much sheep[…
24	*iṯm.mu{i}[d…]*	ITHM … […]
25	*dm.mt.aṣ[ḥ…]*	So to Mot I will cal[l …]
26	*ydd.bqr[b…]*	The Beloved ami[d …]

27	*ṯmm.wlk.[...]*	There and go[...]
28	*[ ]ṯ.lk[...]*	... go[...]
29	*[ ]kṯ.i[...]*	...
30	*[...]*	..."

(About twenty lines are missing.)

Column IV		Column IV
(About twenty lines are missing.)		*(Like the previous column this one is missing its right-hand side. Lines 1-4 are too difficult to translate.)*
1	*[ ].šn[...]*	
2	*wlṭlb.[...]*	
3	*mit.rḥ[...]*	
4	*tṭlb.a[...]*	
		Baal's Visit in the Divine Council
5	*yšu gh[.wyṣḥ ...]*	And he[165] raises his voice [and declares:]
6	*i.ap.bʿ[l...]*	"Where then is Baa[l ...]?[166]
7	*i.hd.d[...]*	Where is Hadd ... [... ?"]
8	*ynpʿ.bʿ[l...]*	Baa[l] arises[... ,]
9	*bṯmnt.[...]*[167]	With eight[...]
10	*yqrb.[...]*	He approaches[...]
11	*lḥm.m[...]*	Food[...]
12	*[ʿ]d.lḥm[.šty.ilm]*	[A]s [the gods] eat, [drink,]
13	*wpqmr[ǵṯm.ṯd]*	A suck[ling of breast is provided,]
14	*bḥrb.[mlḥt.qṣ.mri]*	With a [salted] knife, [a cut of fatling.]
15	*šty.kr[pnm.yn]*	They drink wine [from a goblet,]
16	*bksḥr[ṣ.dm.ʿṣm]*	From go[ld] cups, [the blood of trees.]
17	*ks.ksp[...]*	Cups of silver[...]
18	*krpn.[...]*	Goblets[...]

19	*wtṯn[...]*	And they ... [...]
20	*tʿl.tr[...]*	... new wine (?)[...]
21	*bt.il.li[...]*	The house of El ... [...]
22	*ʿl.ḥbš.[...]*	... [...]
23	*mn.lik.[...]*	Who sent (?)[...]
24	*lik.tl[...]*	Sent ... [...]
25	*tʿddn[...]*	... [...]
26	*niṣ.p[...]*	Reviles ...

(About eleven lines are missing.)

Column V — Column V

(About twenty-five lines are missing.)

1	*[ ]aliyn*	[...] Mightiest [Baal ...]
2	*[bʿl]ip.dprk*	...
3	*[ ]mnk.ššrt*	...

Baal Commanded to Descend to the Underworld

4–6	*[ ]t.npš.ʿgl/[ ]nk.* *ašt.n.bḫrt/ilm.arṣ.*	"[...]life ... calf[...] I will set him in a great pit[168] in the Earth.[169]
6–8	*wat.qḥ/ʿrptk.* *rḥk.mdlk/mṭrtk.*	And you, take your clouds, Your winds, your bolts, your rains;
8–9	*ʿmk.šbʿt/ǵlmk.* *ṯmn.ḫnzrk*	With you, your seven boys, Your eight attendants.
10–11	*ʿmk.pdry.bt.ar/* *ʿmk.{t}ṭly.bt.rb.*	With you, Pidray, Daughter of Light, With you, Tallay, Daughter of Rain.
11–13	*idk/pnk.alttn.* *tkǵr/knkny.*	Then you shall head out For Mount KNKNY.

13–14	*ša.ǵrʿlydm/*	Lift the mountain on your hands,
	ḫlb.lẓr.rḥtm	The hill on top of your palms.
14–17	*wrd/btḫpṯt.arṣ*	And descend to Hell, the House of "Freedom,"
	tsprby/rdm.arṣ.	Be counted among the inmates of Hell;
	wtdʿilm/kmtt.	And you will know, O God, that you are dead."
17–19	*yšmʿ.aliyn.bʿl/*	Mightiest Baal hears;
	yuhb.ʿglt.bdbr.	He makes love with a heifer in the outback,
	prt/bšd.šḫlmmt.	A cow in a field of Death's Realm.[170]
19–22	*škb/ʿmnh.šbʿ.lšbʿm/*	He lies with her seventy times seven,
	tš[ʿ]ly.ṯmn.lṯmnym/	Mounts eighty times eight;
	w[th]rn.wtldnmṯ	[She conceiv]es and bears a boy.
23	*al[iyn.bʿ]lšlbšn*	Might[iest Baa]l clothes him,
24	*i[ ]lh.mǵẓ*	… a gift …
25	*y[ ].lirth*	… to his breast …
26	*n[…]*	…

(About eleven lines are missing.)

Column VI

Column VI

(About thirty lines are missing, including the following tricolon.)

Baal's Death Announced and Mourned

	[idk.lttn.pnm]/	[Then they head out]
	[ʿm.il.mbk.nhrm]/	[For El at the springs of the Rivers,]
	[qrb.apq.thmtm]	[Amid the streams of the Deeps.]

1–2	*[tgly.ḏd.il.w]tb[a]/*	[They come to the mountain of El and] ent[er]
	[qrš.mlk.ab.]šnm	[The tent of the King, the Father of] Years.
3	*[tša.gḫm.w.tṣ]ḥ.*	[They raise their voices and cr]y:
3–5	*sbn/[y].lq*[171]*[ṣm.arṣ]*	"[W]e went to [the edge of the earth,]
	ʿd[172]*/ksm.mḫyt.*	To the limits of the waters.
5–7	*[m]ǵny/lnʿmy.arṣ.dbr/*	We came to the pleasant land of the outback,
	lysmt.šd.šḥlmmt	To the beautiful field of Death's Realm.
8–10	*mǵny.lbʿl.npl.la/rṣ.*	We [c]ame upon Baal fallen to earth;
	mt.aliyn.bʿl/	Dead is Mightiest Baal,
	ḫlq.zbl.bʿl.arṣ	Perished the Prince, Lord of the Earth."
11–14	*apnk.lṭpn.il/dpid.*	Then Beneficent El the Benign
	yrd.lksi.yṯb/lḫdm	Descends from his seat, sits on the footstool,
	[.w]l.ḫdm.yṯb/larṣ[.]	[And] from the footstool, sits on the earth.
14–17	*yṣq.ʿmr/un.lrišḫ.*	He pours dirt on his head for mourning,
	ʿpr.plṯt/lqdqdḫ.	Dust on his crown for lamenting;
	lpš.yks/mizrtm.	For clothing he puts on sackcloth.
17–18	*ǵr.babn/ydy.*	With a stone he scrapes his skin,
	psltm.byʿr	Double-slits with a blade.
19–20	*yḫdy.lḥm.wdqn/*	He cuts cheeks and chin,

	yṯlṯ.qn.ḏrʿh[.]	Furrows the length of his arm.
20–22	*yḥrṯ/kgn.aplb.*	He plows his chest[173] like a garden,
	kʿmq.yṯlṯ/bmt.	Like a valley he furrows the back.
22	*yšu.gh[.]wyṣḥ*	He raises his voice and cries:
23–25	*bʿl.mt.my.lim.*	"Baal is dead! What of the peoples?
	bn/dgn.my.hmlt.	The Son of Dagan! What of the multitudes?
	aṯr/bʿl.ard.barṣ	After Baal I will descend to Hell."
25–28	*ap/ʿnt.ttlk.wtṣd.*	Then Anat goes about hunting,
	kl.ǵr/lkbd.arṣ.	In every mountain in the heart of the earth,
	kl.gbʿ/[lk]bd.šdm.	In every hill [in the he]art of the fields.
28–31	*tmǵ.lnʿm[y]/[arṣ.]dbr.*	She comes to the pleas[ant land of] the outback,
	ysmt.šd/[šḥl]mmt.	To the beautiful field of [the Realm] of Death;
	t[mǵ.]lbʿl.np[l]/[la]rṣ[.]	She com[es] upon Baal fall[en to ear]th.
31–	*[lpš].tks.miz[rtm]/*	[For clothing] she puts on sack[cloth,[174]]

(The rest of the poetic unit continues after the superscription in the next column.)

(The rest of the poetic unit continues after the superscription in the next column.)

	12. *KTU* 1.6	12. Sixth Tablet
	Column I	Column I
		Superscription to the Tablet
1	*lbʿl*	To Baal
		Anat's Continuation of Mourning for Baal
2	*ǵr.bab<n>.td[.]*	With a stone she scrapes her skin,
	p[s]ltm[.byʿr]	Double-[sl]its [with a blade.]
3–4	*tḫdy.lḥm.wdqn.* *t[ṯlṯ]/qn.ḏrʿḫ.*	She cuts cheeks and chin, [Furrows] the length of her arm.
4–5	*tḥrṯ.km.gn/aplb.*	She plows her chest like a garden,
	kʿmq.tṯlṯ.bmt	Like a valley she furrows her back:[175]
6–8	*bʿl.mt.my.lim.*	"Baal is dead! What of the peoples?
	bndgn/my.hmlt.	The Son of Dagan! What of the multitudes?
	aṯr.bʿl.nrd[176]*/barṣ.*	After Baal we will descend to Hell."
8–10	*ʿmḫ.trd.nrt/ilm.špš.*	To her descends the Divine Lamp, Shapsh,
	ʿd.tšbʿ.bk/ *tšt.kyn.udmʿt.*	As she[177] weeps her fill, Drinks her tears like wine.
10–11	*gm/tṣḥ.lnrt.ilm.špš*	Aloud she calls to the Divine Lamp, Shapsh:
12	*ʿmsmʿ.ly.aliyn.bʿl*	"Load on me, please, Mightiest Baal."
13–15	*tšmʿ.nrt.ilm.špš/*	The Divine Lamp, Shapsh, complies;

	tšualiyn.bʿl. *lktp/ʿnt.ktšth.*	She hoists Mightiest Baal, On Anat's shoulders she places him.
15–18	*tšʿlynh/bṣrrt.ṣp<ʿ>n.* *tbkynh/wtqbrnh.* *tštnn.bḫrt/ilm.arṣ.*	She carries him to Sapan's summit, Bewails him and buries him, Sets him in a divine pit in the Earth.
18–20	*ṭṭbḫ.šbʿm/rumm.* *kgmn.aliyn/bʿl*	She slaughters seventy buffalo, An offering (?) for Mightiest [B]aal.[178]
20–21	*ṭṭbḫ.šbʿm.alpm/* *[kg]mn.aliyn.[b]ʿl.*	She slaughters seventy oxen, [An off]ering (?) [for] Mightiest Baal.
22–23	*[ṭṭ]bḫ.šbʿm.ṣin/* *[kgm]n.aliyn.bʿl*	[She sla]ughters seventy sheep, An off[ering (?) for] Mightiest Baal.
24–25	*[ṭṭb]ḫ.šbʿm.aylm/* *[kgmn.]aliyn.bʿl*	[She slaug]hters seventy deer, [An offering (?) for] Mightiest Baal.
26–27	*[ṭṭbḫ.š]bʿm.yʿlm/* *[kgmn.al]iyn.bʿl*	[She slaughters se]venty mountain-goats, [An offering (?) for Migh]tiest Baal.
28–29	*[ṭṭbḫ.šbʿm.]ḥmrm*[179]*/* *[kgm]n.aliyn[.]b[ʿl]*	[She slaughters seventy] asses, [An offer]ing (?) [for] Migh[ti]est B[aal.]
30–31	*[ ]ḫh.tšt bm.ʿ[ ]/* *[ ]zrh.ybm.lilm*	[ ] ... she drinks[180] ... [,] [ ] ... In-law to the gods.

Proposals for Successors to Baal

32–34	*[id]k.lttn[.]pnm.*	[The]n she[181] hea]ds out

	ʿm/[i]l[.]mbknhrm.	For [E]l at the springs of the Rivers,
	qrb/[a]pq.thmtm.	Amid the streams of the Deeps.
34–36	*tgly.ḏd/il.wtbu.*	She comes to the mountain of El and enters
	qrš./mlk.ab.šnm.	The tent of the King, the Father of Years.
36–38	*lpʿn/il.thbr.wtql/*	At the feet of El she bows down and falls,
	tštḥwy.wtkbdnh	Prostrates herself and honors him.
39	*tšu.gh.wtṣḥ.*	She raises her voice and cries:
39–41	*tšmḫht/aṯrt.wbnh.*	"Now Athirat and her sons may rejoice,
	ilt.wṣb/rt.aryh.	The goddess and the band of her brood.
41–43	*kmt.aliyn/bʿl.*	For dead is Mightiest Baal,
	kḫlq.zbl.bʿl/arṣ.	Perished the Prince, Lord of the Earth."
43–44	*yṣḥil/lrbt.aṯrtym.*	Aloud El declares to Lady Athirat of the Sea:
44–46	*šmʿ/lrbt.aṯr[t]ym.*	"Listen, O Lady Athir[at] of the Sea:
	tn/aḥd.b.bnk[.]am{.}lkn	Select one of your sons that I may make him king."
47	*wtʿn.rbt.aṯrtym*	And Lady Athirat of the Sea answers:
48	*bl.nmlk.ydʿ.ylḥn*	"So let us make YDʿ-YLḤN[182] king."
49–50	*wyʿn.lṭpn.ildpi/d.*	And Beneficent El the Benign answers:

50–52	*dq.anm.lyr[ẓ]/* *ʿm.bʿl.lyʿdb.mrḥ/* *ʿm.bn.dgn.ktmsm*	"One so weak cannot run Like Baal, nor handle the lance Like the Son of Dagan, for he is prostrate."
53	*wʿn.rbt.aṯrtym*	And Lady Athirat of the Sea answers:
54–55	*bl{t}.nmlk.ʿṯtr.ʿrẓ/* *ymlk.ʿṯtr.ʿrẓ*	"So let us make Athtar the Strong king, Let Athtar the Strong be king."
56–59	*apnk.ʿṯtr.ʿrẓ/* *yʿl.bṣrrt.ṣpn*	Then Athtar the Strong Ascends the summit of Sapan,
59–61	*yṯb.lkḥṯ[.]aliyn/bʿl.* *pʿnh.ltmǵyn/hdm[.]* *rišh.lymǵy/apsh.*	Sits on the throne of Mightiest Baal. His feet do not reach its footstool, His head does not reach its top.
61	*wyʿn.ʿṯtr.ʿrẓ*	And Athtar the Strong speaks:
62	*lamlk.bṣrrt.ṣpn*	"I cannot be king on the summit of Sapan."
63–65	*yrd.ʿṯtr.ʿrẓ.* *yrd/lkḥṯ.aliyn.bʿl/* *wymlk.barṣ.il.klh*	Athtar the Strong descends, Descends from the throne of Mightiest Baal, And rules over all the great earth.
66–67	*[ ]bn.brḥbt* *[ ]abn.bkknt*	[dr]aw (?) in barrels, [d]raw (?) in casks.[183]

Column II

(About thirty lines are missing.)

Column II

(Lines 1-4 are too difficult to translate.)

1	*l[ ]*	
2	*wl[ ]*	
3	*kd.ʿ[ ]*	
4	*kd.t[ ]*	
		Anat Longs for Baal
4–6	*[ym.ymm]/yʿtqn.*	[A day, two days] pass,
	w[rḥm.ʿnt]/tngṯh.	And [Maiden Anat] seeks him.
6–9	*klb.ar[ḫ]/lʿglh.*	Like the heart of the c[ow] for her calf,
	klb.ṯa[t]/limrh.	Like the heart of the ew[e] for her lamb,
	km.lb.ʿn[t]/aṯr[.]bʿl	So is the heart of An[at] for Baal.
9–11	*tiḫd.m[t]/bsin.lpš.*	She grabs Mo[t] by the hem of his garment,
	tšṣq[nh]/bqṣ.all.	She seizes [him] by the edge of his cloak.[184]
11–12	*tšu.gh.w[tṣ]/ḥ.*	She raises her voice and [cri]es:
12	*at.mt.tn.aḫy*	"You, O Mot, give up my brother."
13	*wʿn[.]bn.ilm.mt.*	And Divine Mot answers:
13–14	*mh/taršn.lbtlt.ʿnt*	"What do you desire, Adolescent Anat?
15–17	*an.itlk.waṣd.*	I was going about hunting
	kl/ǵr.lkbd.arṣ.	In every mountain in the heart of the earth,
	kl.gbʿ/lkbd.šdm.	In every hill in the heart of the fields.
17–19	*npš.ḫsrt/bn.nšm.*	My appetite was lacking humans,
	npš.hmlt./arṣ.	My appetite, the multitudes of Earth.

19–20	*mǵt.lnʿmy.arṣ/dbr.*	I was coming to the pleasant land of the outback,
	ysmt.šd.šḫlmmt	To a beautiful field in Death's Realm.
21–23	*ngš.ank.aliynbʿl/*	Then I approached Mightiest Baal;
	ʿdbnnank.<k>imr.bpy/	I took him like a lamb in my mouth,
	klli.bṯbrn.q<n>y.ḫtuhw	Like a kid crushed in the chasm of my throat."
24–25	*nrt.ilm[.]špš.*	The Divine Lamp, Shapsh,
	ṣḥrrt/la.šmm.	Burns the orb of Heaven
	byd.bnilm.mt	By the power of Divine Mot.
26–27	*ym.ymm.yʿtqn.*	A day, two days pass,
	lymm/lyrḫm.	From days to months,
	rḥm.ʿnt.tngṯh	Maiden Anat seeks him.
28–30	*klb.arḫ.lʿglh.*	Like the heart of the cow for her calf,
	klb/ṯat.limrh.	Like the heart of the ewe for her lamb,
	km.lb/ʿnt.aṯr.bʿl.	So is the heart of Anat for Baal.
30–33	*tiḫd/bn.ilm.mt.*	She seizes Divine Mot,
	bḥrb/tbqʿnn./	With a sword she splits him,
	bḫṯr.tdry/nn	With a sieve she winnows him.
33–35	*bišt.tšrpnn/*	With a fire she burns him,
	brḥm.tṭḥnn	With millstones she grinds him,
	bšd/tdrʿ.nn	In a field she sows him.
35–37	*širh.ltikl/ʿṣrm[.]*	The birds eat his flesh,
	mnth.ltkly/npr[m.]	Fowl devour his parts,
	šir.lšir.yṣḥ	Flesh to flesh cries out.

(Two horizontal lines mark the end of this column.)

	Column III	Column III
	(About forty lines are missing.)	*(El's dream-vision is to determine whether Baal has returned to life, which would be signaled by the appearance of rain. The missing section contains the first possible reading of nature: if the rains have not returned, then El will know that Baal remains dead. The extant text opens with El's description of the second possibility. The narrative then indicates that El has a vision of rain indicating that Baal is alive.)*
		El's Dream Portends Baal's Return
	[widʿ.kmt.aliyn.bʿl]	"[Then I will know that Mightiest Baal is dead,]
[ ]–1	*kḫlq.zb[l.bʿl.arṣ]*	Perished the Pr[ince, Lord of the Earth.]
2–3	*whm.ḥy.a[liyn.bʿl]/* *whm.iṯ.zbl.bʿ[l.arṣ]*	But if Mi[ghtiest Baal lives,] And if the Prince, Lo[rd of the Earth, is alive,]
4–5	*bḥlm.lṭpn.il.dpid/* *bḏrt.bny.bnwt*	In the dream of Beneficent El the Benign, In the vision of the Creator of Creatures,
6–7	*šmm.šmn.tmṭrn/* *nḫlm.tlk.nbtm*	Let the heavens rain oil, The wadis run with honey,
8–9	*widʿ.kḥy.aliyn[.]b[ʿl]/* *kiṯ.zbl.bʿl.arṣ*	Then I will know that Mightiest B[aal] lives, The Prince, Lord of the Earth, is alive."
10–11	*bḥlm.lṭpn.ildp[id]/*	In the dream of Beneficent El the Ben[ign,]

	bḏrt.bny.bnwt	In the vision of the Creator of Creatures,
12–13	*šmm.šmn.tmṭrn/* *nḫlm.tlk.nbtm*	The heavens rain oil, The wadis run with honey.
14–15	*šmḫ.lṭpn.il.dpid/* *pʿnh.lhdm.yṯpd*	Beneficent El the Benign rejoices, His feet on his footstool he stamps.
16–17	*wyprq.lṣbwyṣḥq/* *yšu.gh.wyṣḥ*	He breaks into a smile and laughs, He raises his voices and declares:
18–19	*aṯbn.ank.wanḫn/* *wtnḫ.birty.npš*	"I can sit and I can rest, And my spirit within can rest.
20–21	*kḥy.aliyn.bʿl/* *kiṯ.zbl[.]bʿl[.]arṣ*	For Mightiest Baal lives, The Prince, Lord of the Earth, is alive."
		The Search for Baal
22–23	*gm.yṣḥ.il.lbtlt/ʿnt.*	Aloud El declares to Adolescent Anat:
23–24	*šmʿ.btlt.ʿnt/* *rgm.lnrt.il<m>.šp[š]*	"Hear, O Adolescent Ana[t,] Say to the Divine Lamp, Shap[sh:]
Column IV		Column IV
		El's Message to Shapsh Via Anat (Continued)
1–3	*pl.ʿnt.šdm.yšpš/* *pl.ʿnt.šdmil.* *yštk/bʿl.ʿnt.mḥrṯt*	"Parched are the furrows of the fields, O Shapsh, Parched are the furrows of the grand fields, May [B]aal restore (?) the furrows of the ploughed land.

4–5	*iy.aliyn.bᶜl/* *iy.zbl.bᶜl.arṣ*	Where is Mightiest Baal? Where is the Prince, Lord of the Earth?"
6–8	*ttbᶜ*[185]*.btlt.ᶜnt/* *idk.lttn.pnm/* *ᶜm.nrt.ilm.špš*	Adolescent Anat departs; So she heads out, For the Divine Lamp, Shapsh.
9	*tšu.gh.wtṣḥ*	She raises her voice and declares:
10–11	*tḫm.ṯr.il.abk/* *hwt.lṭpn.ḥtkk*	"Decree of Bull El, your Father, Word of the Beneficent, your Begetter:
12–14	*pl.ᶜnt.šdm.yšpš/* *pl.ᶜnt.šdm.il.* *yš[tk]/bᶜl.ᶜnt.mḥrṯ[t]*	'Parched are the furrows of the fields, O Shapsh, Parched are the furrows of the divine fields, May Baal re[store] (?) the furrows of the ploughed la[nd.]
15–16	*iy.aliyn.bᶜl/* *iy.zbl.bᶜl.arṣ*	Where is Mightiest Baal? Where is the Prince, Lord of the Earth?'"
17	*wtᶜn.nrt.ilm.š[p]š*	And the Divine Lamp, Shapsh, replies:
18–20	*šdyn.ᶜn.b.qbt[.]* *[t]/bllyt.ᶜl.umtk/* *wabqṯ.aliyn.bᶜl*	"... ... And I will seek Mightiest Baal."
21	*wtᶜn.btlt.ᶜnt*	And Adolescent Anat answers:
22–24	*an.lan.yšpš/*	"With strength upon strength, O Shapsh,

	an.lan.il.yǵr[k]/	With strength upon strength may El guard [you,]
	tǵrk.š[pš]	May you, Shap[sh,] be guarded [… ."]
25	*yštd.[ ]*	*(Lines 25-27 are unintelligible. The approximately thirty-five missing lines presumably include Shapsh's successful discovery of Baal returned to the realm of life.)*
26	*dr[ ]*	
27	*r[ ]*	
	(About thirty-five lines are missing.)	

Column V

Column V

Baal's Return to His Throne

1–4	*yiḫd.bʿl.bn.aṯrt/*	Baal seizes the sons of Athirat:
	rbm.ymḫṣ.bktp/	The mighty he strikes with a mace,
	dkym.ymḫṣ.bṣmd/	The attackers he strikes with a weapon,
	ṣǵrym[186].ymṣḫ[187].larṣ	The young of Yamm (?)[188] he drags to the earth.
5–6	*py[ṯb.]b[ʿ]l.lksi.mlkh/*	Then B[aa]l [is enthroned] on his royal throne,
	[lnḫt].lkḫṯ.drkth	[On the resting place], the throne of his dominion.
7–8	*[lym]m.lyrḫm./*	[Day]s turn to months,
	lyrḫm/lšnt.	Months to years,[189]

Mot's Complaint to Baal

8–10	*[mk].bšbʿ/šnt.*	[Th]en in the seventh year,
	w[.b]n.ilm.mt/	[D]ivine Mot [[190]]
	ʿm.aliyn.bʿl.	To Mightiest Baal.
10–11	*yšu/gh.wyṣḥ.*	He raises his voice and declares:
11–12	*ʿlk.b[ʿ]lm/pht.qlt.*	"Due to you, O B[aa]l, I faced shame:

12–14	*ʿlk.pht/dry.bḥrb.*	Due to you I faced splitting with a sword,[191]
	ʿlk/pht.šrp.bišt	Due to you I faced burning with fire.
15–16	*ʿlk.[pht.ṭḥ]n.brḥ/m.*	Due to you [I faced grind]ing with millstones,
	ʿ[lk.]pht[.dr]y[192]*.bkbrt*	Due to you [I fa]ced [winnowing] with a riddle.
17–19	*ʿlk[.]pht.[ ]l[ ]/bšdm.*	Due to you [I faced.].[.][193] in a field,
	[ʿl]k[.]p[ht]/drʿ.bym.	Due to you I faced scattering in the sea.
19–21	*tn.aḥd/baḫk.ispa.*	Give up one of your brothers[194] that I may eat,
	wyṯb/ap.d.anšt.	And my furious anger will turn away.
21–23	*im/aḥd.baḫk.[ ]/*	If you do not [give] up one of your brothers,
	hn.aḫẓ[ ]	Then I will [… ,]
24–25	*[ʿ]nt.akl[y.bn.nšm]/*	[N]ow I will consu[me humans,]
	akly.hml[t.arṣ]	I will consume the multitu[des of Earth."]
26	*w.y[ ].a[ ]*	*(Lines 26-28 are too difficult to translate.)*
27	*[ ]*	
28	*bl[ ]*	

(About twenty-five lines are missing.)

Column VI		Column VI
1–2	*[yṯ]rdh*	*(Lines 1-8 are too damaged to translate.)*
	[yg]ršh	

3	*[ ]ru*	
4	*[ ]h*	
5	*[ ]mt*	
6	*[ ]mr.limm*	
7	*[ ]bn.ilm.mt*	
8	*[ ]šbʿt.ǵlmh*	
		Baal and Mot Battle for Supremacy
9	*[ ].bn.ilm.mt*	[And] Divine Mot [[195]:]
10–11	*p[h]n.aḫym.ytn.bʿl/spuy*[196].	"So look! Baal gave my brothers as my food,
	bnm.umy.klyy/	My mother's sons for my consumption!"
12–13	*yṯb.ʿm.bʿl.ṣrrt/ṣpn*	He turns to Baal on the summit of Sapan,
	yšu(!)[197]*gh.wyṣḥ*	He raises his voice and declares:
14–16	*aḫym.ytnt.bʿl/spuy.*	"My brothers, O Baal, you gave as my food,
	bnm.umy.kl/yy	My mother's sons for my consumption!"
16–17	*ytʿn.kgmrm/*	They eye each other like fighters,[198]
	mt.ʿz.bʿl.ʿz	Mot is fierce, Baal is fierce.
17–19	*yngḥn/krumm.*	They gore each other like buffalo,
	mt.ʿz.bʿl/ʿz	Mot is fierce, Baal is fierce.
19–20	*ynṯkn.bṯnm/*	They bite each other like serpents,
	mt.ʿz.bʿl.ʿz.	Mot is fierce, Baal is fierce.
20–22	*ymṣḫn/klsmm.*	They drag each other like runners,[199]
	mt.ql/bʿl.ql.	Mot falls, Baal falls.

		El Intervenes on Baal's Behalf Via Shapsh
22–23	*ʿln.špš/tṣḫ.lmt.*	Above[200] Shapsh declares to Mot:
23–27	*šmʿ.mʿ/lbn.ilm.mt.* *ik.tmt[ḫ]/ṣ.ʿm.aliyn.bʿl/* *ik.al.yšm[ʿ]k[.ṯ]r/il.abk.*	"Hear now, Divine Mot: How can you fi[gh]t with Mightiest Baal? How will Bull El, your Father, hea[r] you?
27–29	*l.ysʿ.alt/ṯbtk.* *lyhpk.ksa.mlkk/* *lyṯbr.ḫṭ.mṯpṭk*	Surely he will remove the support of your throne, Surely he will overturn the seat of your kingship, Surely he will break the scepter of your rule."
30–31	*yru.bnilm<.m>t.* *ṯtʿ.y/dd.il.ǵzr[.]*	Divine <Mo>t is afraid, The Beloved of El, the Hero, is scared.
31–32	*yʿr.mt/bqlh.* *y[ ]*[201]	Mot trembles at her voice, He [… :]
33–35	*bʿl.yṯṯbn[.lksi]/mlkh.* *l[nḫt.lkḥṯ]/drkth[.]*	"Let Baal be enthroned on [his] royal [throne,] On [the resting place], [the throne] of his dominion."
35	*[ ]*	
36	*[ ]d[ ]*	*(Lines 35-42 are unintelligible. They apparently complete the preceding episode of Baal's interaction with Mot and perhaps introduce the following speech, which evidently refers to the sun goddess's journey through the underworld in a sacrificial setting of some sort. The speaker, addressee, and larger context are unclear.*[202]*)*
37	*[ ].hn[ ]*	
38	*[ ]šn[ ]*	
39	*[…]it*	
40	*[…]qbat*	
41	*[ ]inšt*	
42	*[ ]u.*	
42–45	*ltštql/[ ].ṭry.*	"So get yourself to …

	ap.ltlḥm/[l]ḥm.trmmt.	So you may eat the sacrificial [me]al,
	ltšt/yn.tǵẓyt.	You may drink the offertory wine.
45–47	*špš/rpim.tḥtk/*	Shapsh rules the Rephaim,[203]
	špš.tḥtk.ilnym	Shapsh rules the Gods.[204]
48–49	*ʿdk.ilm.*	Your company are the Divinities,
	hn.mtm/ʿdk.	See, the Dead are your company.
49–50	*kṯrm.ḥbrk/*	Kothar is your magician,
	wḫss.dʿtk	And Hasis your diviner.[205]
51–53	*bym.arš.wtnn/*	On the day[206] of Desire and Tunnan,[207]
	kṯr.wḫss.yd/	Kothar wa-Hasis banishes,
	ytr.kṯr.wḫss	Kothar wa-Hasis shakes (?)."[208]

Scribal Colophon

(Two horizontal lines demarcate the following colophon:)

54	*spr.ilmlkšbny*	The scribe is Ilimalku the Shubanite,[209]
55	*lmd.atn.prln.*	Student of Attenu the diviner,[210]
55–56	*rb/khnm*	Chief of the priests,
56	*rb.nqdm*	Chief of the shepherds,
57	*ṯʿy.nqmd.*	The Thaite[211] of Niqmaddu,
57	*mlkugr[t]*	King of Ugar[it,]
58	*adnyrgb.*	Lord of YRGB,
58	*bʿl.ṯrmn*	Master of THRMN

Notes

1. For an optimistic view of the archaeological evidence, see Petersen 1994: 50.
2. Professor J. A. Hackett, personal communication.

3. For lists of alternative interpretations, readers are invited to consult Caquot, Sznycer, and Herdner 1974, or Gibson 1978 in tandem with Pardee 1980: 270–84. For alternative views of lines in 7–8 since 1980, see Smith 1994b.

4 Athirat is the conventional spelling of the goddess's name. RS 20.24 (cf. 20.123 + IVb:8) provides Akkadian syllabic spellings of Ugaritic divine names, including Ashratu for Athratu (with the case ending).

5. The end of the cycle may also connect the Ugaritic monarchy with the Rephaim, the ancient line of deceased heroes (see n. 203 below). The other two great Ugaritic literary works, Kirta and Aqhat (1–3 and 4–6), likewise reflect connections with the Ugaritic monarchy. Kirta not only represents the values of kingship as well as the challenges posed to it (need for an heir, illness, and rebellion); he is also identified as an ancient monarch of the line of the Rephaim which the Ugaritic monarchy saw as its ancestors (2 III 3–4, 14–15). Similarly, Daniel is viewed as an ancient clan leader who not only epitomizes the values of just rule and family piety; he also is called "a man of Rapiu" (4 I 1, 17, 35, 42; II 28; V 4–5, 14, 33–34), a title that would link Daniel, and by extension, his son, Aqhat, to the line of old tribal heroes and kings who were understood as the ancient ancestors of the Ugaritic monarchy in *CAT* 1.161.2–12 (cf. the figure of Rapiu in *CAT* 1.108.1).

6. This is the name of Baal's holy mountain. Other deities such as Anat (see 9 II below) have their own sanctuary-mountains. High places may have represented the meeting point between the heavens, the realm of the deities, and earth, the realm of humans. (The building of temples on the highest point, the acropolis, of a place evidently drew on this idea.) As with Baal and Anat, Yahweh's home on earth is located on a "holy mountain" (Exod 15:13, 17-18). In one biblical passage (Ps 48:2-3), the name of Baal's mountain, Sapan, is incorporated into the description of Yahweh's mountainous home. See also Isa 14:13 for a different usage of Sapan in biblical tradition.

7. The clichés of the first two lines are known elsewhere, suggesting that "his dominion" (*drkth*) is the end of a line, which would imply a third line of unknown length. This third line may describe the reward of gaining kingship (in contrast with the following two bicola).

8. The possible length of line 27 and the norms of poetic structure would suggest that a third line is to be reconstructed for this colon, perhaps containing a second image of destruction.

9. Messengers are to repeat verbatim the message given to them by their master, in this case El.

10. The word for "earth" is used here and elsewhere as a term for the underworld. It is rendered as "Hell," both for reasons of familiarity to English readers and for its alliteration with "Heaven." This "Hell" is, however, a place of neither fire nor devils, but the home of the god of Death. The "Deeps" (next line) refers to the cosmic ocean beneath the inhabited world.

11. This lacuna originally contained the name of the mountain, presumably Mount KS, as suggested by lines 11-12 above.

12 The word refers to a young woman, married or unmarried, who has not yet given birth.

13. Reading for *ilk*.

14. Reading for *dl*.

15. The structure of this colon is rendered here in accord with Ginsberg (1969: 129) and others. For an alternative view, see Parker 1989: 9-10.

16. This lacuna presumably contained a speech-opening formula.

17. The reconstructions for this colon are based on 12 VI 27–29.

18. The reconstruction and translation assume an idiom, **šmḫ lb*, "the heart rejoices." See Smith 1994b: 283. Cf. *CAT*'s reading *šm[m*.

19. Based on parallelism, interpreting as *w<a>ʿnnh*, with <a> lost due to sandhi. "And his servants" is another possible translation.

20. Reading for *phr*.

21. Parallel passages read *llḥm*, and so *lḥm* here might reflect a haplography. However, it is possible that this is a variant without the preposition *l*.

22. Reading of g based on line 24.

23. Reading for *hlm*.

24. *[ym]nhm*, "their right hand," is another plausible reconstruction.

25. Context requires a verb of speech (perhaps **ʿny*).

26. A speech-opening formula is perhaps to be reconstructed here.

27. For a modification of this divine title in the Bible, see Ps 68:5. See also Yahweh's titles in Deut 33:26 and Ps 104:3.

28. For a similar call to Yahweh, see Ps 92:10; cf. Judg 5:31.

29. Actually only one weapon is made at a time.

30. In accordance with its function, the name means "may he drive."

31. In accordance with its function, the name means "may he expel all."

32. This word is the same as Baal and may be regarded as a pun. It is also possible that the title is to be translated "Prince Baal of the Earth" (cf. Athirat's title, *aṯrt ym*, "Athirat of the Sea").

33. The form with *w* is unusual and might involve an error (for *n*?).

34. For the expression, cf. Josh 22:10 and 1 Sam 16:12 (Pardee 1988a: 19).

35. See Pardee 1988a: 19. Other scholars render "goddess," based on the appellative use of Ishtar in Akkadian (Ginsberg 1969: 136 n. 1). Or does this sentence express a superlative (a goblet not even the goddess, or specifically the goddess, Athirat, may see), or the exclusion of females (here goddesses) from a religious ceremony (Caquot, Sznycer, and Herdner 1974: 155 n. n; de Moor 1987: 3 n. 13)?

36. This view of the noun *nʿm* (<**nǵm*) is held by Cassuto and Cross (see Smith 1994b: 65 n. 126: Lewis 1989: 52). The noun may also be translated "the pleasant one" (<**nʿm*) or the like, which is perhaps used in a sense similar to "good (*ṭb*) of voice" in the next colon (suggested as a possibility by B. Zuckerman, personal communication); or, if the first etymology is correct, perhaps both senses were viewed as being within the word's range. Cf. the description of David in 2 Sam 23:1.

37. D. Pardee (personal communication) indicates that a trace of this word–divider is visible under a microscope. A number of other readings below are clarified thanks to Pardee's personal communications. (I wish to express my deep gratitude to Professor Pardee for access to his notes on text 9 and for his permission to cite them. The format of this volume precludes extensive use of his notes.)

38. The preposition denotes the singer's song about Baal, but the context might also evoke the singer's physical posture before Baal (cf. *qm ʿl*, "to stand before," in 8 I 21).

39. Possibly a title of Baal. Or, perhaps a haplography is involved: *pdr<y>.ydʿ*, "Pidray he [Baal] knows" (cf. de Moor 1987: 4 n. 19).

40. Possibly in the "biblical sense" of knowing, i.e., sexual relations.

41. Elsewhere the expression refers to Pidray, Tallay, and Baal's third "daughter" (or "maiden"), Arsay.

42. For parallels between this column and *CAT* 1.7, see Dijkstra 1983: 26–28.

43. Anat's "house" here presupposes a fortified temple located on her sanctuary-mountain (or more specifically, an acropolis?). Cf. Yahweh's sanctuary or "holy mountain" in Exod 15:13, 17-18; Ps 48:2-3.

44. For the reading, see Pardee 1980: 275 and *CAT*.

45. Terms for west and east respectively, perhaps a merismus suggesting the world-wide extent of her fighting.

46. There is hardly any room for *[l]* and perhaps it was omitted by mistake (Gibson 1978: 47).

47. For this translation, see Good (1982), who notes biblical passages using harvest and gleaning as expressions for warfare (Judg 8:1-2; 20:44-46; Jer 49:9; Obad 5). Good also cites *KTU* 1.13.4-7 as another passage that describes Anat's battle with this sort of imagery.

48. As read by *CAT*, the three heads of the wedges of *n* are visible (cf. Pardee's reading *mdat*).

49. The furniture suggests a feast with the captives as Anat's main course rather than her continued battling. This section accordingly uses the language of warfare to convey the goddess' consumption of her captives.

50. Not "[She] washes from her hands warrior-blood," which would require **bydh dm ḏmr* instead of the text's *ydh bdm ḏmr*. Accordingly Pardee (1980a: 276) compares Ps 58:11-12. Washing in the enemies' blood is perhaps a ritualistic custom denoting Anat's complete victory over them.

51. In accordance with the other plural forms. See also line 21.

52. Reading for *a*, apparently an oral error.

53. Only one horizontal wedge is visible for the first letter, which is the basis for the reading *t* (Virolleaud, Gaster, Gordon [*CTA*, p. 16 n. 4] and Pardee), but the lacuna to the left of this wedge has room for two additional horizontal wedges of *n* (as read by Cassuto, Ginsberg, *CTA*, and *CAT*). The latter is read here on the basis of the one parallel text, though with hesitation.

54. So *CAT*. The reconstruction is offered tentatively; it is based on the possible parallel in *CAT* 1.101.16.

55. The reconstruction is uncertain. Pardee (personal communication) records a single vertical wedge before *št*, which would call the reconstruction here into question.

56. Perhaps a stringed musical instrument in the shape of a bull's head (hence *rimt* related to *rumm*, "bulls" or "buffalo"), according to J. C. Greenfield (personal communication cited in Pope 1977: 294).

57. So emending *m* in accordance with *tšr* in the parallel passage from *CAT* 1.101.17. Pardee (1980a: 276–77) notes the possibility that *tšr* might represent the correct reading. The reading *mšr* would represent a noun issuing in the translation "(with) a song about the love of Mightiest Baal" or the like.

58. If correctly interpreted, "wide world" is an expression for the underworld, in accordance with Baal's chthonic experience in 11-12 (just as Pidray and Tallay's titles correspond to Baal's character as a god of the rainstorm).

59. The opening of this section assumes a switch in scene back to Baal on Mount Sapan, last mentioned in 9 I.

60. Reading for *ymmt*, apparently an oral error involving bilabial consonants.

61. The word involves a pun on the Ugaritic word for "food."

62. Read also by *CTA* and *CAT*, this word–divider is visible only at the left–hand edge of its head, according to Pardee's drawing.

63. The word involves a pun on the Ugaritic word for "peace-offering" and thereby evokes the impression of a ritual act.

64. These titles for the holy mountain of Yahweh appear in Exod 15:17; Ps 78:54. For a comparable concentration of titles for Yahweh's mountain, Jerusalem/Zion, see Ps 48:2-3.

65. Anat fears that this unexpected visit presages bad news (cf. 6 II 44-47; Ezek 21:11-12; Dan 5:6; see Ginsberg 1969: 132 n. 18).

66. For the readings in lines 37–51, see Pardee 1984.

67. Or, "the God of the Great Waters," if *rbm* were elliptical for *mym rbm*, "mighty waters" referring to the cosmic waters (cf. Pss 29:3; 93:4; so Caquot, Sznycer, and Herdner 1974: 167 n. h).

68. The reading is highly debated. The translation here assumes *ištm[d]h*. See Pardee 1984: 252–54.

69. The same figure is named as Yahweh's enemy in Isa 27:1.

70. Cf. the figure named as Yahweh's enemy in Ps 74:13 and Rev 13:1.

71. Like "beloved and "daughter, "calf" and "dog" may be applied as titles to someone to denote his or her subservience and belonging to another person (as known from some Mesopotamian proper names and from the El-Amarna letters). These particular animals serve this purpose apparently because they are domesticated species.

72. This line and the following three have been taken as the continuation of the description of Baal's enemy in the previous colon. A purpose clause, such as the one ending the previous colon, would normally mark the end of a unit and therefore militate against such a hypothetical continuation. Furthermore, according to the extant context Anat does not yet know that Baal has defeated Yamm, the apparent referent of these lines. For the same reason these lines are probably not declarative sentences claiming that Baal "banished from the summit of Sapan, The one who pecks like a bird his ear," etc. (so Caquot, Sznycer, and Herdner 1974: 169).

73. The two letters are unclear. One vertical wedge and perhaps part of the head of a second vertical wedge to its left are visible, permitting the readings either *l* or *ṣ*. Then there is a horizontal wedge, perhaps with another horizontal wedge above it, followed by the rest of the letter *r* on the tablet's edge. The translation assumes the reading *kʿṣr* (so also *CAT* and Pardee with qualifications).

74. *CTA* reads *[–]ʿn* while *CAT* reads *yʿn*. Pardee's drawing shows the bottom of a vertical wedge.

75. Pardee reads *k*; if correct, it is an error for *n*, which is read by *CTA* and *CAT*.

76. This reconstruction, advocated by Driver (1956: 88), Good (1984: 81), and

CAT, is supported by Pardee's reading of the first two wedges. Pardee's drawing shows the horizontal letters of the first letter and the head of the left–hand wedge of the second letter.

77. See Good 1984: 81 and *CAT.*

78. A title of Baal would seem to belong here, but "Cloudrider" (*rkb ʿrpt*), one of his standard epithets, especially appropriate to this sort of meteorological setting, would require too much space (cf. *CAT*). Perhaps Hadd is to be reconstructed here.

79. The word "horns" might refer here metaphorically to Baal's double-lightning, in view of *qarnayim*, "(double-)horns," in Hab 3:4 (Good 1984: 81).

80. Given line 22, *[an.]* might be reconstructed, but line 22 is itself partially reconstructed. For the highly damaged area of this line, Pardee reads *ak[.]an[k.] CAT* reads *an[k].*

81. Reading for *awṣ* (one horizontal wedge omitted).

82. The form is exceptional, and the nominal phrase may involve a scribal error for either *ybmt limm* or *bt abh* (Pardee 1980: 279). Did the scribe begin to write the former and then switch to the latter?

83. That is, Anat. According to Lichtenstein (1979: 35-37), the scene assumes that a feast ensues (for the same wording, with the feast made more explicit, see 10 V 44-48). The banquet finishes with Anat anointing herself. Lichtenstein notes that in Mesopotamian banquet accounts the anointing of guests follows the feast.

84. Cf. Yahweh's title in Deut 32:6: "Is not he [Yahweh] your father who created you, who made you and established you?" (RSV)

85. *CTA* reads *–d, CAT* and Pardee *kd.* A single horizontal wedge is clearly visible.

86. A drinking mug excavated at Ugarit depicts the following scene with Anat as a bird (Pope 1971). Possibly the same verb in 15 II 10-12 may express the idea that Anat turns (**twr*) or shoots (**yry*) into the air in the form of a bird, which would provide the basis for Pope's translation, "[Anat] shot (from) earth" (1971: 402). The translation here presupposes the same image of Anat but without an explicit description of her takeoff.

87. *CTA* reads *qn[-?](a/w)–n[—lt,* while *KTU* has *q*(?)ny*[ ]wb*nxxlt**. In view of these readings, it would be tempting to reconstruct *qn[y].[ ].n[ḥ]lt* and translate "(which) he established as [an inhe]ritance" (cf. *CTA* p. 18 n. 11, which compares *dyqny ḏdm* in 6 IV 58; Exod 15:18). However, caution is in order. *CAT* now reads *qny[.w]adn.[bni]lm.*

88. The parallels suggest the reconstruction *y[ʿn.i]l,* but Pardee reads *y[ʿn]y.* The only remains of the final letter, the top edges of the heads of two (?) vertical wedges, support either reading.

89. See below lines 25–27.

90. Perhaps the firmament of the heavens?

91. So according to the parallels, but Pardee reads *by[d.]m[dd.ilm.m]t.*

92. Or the epithet may mean "Son of El," reflecting his status as El's progeny.

93. *CTA* reads *ašplk,* which is contextually possible.

94. The meaning of the phrase is debated. Renfroe (1992: 52-56) translates the expression: "declaration of *fate.*"

95. Based on the parallels, reading for *arḫb.*

96. It is possible that rather than place-names, these nouns represent topographical features, "mountain" and "height," respectively.

97. Based on the spelling of the word in the following bicolon, *CTA* and *CAT* emend to *ḫkpt*. Variant spellings of foreign proper names is common, however.

98. There is room for a line between lines 5 and 6, but there is no evidence of any writing in this space.

99. Reading for *id*.

100. If *tʿlt* is the verb (<*ʿ*ly*) governing this line, the expected form would be either a suffix form *ʿlt* or a prefix form *tʿl*. Should the line read *plkt.>lt. ymnḫ* or *plk.t>lb(!?)ymnḫ*? Given the anomaly, the form is understood as a *t*– preformative noun. Yet some read *qlt*.

101. Line 5 is here transposed after lines 6–7. The reference to garments in line 5 does not fit with the two preceding lines (2–4) involving the spindle. Rather, it belongs with the reference to garments in lines 6–7. The placement of line 5 before lines 6–7 might be explained as an unusually long *casus pendens* ("as for her robes, the covering of her skin, ..."), but the customary poetic pattern would suggest that line 5 was the third line in the tricolon with lines 6–7.

102. The verbs in this context express Athirat's attitude toward El as she performs her domestic chores (see O'Connor 1989: 27). Below (10 III 26) the second verb is used for entreaty of Athirat by Baal and Anat and perhaps anticipates Athirat's entreaty of El on their behalf in 10 IV-V.

103. Is this a misspelling with *ʿṯtrt* in mind (Gibson 1978: 56)?

104. Reading for *[p]np* (scribal omission of a horizontal wedge).

105. *CTA* reads *n[ ]t. n[r]t*, "light" (see *CTA* p. 23 n. 9) is one possible reading, assuming that *ẓl*, "gleam," is the correct reading and interpretation of the first word in the colon (rather than *pʿl*, "work" as understood by some). *CAT* reads *nr*.

106. This title of her servant apparently reflects the nature of the mistress, Athirat, as suggested by her longer appellation, "Lady Athirat of the Sea."

107. Context suggests a verb of speech here. The most common proposal is *y[ṯ]b*, literally "returns," perhaps in the sense of giving an answer. However, the tablet does not show the right-hand vertical wedge of *b*, but a horizontal wedge. The other proposed reading is *y[ʿ]n*, "he answers," which is assumed in the translation.

108. De Moor (1987: 49 n. 220) compares the offense of spitting in the assembly in the Dead Sea Scrolls (1QS 7:13).

109. Reading for *bm*. The width of the sign comports with *b*, in which case the letter may be a scribal error for *d*.

110. Given the form *tdmmt* in the following bicolon, *tdmm<t>* might be reconstructed here, except that parallelism of the same word in different genders may be involved, given the parallelism of the two bicola, lines 18–21 and 21–22.

111. The complaint here has the force of a saying. Cf. *Pirqe Abot* 2:8: "The more maidservants, the more lewdness" (Gibson 1978: 58 n. 6).

112. Although El and she may make joint decisions (as in 12 I), Athirat's question shows that she recognizes El's ultimate authority in the pantheon.

113. The head of a vertical wedge is visible. The attested wedge is compatible with *u*, which is reconstructed by commentators and assumed in the translation.

114. Given the parallel in lines 12–13, it is tempting to reconstruct *wḫbq qdš wamrr* before this line.

115. Based on late-second-millennium iconographic evidence, Good (1984)

doubts that this passage presupposes a saddle rather than ropes for riding. The word *gpn*, literally "vine," is used for rope (as translated here in the second line) or a riding-strap in Gen 49:11 (Greenfield 1964: 527 n. 2).

116. Or: "takes a torch."

117. That is, Athirat.

118. This generally accepted emendation is based on 4 VI 6, but is it possible that *bk* (<**bbk*, "from a cup") here is a variant?

119. A metaphor for wine.

120. Ugaritic *yd*, "hand," is an euphemism for penis as well as a word for "love, passion" (the Ugaritic word reflects a coalescence of two originally distinct lexemes; see Caquot, Sznycer, and Herdner 1974: 205 n. i; Seow 1989: 110 n. 88).

121. Reading for *ṯkt* ("ship" or "barque"), as this image would seem out of place in this context (see Smith 1994b: 53).

122. A poetic term for thunder. See also 2 Sam 22 (Ps 18):14; Ps 29:3-9.

123. For a comparable biblical usage, see Job 37:3.

124. Reading for *bbhmk* (a scribal error due to an extra verical wedge). See lines 29–31 and 36–37 below.

125. Reading for *lḥmd*. See above lines 16 and 33.

126. This scribal instruction, demarcated by horizontal lines, may tell the reader to assume the standard description of sending messengers, the standard instructions for the addressee to come to the speaker, and perhaps the standard description of the addressee's journey as well (cf. Ginsberg 1969: 134 n. 24).

127. That is, Baal serves Kothar.

128. The parallel context in 8 III 8-10 commands Kothar to depart and build a palace for Yamm; perhaps a similar instruction is to be understood here.

129. Cf. 10 V 61–62.

130. Baal seems to be referring to an episode involving Yamm's abuse, perhaps mentioned in 10 III 12-13 as well.

131. Literally, "consumes."

132. Reading for *kbᶜ* (haplography of two horizontal wedges).

133. As in one ritual text, here the verbs may refer specifically to the preparation of the animals for the feast (so Levine and de Tarragon 1993: 81, 95), described in more detail in the following lines.

134. Read *il<m>*? Cf. 1.22 I 12–14 below 22 Side Two (*CAT*).

135. Seventy is a conventional number for a generally large group (see Judg 9:5; 2 Kgs 10:1; cf. Exod 1:5). In the narrative of Elkunirsa, a West Semitic myth written in Hittite, Ashertu's children number 77//88 (Hoffner 1990: 69). The number of gods perhaps survives in the later Jewish notion of the seventy angels, one for each of the seventy nations (*Shabbat* 88b; *Sukkah* 55b; Caquot, Sznycer, and Herdner 1974: 214 n. k).

136. The tail of a horizontal wedge seems visible, which might lend support to the reading *yn*, as read by some commentators. Perhaps a vertical dittography from line 53 is involved. In any case, there is no evidence for the reconstruction *y[n]* in lines 47 and 49, which casts doubt on the reading or reconstruction of *yn* here.

137. *CAT: dkr<t yn>*.

138. Reading instead of *ᶜdr* resulting from haplography.

139. There may be enough room for the reconstruction, *b[kmyṯ]b* (cf. *CTA* 29 n. 5; see line 42). Cf. *CAT*'s reading: *b bt [ʿ]rb*.

140. As the next two bicola indicate, the window is imagined as installed in the clouds so that Baal's thunder and rains can reach earth. For the same motif, see 2 Kgs 7:2, 19. For the window viewed as a gate installed in the heavenly firmament, see Gen 7:11; cf. Mal 3:10 (Caquot, Sznycer, and Herdner 1974: 211 n. g).

141. "The Warrior" is a title of Baal.

142. Renfroe (1992: 33-34) takes the unit as a bicolon, with "eye" not as a verb but a noun serving as the feminine antecedent of the verb: "The Lord's eye is in front of his hand, When it *speeds* the cedar from his right."

143. Many commentators believe that a haplography of *y* occurred at the end of this word. If so, the bicolon might be rendered: "Will either king or commoner/occupy the land of <my> dominion?" (see Gibson 1978: 65).

144. The volitive form of the verb rules out the interpretation of this sentence as a declaration or speech-opening formula on Mot's part (cf. Ginsberg 1969: 135). For comparable syntax, see 11 III 18-19, 25-26.

145. Some commentators suggest reading *dymru*. See *UT* 9.10; Gibson 1978: 66; Seow 1989: 133; *CAT*.

146. This expression conveys a double entendre of "rules" (in accordance with the parallelism with "reigns" in the preceding line) and "feeds" (in keeping with the parallelism with "satis[fies]" in the following line). Suggestion, courtesy of S. Parker.

147. For reconstructions and corrections in lines 52–58, see 14.5–12; Dijkstra 1983: 30.

148. The parallel words *b<n>//bn* suggest titles, but the sense of these epithets is unclear. It is not even evident that these titles belong to the messengers; rather, they may name personages whom the messengers are commanded to see (cf. 10 II 30-31).

149. An antiphrastic expression for a prison-house. A house for lepers is given this label in 2 Kgs 15:5. For Sheol as a prison, see Jonah 2:7; and as a place of entrapment, 2 Sam 22 (Ps 18):5-6.

150. According to Gibson (1978: 67), the two scribal lines indicate that the text omits the narration of the messengers' journey to Mot. If so, the text moves almost immediately to the beginning of Mot's reply to Baal reconstructed below on the basis of the repetition of the speech in the next column.

151. Cf. the cosmic size of the appetite of Sheol (the Underworld) in Isa 5:14.

152. Continuing from the previous bicolon, Mot asks if his appetite is like that of a thirsty buffalo or hind who goes to a water-source to drink.

153. This line has often been compared with Ps 42:2, where the speaker compares human desire (**npš*) for Yahweh to the longing of a deer (*ʿyl*, cognate with Ugaritic *aylt* here) for channels of water.

154. See 3 VI 59 and 12 VI 54–58.

155. On this title, see n. 211 below.

156. The same cosmic enemies oppose Yahweh (Isa 27:1; Ps 74:13–14).

157. Mot contrasts Litan's fate at the hands of Baal with his own intention to devour Baal.

158. Probably a scribal addition, given the standard formula *ydd il* elsewhere and the length of line.

159. The length of this line militates in favor of the common view that a dittography is involved here.

160. Other passages with parallelism of **ary*– and **aḫ*– (as in the previous bicolon) would suggest haplography here.

161. An expression for Mot's boundless appetite.

162. Or, perhaps "because he [Mot] was scorching the olive" (so de Moor 1987:72).

163. Reading for *waṣḫ*.

164. SHGR and ITHM (see below) are two deities who receive an offering together in *CAT* 1.148.31. Little is known of either deity. It would seem that SHGR is a minor deity, perhaps associated with Baal, and either representing or having charge over animals (Caquot, Sznycer, and Herdner 1974: 246). ITHM is perhaps associated with Baal as well, but nothing else is known of this figure.

165. El?

166. The name of Jezebel, the daughter of a king of Tyre as well as a follower of the Phoenician god Baal (1 Kgs 16:31; 18:4, etc.), similarly means "Where is Baal?" See also 12 IV 4-5, 15-16.

167. Based on 11 V 8–9, it is tempting to reconstruct: *ynpᶜ.bᶜ[l.bšbᶜt. ǵlmm]/bṯmn{t}.[ḫnzrm]*, "Baal arises [with (his) seven boys], With (his) eight [attendants]." As an emendation is required, this proposal must be regarded with caution. Note also *CAT*'s reading of *a[* after *btmnṯ*. Dijkstra (1983: 31) suggests a reconstruction based on 9 V 10–12. Though free of textual difficulty, this reconstruction assumes that Baal has a home with seven rooms//eight chambers, an architectural detail otherwise attested only of El's abode.

168. Perhaps reflecting a type of burial. Cf. 12 I 17-18. The adjective "great" translates *ilm* ("divine"), used here apparently as a superlative as in 9 I and elsewhere.

169. As the Ugaritic word for "earth" and "Hell" (or underworld) is the same, the connotation of underworld should be borne in mind whenever "Earth" is used in the rest of the Baal Cycle.

170. For Baal's sexual relations with a cow, see also texts 15 and 16 below (*CAT* 1.10 and 1.11) and *CAT* 1.13. For biblical evidence to this effect, see Smith 1990: 51. Cf. the myth of "Sin and the Cow" known in Akkadian sources (Veldhuis 1991). The cow in the Ugaritic passages is apparently not Anat, as has been argued on occasion.

171. One horizontal wedge is visible, and so *q* is read here on the basis of the parallel. Cf. *CAT*.

172. See *CTA* p. 36 n. 7; Gibson 1978: 4.

173. Literally, "the opening of the heart."

174. This poetic unit is continued in lines 2-3 of the next column.

175. The customary speech-opening formula ("She raises her voice and cries") is omitted here.

176. Perhaps with Bauer emend to *ard*, "I will descend" (cf. 11 VI 25; *CTA* p. 38 n. 3; Gibson 1978: 74)?

177. That is, Anat.

178. The translation here is inferred from context. For the problems in interpreting *gmn*, see Watson 1989.

179. For the ass as a sacrificial offering, cf. *ʿr* in *CAT* 1.40.26, 34, 43 (but the reading in some cases is questionable; see *CTA* p. 114 n. 5). Ginsberg (1973: 131 n. 3) reconstructs *[y]ḫmrm* ("roe-bucks"), which seems to fit better with the other animals in this context. For criticism, see *CTA* p. 39 n. 1. According to P. Wapnish (personal communication), the roe-buck (*Capreolus capreolus*) is attested in Levantine sites. Cf. Deut 14:5; 1 Kgs 5:3 (Caquot, Sznycer, and Herdner 1974: 255 n. e').

180. If the word means "to drink" and not "to place," Anat perhaps consumes either part of the sacrifice or perhaps less likely even some of her deceased brother, an act more explicitly described in 26.4-5.

181. That is, Anat.

182. The name consists of two verbs meaning "he knows, he understands." The relation between this name and the character is unclear.

183. The verbs assume some form of the verb **šab* in both lines. This may be a reference to Athtar as a god of irrigation.

184. A gesture of supplication (Greenstein 1982b).

185. Given that the **qatala* form for this verb commonly begins descriptions of travel elsewhere in the Baal Cycle, a dittography might be suspected in this instance.

186. The wedges between *r* and *m* appear to be the heads of the top left-hand, bottom left-hand and right-hand wedges of *y*. Therefore, *ṣǵrym* is tentatively read here. Cf. *CAT*'s reading *ṣǵrm*.

187. Reading for *ymṣi*.

188. If this phrase is correctly understood, the direct objects in the two preceding parallel lines might be interpreted as "the Great (God)" (cf. 9 III 39) and "crushers of Yamm" (cf. Ps 93:3). In both 9 III 39 and Ps 93:3, the term in apposition is River(s), a title of Yamm in both Ugaritic and biblical literatures.

189. Elsewhere this bicolon is prefaced by *ym ymm yʿtqn*, "one day, two days pass."

190. It is possible that a verb of speech is to be reconstructed in this lacuna, in which case the following line is to be understood as part of this colon. However, verbs of speech with the preposition *ʿm* ("with, to") are rare in Ugaritic poetry. Another possibility is a form of the verb **ṯwb*, "to turn," as this verb is used with *ʿm* in a comparable context in 12 VI 12-13 prior to a speech-opening formula. The difficulty is that the prefix form of the verb that would be expected is *yṯb*, but the lacuna seems to have room for only two letters.

191. These lines and the following two bicola use agricultural imagery to describe the destruction of Mot (cf. Exod 32:20). Healey (1984: 248) suggests that "sword" here may be a "threshing-sledge," perhaps of the sort with sharp metal wheel-blades. The line may then refer to threshing.

192. On the basis of 12 II 31–33 some scholars reconstruct plausibly *<bḫṯr ʿlk pḫt bqʿ>*, "<by the sieve, Because of you I faced cleaving>" (Caquot, Sznycer, and Herdner 1974: 266 n. f; Greenstein 1982a: 203 n. 53).

193. 12 II 35 and the parallelism would seem to call for a verb meaning "to scatter" or the like. *CTA* reads *ǵly*, which might mean, in the words of Healey (1984:

248), "'boiling' ... , referring to the outdoor boiling of grain to make *burgul.*" Cf. Greenstein 1982a: 203 n. 53.

194. The identity of Baal's brothers is unclear. These "brothers" might be the various Baals listed after Baal Sapan in *CAT* 1.118.5-10 (suggested as a possibility by Caquot, Sznycer, and Herdner 1974: 80) or the *bʿlm*, "the Baals" (*CAT* 1.119.6; 1.148.11-12), or both, but they are not to be identified with his meteorological vanguard in 11 V 7-9 (=? "Baal's divine helpers," *il tʿḏr bʿl* in *CAT* 1.84.8, 47, 1.118.25 and 1.148.8 [cf. 1.109.21]).

195. The lacuna perhaps contained a verb opening the following speech.

196. The heads of only two wedges are visible at the top of the first sign, which would suggest *s* rather than *l*. The lower part of the sign is damaged.

197. Reading for *yšl* (haplography of a horizontal wedge).

198. Perhaps some sort of animal as in the following two bicola. Cf. Ethiopic *gomari*, "hippopotamus" (Leslau 1987: 194, 195; Caquot, Sznycer, and Herdner 1974: 268 n. b).

199. Perhaps some sort of animal, as in the preceding two bicola. Alternatively, a group of men.

200. For syntax and context, cf. *CAT* 1.161.19.

201. Some wedges are visible which apparently jeopardize the full reconstruction of *y[šu.gh.wyṣḥ]* (which is to be translated: "And he raised his voiced and declared:").

202. The passage has been generally understood as a hymn praising Shapsh on her nightly circuit through the underworld, where the Rephaim dwell. The verbs in the second colon below have been interpreted accordingly as second person invoking Shapsh. Summoning the sun goddess to partake of a feast would be unusual, which suggests another line of interpretation. The verbs may be understood as third person forms, as rendered here. For speculations on the cultic context of this final piece, see Dijkstra 1986. *CAT* 1.161.18-26 may refer to the ritual descent of the king to the underworld, in the presence of Shapsh (Levine and de Tarragon 1984: 657-58); a comparable ritual may be involved here. If so, it is the king who is invoked. For the associations between the Ugaritic monarchy and the Rephaim mentioned in the hymn, see the following footnotes. See also n. 5 above.

203. As the parallel terms "gods," "divinities," and "dead" suggest, the Rephaim here are deified ancestors. The Rephaim (*rpum*) appear in *CAT* 1.161 as the tribal ancestors of Ugarit's royal line. For biblical parallelism between the Rephaim and the dead (*mētîm*), see Ps 88:11; Isa 26:14, 19. See also *KAI* 177:1.

204. For the biblical use of "god" (*ʾĕlōhîm*) for the dead, see 1 Sam 28:13 and Isa 8:19 (Lewis 1989: 35-36, 49-50). The Ugaritic word "god" (*il*), is used with the names of deceased kings in *CAT* 1.113.13-26. If the final passage of the Baal Cycle was addressed to the living king, the "Rephaim" and "gods" would refer to his putative tribal and royal ancestors and not to the dead in general. For Rephaim as deceased kings in Israelite tradition, see Isa 14:9.

205. That is, one who casts spells. This understanding is based on the apparently magical use of these parallel terms in a Ugaritic incantation, Ras Ibn Hani 78/20.9-10 (Smith 1984; Dijkstra 1986: 150). The terms have generally been translated "your companion" and "your intimate," respectively.

206. Perhaps "In the sea"(?), in which case the sun goddess may be regarded as

making the westward journey which leads to the underworld. For the association of the cosmic waters with the Rephaim of the underworld, see Job 26:5.

207. Two cosmic enemies whom Anat speaks of having defeated in 9 III above. They may also be the demons here subject to Kothar's magic. Cf. Ps. 91:13 (Dijkstra 1986: 151).

208. These verbs have also been interpreted as verbs of travel, the lines then suggesting Kothar's protection on the journey.

209. A clan name (cf. the place-name *šubānu*)?

210. Or possibly a personal name.

211. This title may be not a family name but a title denoting either a cultic officiant, perhaps an "offerer" (see Freilich 1992) or a social-political rank meaning "lord, master" (Greenfield 1969: 60-61). Caquot, Sznycer, and Herdner (1974: 221 n. k) entertain the possibility that the word is not a title but a verb. The syntax seems to militate against this approach.

Variant Version

13. *CAT* 1.133

The text contains two sections demarcated by a scribal line between lines 11 and 12. Lines 1-11 represent a variant version of a passage well known from the Baal Cycle (11 I 11-22, except 18-20a). Lines 12-19 are highly debated. Like lines 1-11, lines 12-19 refer to Mot. Otherwise, they are unclear, which complicates their interpretation as well as the understanding of the text as a whole. Do lines 12-19 draw on a well-known text (11 II 20)? Or were these lines part of a scribal creation attached to the older first part?[1]

Front side of the tablet

		Mot's Speech to Baal
1–2	*wyʿny.bn/ilm.mt.*	And Divine Mot answers:
2–5	*npš[ ]/npš.lbim/thw.*	"Is my appetite the lion's appetite in the wild,
	wnpš/anḫr.bym	The appetite of the dolphin in the sea?
6–8	*brkt.[ ]šbšt/krumm.*	Does it[2] go[3] to a pool like a buffalo,
	hm/ʿn.kd̲d.aylt	Or travel to a spring like the hind?
9–11	<*i*>[4] *mt.hm.ks.ym/sk.nhr*	Or will my cup contain a whole river,[5]
	hm/šbʿ.ydty.bṣʿ	Or my portion amount to seven bowls' worth?"
	———————	
		Mot's Feast (?)
12	*[ ]*[6] *bʿrbt*	... sated/seven...great ones
13	*[ ].qbẓ.t̲m[ ]*[7]	... assembly of eight ...

Bottom edge of the tablet

14	*[ ]m.ẓbm.t̲r*	... gazelles, bull ...[8]

Back of the tablet	**Mot's Demise (?)**
15–17 *[[9]]bn.ilm/m[t.]šmḥ.*[10]	[So] Divine Mot is wiped out (?),[11]
pydd/il[.]ǵzr	Indeed, the Beloved of El,
18–19 *bab*[12] *n.ʿz*[13].	By the stone (?) of the Strong One,
w/rgbt.zbl	And the mound (?) of the Prince.[14]

Notes

1. For these questions, see Pardee 1988b: 163–64.

2. That is, Mot's appetite. This bicolon seems to be dependent on "appetite" (*npš*) in the previous bicolon (lines 2–5). Cf. 11 I 16–17, which likewise depends for its governing subject on *npš* in the previous bicolon in lines 14–16.

3. The translation assumes **šbš* and **kd̲d* as verbs of travel (see Pardee 1988b: 159–60 for the philogogical defense of this view). The apparent literary parallel in Ps 42:2 (cf. Lam 1:6) would seem to favor this approach. For an alternative, see Pardee 1988b: 159–60.

4. See the parallel context of 11 I 18–22. Renfroe (1992: 100) refers here to an "apparent truncation of *ʾmt* to *mt.*"

5. Mot's appetite (continuing from the previous bicolon) is not the subject, given the lack of agreement in gender between the putative subject and verb. See 11 I 20–22 for the reversed form of this bicolon.

6. Further wedges are visible which Pardee read as part of *š*.

7. Another wedge is visible, which Pardee reads as part of *t*.

8. Dijkstra (1983: 31) sees in these lines "seven ladies" followed by an "assembly of eight," and then references to animals. If so, the animal words may refer either to animals eaten in the context of a divine assembly or to ranks among the deities. For comparison with 2 IV 5–8, see, among others, Renfroe 1992: 100; for the use of animal names for leaders, see Miller 1970.

9. Evidence that this passage is a citation or variant of 11 II 20 is lacking, as the two passages differ significantly. It is therefore difficult to follow Dijkstra in reconstructing [*ṣḥq*] with confidence. Perhaps a two-letter particle (such as *hl* or *ap*) with a word-divider begins this clause, as presumed by the translation.

10. Dijkstra (1983: 31, following others) reads *ḫ* for *ḥ*, on the assumption that this line imitates 11 II 20. The emendation is rejected by Pardee (1988b: 162, esp. n. 22).

11. The verb is governed by the preceding noun clause (so Pardee) rather than the following one (so Dijkstra), as the particle *p* begins a clause and does not stand between a subject and the verb governed by it. With Dijkstra's emendation (see n. 12), he renders "rejoices," in which case the section refers to Mot's victory over Baal—"Ambiguïté assez déroutante" (Pardee 1988b: 163).

12. Following Pardee's reading. Dijkstra (1983: 31) emends to *badn*.

13. Dijkstra (1983: 31) reads {.} between these two letters, but Pardee (1988b) shows no such reading.

14. If correct, the passage would present another version of Baal's victory over Mot. The obscurity of the meaning might be viewed as militating in favor of Dijkstra's emended version, in which case the text may be rendered: "In (his) strong lordship/And awesome nobility."

Variant Version

14. *CAT* 1.8

The text contains copies and/or variants of lines from the fourth tablet of the Baal Cycle, 10 I 20–22 (or III 28–30), IV 62–V 1, and VII 52–59. The tablet may constitute a scribe's practice text.

1–2	*[[1]]k.mgn.rbt.aṯrt/[ym[2]].*	"[...]. a gift for Lady Athirat of the [Sea,]
	mǵẓ.qnyt.ilm[3]	A present for the Creatress of the Gods."
3–5	*wtnbt.lbᶜl.km/[i]lm*	"Let a house be given to Baal like the [g]ods,
	wḥẓr.kbn/[a]ṯrt.[4]	A court, like [A]thirat's sons."
5-6	*gm.lǵlmh/bᶜl.yṣḥ.*[5]	Aloud to his l[a]ds Baal declares:
6-9	*ᶜn.gpn/wugr.*	"See, Gapn and Ugar,
	bn.ǵlmt/ᶜmmym.	Sons of the Lass, Kinsmen of Sea (?),
	bn.ẓlm[t]/rmt.prᶜt.	Sons of..[.,] the Exalted Firstborn (?).[6]
9	*ibr[.mnt]*	
10	*ṣḥrrm.ḥbl[ ]*[7]	*(The rest of the text is extremely difficult to interpret.)*
11	*ᶜrpt.tḥt.*[8]*[ ]*	
12	*mᶜṣrm.ḥ[ ]*	
13	*glṯ.isr[ ]*	
14	*m.brt[ ]*	
15	*ymt[m]*	
16	*ši[ ]*	
17	*[m]*	

Notes

1. *CAT* and del Olmo Lete (1981: 501) read *ik*. If correct, this variant contains no main verb, which seems unlikely. If *šskn* in 10 1 20 were to be taken from **nsk*, "to pour" (see del Olmo Lete 1981: 595) and if it were possible to reconstruct two letters here, it may be preferable to restore *[šs]k* ("cast") as a shorter form of the same verb.

2. *CAT* reads the *m* and the first letters of lines 4 and 5. Parallel passages from 10 ensure the reconstructions.

3. See 10 I 21-22, III 28-30.

4. See 10 IV 50-51.

5. For reconstructions and corrections in lines 5-17, see 10 VII 52-59; Dijkstra 1983: 30.

6. The parallel words, *bn//bn,* suggest titles, but the sense of these epithets is unclear. It is not even evident that these epithets belong to the messengers; rather, they may name personages whom the messengers are commanded to see (cf. 10 II 30-31).

7. To judge from the parallel text in 10 VII 57-58, the gaps at the ends of this line and the following one are relatively short.

8. Two further vertical wedges are visible, but the readings of the letters are uncertain.

Shorter Texts

Baal Fathers a Bull

15. *CAT* 1.10

Translated by Simon B. Parker

This narrative is inscribed in three columns, none complete, on one side only of a large tablet. No narrative sense can be made of the first column. The middle column has the longest completely preserved text, extending over about thirty lines. Having arrived at Baal's house, Anat is informed that Baal has gone hunting in a grassland where bulls are plentiful. Anat flies to him. He proposes that they "lengthen life"(?) (by begetting offspring?) and fight his enemies. Anat's attention is caught by a cow, and evidently she suggests that Baal produce bovine offspring, because the third column begins with a reference to cows bearing—including a calf for Anat. Baal then goes up his mountain and sits on his royal throne, while Anat apparently presides over the birth of a bull for Baal. She too then goes up Baal's mountain and proclaims to him the good news of the birth. The condition of the tablet and the difficulty of many parts of the preserved text preclude a general interpretation of the story.

	Column I	Column I
	(Ca. twenty lines missing.)	(*Ca. twenty lines missing.*)
1	*[b]tlt.ʿnt*	[ ] Anat the Girl
2	*[ ]h*[1]*p.hẓm*	[ ]…
3–5	*[ ]ḥ dlydʿ bn il* *[ ]pḫr kkbm* *[ ]dr dt šmm*	[ ] which the gods do not know, [ ] the assembly of the stars, [ ] the circle of those in the heavens.
6–7	*[al]iyn bʿl* *[ ].rkb ʿrpt*	[ ] Baal the [Al]mighty [ ] the Rider of Clouds
8–9	*[ ]ǵš.llimm* *[ ]lyṯb.larṣ*	[ ] to the peoples, [ ] not(?) return to the Earth.
10	*[ ].mtm*	[ ] men/the dead
11	*[ ]t?y*[2]*d mhr.ur*	[ ]…
12	*[ ]yḥnnn*	[ ] they show him favor (?)
13	*[ ]t?t.ytn*	[ ] he gives
14–15	*[btlt] ʿnt* *[ybmt] limm*	[ ] Anat [the Girl] [the Sister] of Peoples
16–17	*[ ]l.limm* *[yṯ]b.larṣ*	[ ] to the peoples, [not(?) retu]rn to the Earth.
	(About twenty-three lines are almost or completely missing. The end of line 24 may be restored *r]umm.*)	(*Ca. twenty-three lines almost or completely missing. One line apparently ends with a reference to bulls.*)

Column II		Column II
(Ca. twenty lines missing)		(*Anat is inquiring after Baal's whereabouts.*)
1–2	*[bʿl bbhth]* *[il hd bqr]b.hklh*	["Is Baal in his house?] [Hadd, the god, in] his palace?"
(One line left vacant)		
3	*wtʿnyn.ǵlm.bʿl*	Baal's pages reply:
4–5	*in.bʿl.bbhth{t}* *il hd.bqrb.hklh*	"Baal is not in his house, Hadd, the god, in his palace.
6–7	*qšthn.aḫd.bydh* *wqṣʿth.bm.ymnh*	He took his bow in one hand, His arrows up in the other;
8–9	*idk.lytn.pnm* *tk.aḫ.šmk.mla[t r]umm*	Then he set his face For the grassland of SHMK, aboundi[ng in b]ulls."
10–12	*tšu knp.btlt.ʿn[t]* *tšu.knp.wtr.bʿp* *tk.aḫ šmk.mlat rumm*	Anat the Gir[l] raises her wings, Raises her wings and sets off, flying, For the grassland of SHMK, abounding in bulls.
13–16	*wyšu.ʿnh.aliyn.bʿl* *wyšu.ʿnh.wyʿn* *wyʿn.btlt.ʿnt* *nʿmt.bn.aḫt.bʿl*	Baal the Almighty raises his eyes, Raises his eyes and catches sight, Catches sight of Anat the Girl, Loveliest of the sisters of Baal.
17–18	*lpnnh.ydd.wyqm* *lpʿnh.ykrʿ.wyql*	Before her he steps and stands, At her feet he bends and bows.
19	*wyšu.gh.wyṣḥ*	He raises his voice and cries:
20	*ḥwt.aḫt.wnark*	"Sister, let us lengthen life!(?)
21–23	*qrn.dbatk.btlt ʿnt* *qrn.dbatk.bʿl.ymšḥ* *bʿl.ymšḥ.hm.bʿp*	Your powerful(?) horns, Anat the Girl, Your powerful(?) horns let Baal anoint,

		Let Baal anoint them in flight (?).
24–25	*nṭʿn.barṣ.iby* *wbʿpr.qm.aḫk*	In the Earth, let us gore my foes, In the Dust, those opposing your brother."
26–29	*wtšu.ʿnh.btlt.ʿnt* *wtšu.ʿnh.wtʿn* *wtʿn.arḫ.wtr.blkt* *tr.blkt.wtr.bḫl*	She raises her eyes, Anat the Girl, She raises her eyes and catches sight, Sight of a cow, and sets off walking, Sets off walking, and sets off trembling (?).
30	*[b]nʿmm.bysmm.ḥ[ ] k[ ]t*	[Among] the lovely, among the shapely, . . .[3]
31	*[ql].lbʿl.ʿnt.ttnn*	Anat [calls] loud and clear to Baal:
32–33	*[ ].bʿlm.dipḥ/i[ ]* *[il] hd dʿnn n[ ]*	"[ ], Baal, what I see [ ] Hadd [the god], what our eyes [."]
34	*[ ]aliyn.b[ʿl]*	B[aal] the Almighty [replies:?]
35	*[btl]t.ʿn[t]ph*	"[ ] Ana[t the G]irl, [I?] see!"
(Ca. five lines without a clearly preserved word.)		(*It is unclear what develops in the remaining five lines.*)
Column III		Column III
(Ca. twenty lines missing.)		(*After the missing first twenty lines, Baal and Anat are again in conversation.*)
1–3	*[ ]m(?) arḫt.tld[n]* *a?l?p.lbtlt.ʿnt* *wypt.lybmt.li[mm]*	"[ ] the cows will bear An ox(?) for Anat the Girl, A heifer for the Sister of Peo[ples."]
4	*wyʿny.aliyn [bʿl]*	Then [Baal] the Almighty replies:
5–6	*lm.kqnyn.ʿl[ ]* *kdr{d}.dyknn [ ]*	"Why, like our creator(s), . . [ ] Like the circle that produced us [?"]

7–8	*bʿl.yṣǵd.mli?[ ]*	Baal marches, full of [ ]
	il hd.mla.uṣ/l[ ]	Hadd, the god, with full [ ]
9–10	*btlt*[4]*.pbtlt.ʿn[t]*	The Girl, yes, Ana[t] the Girl,
	wp.nʿmt.aḫt.[bʿl]	And yes, [Baal]'s loveliest sister—[5]
11–12	*yʿl.bʿl.bǵ[r]*	Baal ascends the moun[tain,]
	wbn[6]*.dgn.bš[mm?]*	Dagan's son the he[avens(?)];
13–14	*bʿl.yṯb.lks[i mlkh]*	Baal returns to [his royal] thro[ne,]
	bn.dgn.lkḫ[ṯ drkth]	Dagan's son to [his sovereign] sea[t,]
15–16	*lalp.ql.ẓ[ ]*	. . . a cry for/to the ox,
	la<l>p.ql.nd.[ ]	Uttered a cry for/to the ox ...
17–18	*tlk wtr.b[ḫl]*	She goes and sets off [trembl]ing(?),
	bnʿmm.bys[mm]	Among the lovely, the sha[pely .][7]
19	*arḫ arḫ.[ ]*	The cow, the cow [ ]
20–21	*ibr.tld? [lbʿl]*	It bears a bull [for Baal,]
	wrum.l[rkb ʿrpt]	An ox for [the Rider of Clouds.]
22–23	*tḫbq.[ ]*	She embraces [the cow(?)]
	tḫbq.[ ][8]	She embraces [the cow(?)]
24	*wtks[y]nn.b[ ]*	She covers it with [ ]
25–26	*yʿ?l?.šrh.wšḫph*	. . . its cord and milk,
	[ ]b? šḫp ṣǵrth[9]	[ ] its youthful milk.
27–28	*yrk.tʿl.b[ ]*[10]*ǵr*	She goes up the mountain's flank,
	mslmt.bǵr tliyt	Up the mighty mountain's ridge.
29–31	*wtʿl.bkm.barr*	She goes up the rise, up Araru,
	bm.arr.wbṣpn	Up Araru, yes and up Zaphon,
	bnʿm.bǵr.tliyt	Up the lovely, the mighty mountain.
32	*ql.lbʿl.ttnn*	She calls out loud and clear to Baal:

33–34	*bšrt.il.bš[r b]ʿl* *wbšr.ḥtk.[dgn]*	"Great news!—welcome it, Baal, Welcome it, offspring of Dagon,
35–36	*k.ibr.lbʿl [yl]d* *wrum.lrkb ʿrpt*	For a bull is born to Baal, A wild ox to the Rider of Clouds!"
37	*yšmḫ.aliyn.bʿl*	Baal the Almighty rejoices!

Notes

1. Or *p*.
2. Or *ḫ*.
3. Some see here traces of *ḥbl kṯrt* "the band of the Katharat."
4. The *t* and *l* are superimposed.
5. This bicolon may be misplaced. It would fit well after the next three bicola, where an introduction of Anat seems desirable.
6. The *w* and *b* are superimposed.
7. Cf. II 29–30.
8. Some see traces of the word *arḫ* following *tḥbq* in both lines.
9. The *ṣ* is superimposed over a horizontal wedge. Perhaps the scribe started to write *h* after *šḫp,* as in the previous line.
10. Traces of two or three superimposed letters between *b* and *ǵ*.

A Birth

16. *CAT* 1.11

Translated by Simon B. Parker

This fragment, the upper right corner of a tablet, is more obscure than is sometimes supposed. (How much is missing from the left of the column is unknown.) There are clear references to a birth, to the Katharat goddesses, and to Baal and Anat. Many have assumed that it is Baal and Anat who are the subject of the sexual encounter in lines 1–2, but Walls (1992) and P. L. Day (1992) have argued cogently that Anat is not sexually active. Walls has even questioned whether lines 1–2 refer to sexual activity at all (1992: 134–39).

1	*[ ].yṯkḫ.wyiḫd.bqrb[ ]*	[he] ... and he grasps the vagina[
2	*[t]ṯkḫ.wtiḫd*[1]*.bušr*[2]*[ ]*	[she] ... and she grasps the penis/-testicles[
3	*[b]ʿl.yabd*[3]*.lalp*	[B]aal ... to/for the bull/a thousand
4	*[bt]lt.ʿnt*	[ ] Anat the [Gi]rl
5	*[nš?]q.hry.wyld*	[embra]ce, conception, and birth
6	*[ ]m.ḫbl.kṯ[rt]*	[ ] the band of the Kath[arat]
	[bt]lt.ʿnt	[ ]Anat the [Gi]rl
8	*[ali]yn.bʿ[l]*	[ ]Baa[l the Mig]hty
9	*[ ]mʿn[ ]*	...

(The remainder of the fragment—lines 9–18—preserves only odd letters.)

Notes

1. In this and the preceding line *kyiḫd* is a possible reading instead of *wyiḫd.*
2. Or *bušk.*
3. Or *ynbd.*

The Wilderness

17. *CAT* 1.12
Translated by Simon B. Parker

The bottom thirty lines of two columns are preserved. The full size of the tablet cannot be determined, but the reverse of the preserved part is not inscribed. The narrative is too fragmentary and the language too difficult or ambiguous to permit an authoritative translation or interpretation.

This much seems clear. In the remains of the first column, two women complain that something inside them is eating them. El sends them off into the marginal land, where they are to bear tauromorphic "Eaters" and "Tearers." Baal then prowls in the same general area, looking for these newborn creatures. In the incomplete lines in the middle of the second column, it seems that Baal then destroys them. But after seven years, he still carries their blood, so that the leaders of his kin come after him, and he in turn falls. (Presumably the "Eaters" and "Tearers," who were to "have the face of Baal," were Baal's offspring, so that his kin bear some responsibility for avenging their death.) Unfortunately, the conclusion of the narrative is among the least comprehensible lines.

Column I		Column I
(Only the ends of the first six lines are preserved.)		(*As the text becomes clear, two females are addressing El.*)
7–8	*[ ]rn.km.šḥr/* *[ ]ltn.km.qdm/*	"[ ] like dawn, [ ] like the east.
9–11	*[k]bdn.il.abn/* *kbd kiš<t>?.tikln/* *ṯdn.km.mrm.tqrṣn/*	Our liver, El, our father, Our liver they eat like fire, Our breast they bite like . . ."
12–13	*il.yẓḥq.bm/lb.* *wygmḏ.bm kbd/*	El laughs in his heart, Quivers and shakes in his liver:[1]
14–17	*ẓi.at.* *ltlš/amt.yrḫ./*	"Out you go, Tulisha, maid of Yarikh,

	ldmgy.amt/atrt.	Damgaya, maid of Asherah;
17–18	*qḥ/ksank.ḥdgk/ḥtlk.*	Take your stool, your satchel, your swaddle,[2]
19–22	*wẓi./baln.tkm/* *btk.md!br*[3]*. /il.šiy./*	Off into the woods of TKM, Into the god-awful wilderness.[4]
23–25	*kry amt/ʿpr.* *ʿẓm yd/ugrm.*	Dig, maid, the dust, with strong hand, the fields.
25–29	*ḫl.ld/aklm.* *tbrkk/* *wld.ʿqqm./* *ilm.ypʿr/šmthm/*	Writhe, give birth to the Eaters —may they bless you,[5] Give birth to the Tearers —may the gods name them.[6]
30–33	*bhm.qrnm/km.trm.* *wgbtt/km.ibrm/* *wbhm.pn.bʿl./*	They will have horns like oxen, Bulk like that of bullocks; They will have the face of Baal."[7]
34–35	*bʿl.ytlk.wyṣd* *yḥ pat.md!br*[8]	Baal roams around hunting, Prowls the edge of the wilderness,
36–37	*wn.ymǵy.aklm* *wymẓa ʿqqm*	That he might reach the Eaters, That he might meet the Tearers.
38–39	*bʿl.ḥmdm.yḥmdm* *bn dgn.yhrm*	Baal is intensely intent on them, The son of Dagan fixed on them.
40–41	*bʿl.ngthm.bpʿnh* *wil hd.bḫ?r?ẓʿh*	Baal seeks them on foot, Haddu the god . . .

Column II

(Only the first few letters of each of the first thirty lines are preserved. The first few letters of Col. I, 40 and 41 reappear in the

Column II

(*Some words of Col. I, 40–41 appear in lines 5–6 and 21–22 and of Col. I, 38–39 in lines 8–9, and line 7 seems to reappear in line 23. Apparently Baal continues or*

	preserved beginnings of Col. II, 5 and 6, 21 and 22, and the remains of Col. II, 8–9 recall Col. I, 38–39. Lines 24–25 read: *yisphm b[ʿl]/bn.dgn[ ]*.)	*repeats his intent search for the Eaters/ Tearers. Otherwise what happens in the largely lost first thirty lines is unknown—as is most of what happens in the rest of the column. Lines 24–25 begin:* Ba[al] rounds them up [ ]/ The son of Dagan [ ].)
31–33	*ʿn.bʿl.aḫ?ḏ?[ ]/* *ẓrh.aḫḏ.qš[t]/* *pʿn.bʿl.aḫḏ[ ]/*	At Baal's eyes [ ] At his back, grasping [ ] At Baal's feet, grasping [ ][9]
34	*wṣmt.ǵllm[ ]/*	And destroyed . . .
35	*aḫḏ.aklm.k/w?[ ]/*	Grasping the Eaters [ ]
36	*npl.bmšmš[ ]/*	They fell in confusion(?)
37–38	*an pnm.yḥr[ ]/* *bmtnm.yšḫn.[ ]/*	In the strength of his face he grew hot [ ] In his loins he became warm [ ]
39–40	*qrnh.km.ǵb[ ]/*	His horns are like [ ]
	hw.km.ḥrr[ ]/	As he grew hot [ ]
41	*šnmtm.dbṭ[ ]/*	. . .
42–43	*trʿ.trʿn.a[ ]/* *bnt.šdm.ṣḥr[ ]/*	We have finally broken through (?) . . . The daughters of the fields have pierced (?) . . .
44–45	*šbʿ.šnt.il.mla/* *wṯmn.nqpnt.ʿd/*	Seven long years have been filled, Eight slow-passing cycles:
46–47	*klbš.km lpš.dm.a?[ḫh]/* *km.all.dm.aryh/*	He was garbed in his siblings' blood like a garment, His fellows' blood like a mantle.
48–49	*kšbʿt.lšbʿm.aḫh.y?m[ ]/* *wṯmnt.lṯmnym/*	When his seven and seventy siblings [ ] All eight and eighty of them,

50–51	*šr.aḫyh.mẓah/* *wmẓah.šr.ylyh/*	The chief (?) of his siblings met him, He met the chief (?) of his kin,
52–53	*bskn.sknm.* *bʿdn/ʿdnm.*	In the direst danger, In the most critical time,
53–55	*kn.npl.bʿl/km ṯr.* *wtkms.hd./km.ibr.*	So Baal fell like an ox, Haddu crumpled like a bullock
55	*btk.mšmš.bʿl?*[10]*/*	In the confusion . . .
56–57	*i<š>?ttk.lakl*[11]*/* *išttk.lm.ttkn(?)/*	. . . . . .
58–59	*štk.mlk.dn/* *štk.šibt.ʿn/*	. . . the mighty/just king . . . . . . the women drawing water
60–61	*štk.qr.bt.il/* *wmṣlt.bt.ḥrš/*	. . . the spring of the house of El And the "deep" of the house of the diviner.

Notes

1. "In his heart" is the equivalent of English "to himself." "Liver" here corresponds to English "belly."

2. The three are items used in childbirth.

3. The tablet reads *l*.

4. Or: "the wilderness of IL SHIY."

5. Or: "Let them bring you to your knees." "The gods" of the next line might be anticipated as the subject of the verb in "may they bless you."

6. Or: "let El pronounce their names."

7. Or: "But Baal will face them out."

8. The tablet reads: *mlbr*.

9. As much as a third of each line may be missing, so that the prosody—and hence the syntax—is quite uncertain.

10. With *CAT*. Herdner: *d(ṣ/l);* Virolleaud: *dš*?

11. Or possibly: *lawl*.

The Binding of a Monster

18. *CAT* 1.83

Translated by Simon B. Parker

This fragment—the reverse and beginning of the obverse of the tablet are missing—is apparently an account of the threat posed by one of the sea monsters that Anat boasts of having defeated in 9, col. III above (*CAT* 1.3 III). The address to Yamm in lines 11–13 suggests that lines 8–10 are also a second person address (rather than an account of an action in the third person)—and possibly lines 5–7 also. Indeed, the sequence of verses makes most sense if read as part of a single speech. In this text, then, an appeal is made to Yamm himself to restrain the monster and relieve the people's plight.

This little fragment may have been used for some ritual purpose, or simply been a scribal exercise. I owe the reading of the original text to the collation and photography of Dr. Wayne Pitard.

1	*]r [*	
2	*]il.[*	[ ]god [ ]
3	*]un.barṣ*	They [ ] in/from the earth
4	*mḫnm.ṯrp ym*	. . . the sea.
5–7	*lšnm.tlḥk./šmm* *tṯrp/ym.ḏnbtm.*	The forked tongue licks the heavens,[1] The forked tail thrashes(?) the sea.
8–10	*tn![2]n.lšbm/tšt.* *trks/lmrym.lbnn*	Put the Dragon on high/in check(?), Bind it to Lebanon's height.
11–12	*pl.tbṯn.yymm* *hmlt ḫt.ynhr*	They are humiliated, Yamm, The multitudes terrified, River;
13–14	*ltph.mk/tḥm r.[ ]*	They see abasement . . .

(Only odd letters are preserved on the reverse of the tablet.)

Notes

1. Cf. the description of the voracious Mot (Death) in 11 (*CAT* 1.5) II 2–3.
2. The tablet reads: *a*.

El's Divine Feast

19. *CAT* 1.114
Translated by Theodore J. Lewis

This text is typical of many Ugaritic tales which tantalize the imagination with the fascinating escapades of the deities, yet bristle with so many problems of interpretation that readers are left uncertain about many crucial turns. Perhaps the Ugaritic bards knew that the best story should leave an audience thirsting for more.

Banquet scenes occur often in the Ugaritic myths. This text describes the god El, the head of the pantheon, arranging a banquet for the gods in which he himself participates to excess. The fare consists of choice pieces of game and enough drink to rival any Greek bacchanal.

The beginning of the text finds El preparing the cuts of meat for the mess which is to take place at his residence. At his invitation, the gods feast and drink to the point of inebriation. We then meet up with the moon god Yarikh, although scholars debate his role in the tale (a few would remove the deity completely, preferring to see reference to a monthly [*yrḫ*] feast instead). He seems to be skilled in the culinary art of meat preparation, as he cooks and carves portions for deities he favors. Other interpretations (based in part on reconstructing the word "dog" in line 5) see Yarikh in a far more debased role crawling around under the tables like a dog and receiving either scraps of food or beatings.

The goddesses Anat and Athtartu prepare the choicest of cuts for Yarikh and are then rebuked by El's gatekeeper (identity not disclosed). He thinks such fare should not be wasted on an inferior deity who is no better than a dog. The best should be reserved for El, the chief god of the pantheon, who is, after all, the host of the party. He also rebukes the god El perhaps for a party that is getting out of control.

The tale then focuses on El's behavior at the banquet, which is called a *marziḥu*, an institution known for its drinking throughout much of the ancient Near East (cf. Amos 6:7; Jeremiah 16:5). El drinks to inebriation and staggers home with the help of two little-known deities (Thukamuna and Shunama), who have to carry him. A mysterious (at least to us) figure, Habayu, known as "he of two horns and tail," berates El for his behavior. El collapses dead drunk, falling in his own waste.

The chided goddesses Anat and Athtartu set off to hunt. The text breaks off without stating the object of their quest. Scholars suggest that they are in search of either more game to replenish El's table or a cure for El's condition.

The back of the tablet describes the return of the goddesses, who bring back ingredients for some type of healing procedure. Many have reasoned that the recipe must be a cure for patients suffering from hangovers and thus the intimate connection with a tale of El's overindulgence. Once again, readers are teased. All of the ingredients of this wonder potion are clear, except one. What is a *pqq*-plant and where does one find it?

For the most part the tablet, which measures 17.9 cm by 14.1 cm, is complete. There are a few lines damaged and missing at the bottom of the recto and the top of the verso. There are two areas (middle of lines 4–5 and near the beginning of lines 15–17) where the text is damaged.

Recto		Side 1
1–2	*il dbḥ.bbth.mṣd.* *ṣd.bqrb / hklh.* *sḥ.lqṣ.ʾilm.*	El slaughters game in his house, Butchers beasts in his palace, Bids gods to the cuts of beef.
2–4	*tlḥmn / ilm.wtštn.* *tštn.y<n> ʿd šbʿ /* *trṯ.ʿd [škr].*	The gods eat and drink, Drink wine till sated, Vintage till inebriated.
4–6	*yʿdb.yrḫ / gbh.km [. . .]*[1] *yqṯqṯ.tḥt / ṯlḥnt.*	Yarikh grills the haunch like a [,] Grabs the hind-quarter beneath the tables.
6–8	*il.d ydʿnn /* *yʿdb.lḥm.lh.*[2] *wd l ydʿnn /* *ylmn.ḥṭm.tḥt.ṯlḥn*[3]	As for the god whom he knows, He grills fare for him to feast; As for the god he does not know, He strikes with sticks beneath the table.

9–11	*ʿṯtrt.wʿnt.ymǵy /* *ʿṯtrt.tʿdb.nšb lh /* *wʿnt.ktp [.]*	He nears Athtartu and Anat, Athtartu grills a steak for him, Anat roasts a rack of ribs.
11–14	*bhm.ygʿr.ṯǵr / bt.il.* *pn.lm.k!lb*[4]*.tʿdbn / nšb.* *linr.tʿdbn.ktp /* *bil.abh.gʿr.*	The porter of El's house chides them, Not to grill a steak for a dog, Not to roast a rib for a cur. He chides El, his father, too.
14–15	*yṯb.il. [. ./.] .* *il.yṯb.bmrzḥh*	El sits . . . El settles into his bacchanal.
16	*yš[t].[y][n].ʿd šbʿ.* *trṯ.ʿd škr*	El drinks wine till sated, Vintage till inebriated.
17–18	*il.h[l]k.lbth.* *yštql. / lḥẓrh.*	El staggers to his house, Stumbles in to his court.
18–20	*yʿmsn.nn.ṯkmn / wšnm.* *wngšnn.ḥby. /* *bʿl.qrnm.wḏnb.*	Thukamuna and Shunama carry him, Habayu then berates him, He of two horns and a tail.
20–22	*ylšn / bḫrʾih.wṯnth.* *ql.il.km mt /* *il.kyrdm.arṣ.*	He slips in his dung and urine, El collapses like one dead El like those who descend to Earth.[5]
23–24	*ʿnt / wʿṯtrt.tṣdn.* *[š][. . .] / q[d]š.bʿ[. . .]*	Athtartu and Anat march off to hunt ...

Verso — Side 2

25'	*[ ][n] . d[. . .]*	
26'–28'	*[ʿṯ][t]rt.wʿn[t][. . .] /* *[w]bhm.tṯṯb.[m]dh[...] /* *km.trpa.hn nʿr*	Athtartu and Anat . . . And with them they brought back . . . As when one heals to return to youth.

29'–31' *d yšt.llṣbh.šʿr klb /*	On his brow one should put:
[w]riš.pqq.wšrh /	—hairs of a dog —the top of a *pqq*-plant and its stem
yšt aḥdh.dm zt.ḫr[p]at	Mix it with the juice of virgin oil.

Notes

1. Some scholars see indications that the text reads ***klb***. This is far from certain.
2. In between lines 7 and 8 the gloss *d mṣd* ("of the game") is written in a smaller script.
3. In between lines 8 and 9 the letters *bq[ ]* are written in a swaller script.
4. The text reads *rlb*.
5. "Earth" here designates the underworld.

The Rapiuma

20–22. *CAT* 1.20–22
Translated by Theodore J. Lewis

These three fragmentary texts describe El's banquet for and with the Rapiuma, who have been viewed as representing (a) minor deities, (b) heroic warriors, (c) a tribal group, (d) the shades of the dead, or (e) some combination of (a)–(d). While the exact identification of the Rapiuma will continue to be debated, most scholars emphasize their connection with the cult of the dead especially in view of the Ugaritic Funerary Text (*CAT* 1.161), which invokes the Rapiuma in the context of what seems to be an elaborate funerary ritual. The cognate term for Rapiuma is amply attested in unambiguous contexts in Phoenician inscriptions (*rpʾm*) and biblical texts (*rĕpāʾîm*) to designate the shades of the dead.

The Ugaritic Rapiuma were perceived to be quite active. Here we have them hitching horses, galloping on stallions, and riding for three days to a banquet where they dine on what seems to be sumptuous fare. In contrast, the biblical texts argue against ascribing any power to the Rephaim. While the biblical Rephaim may engage in some activity (Isa 14:9; cf. 1 Samuel 28), for the most part they are stripped of any power (cf. Isa 26:14; Ps 88:11).

Scholars are at a loss at pinning down the speakers/participants in these texts, and interpretations vary. We seem to have alternating speakers, as indicated by first person discourse (by El or Daniel) in some sections and the lack thereof in others. The identifications of speakers (placed in parentheses) are not in the Ugaritic original and serve only as a guide to help the reader distinguish different voices in the texts. The term "narrator" has been chosen to designate those passages lacking first person discourse. While this is not the most desirable term, greater precision is beyond our grasp. To call this person an "officiant" may imply too cultic a role. Ultimately this depends on what one sees going on in the text. Should we envisage a performance of this work with a respondent of some kind (the community? a liturgical leader?). Is this speaker in the second person the same as the "person" who speaks of the spirits in the third person elsewhere? At present, the texts do not yield definitive answers.

Some scholars have suggested that these texts represent a continuation of the Aqhat narrative (texts 4 to 6 above). This suggestion is based on the mention of Daniel in 20.1.7–8 and, even more so, on the assumption that Aqhat must have been restored to Daniel (assuming the Aqhat tale to follow the same mythic pattern as the Baal myth). Yet there is no hard evidence to support the revivification of Aqhat and the mention of Daniel in 20 may only mean that Daniel was a well-known figure whose episodes were recounted in numerous tales.

The text, including the order of the tablets, is based, for the most part, on the new edition by Pitard (1992).

20. *CAT* 1.20 First Tablet

CAT 1.20 I Side 1

(The left side of this tablet is damaged. The width of this column is not known. No single line is complete enough to estimate the average number of letters per line.)

		(Narrator:)
1–3	*rp]um.tdbḥn*	[The sh]ades will feast,
	š]bʿd.ilnym	The spirits [seven]fold,
	] kmtmtm	[ ] like the ancient dead.
4–5	*]b.kqrb.sd*	[ ] when the assembly draws near,
	]n bym.qẓ	[ ] on the festive summer day.

6–7	*iln]ym.tlḥmn* *]rm.tštyn*	[The spi]rits will eat, [ ] will drink.
8–9	*]il.dʿrgzm* *]dt.ʿl.lty*	The god of the ... [ ], [ ] who is in charge of ...
10	*]tdbḥ.amr*	[ ] the sacrifices of ...
11	*]y[*	[. . .]

(The text breaks off. No part of the bottom portion of the tablet is preserved to allow one to estimate the length of the ongoing narrative.)

CAT 1.20 II		Side 2
		(El:)
0–1	*[šbʿ.bbty]* *ṯmn.bqrb.hkly.*	["Seven in my house,] Eight within my palace."
		(Narrator:)
1–2	*r[pum.aṯrh.] / tdd.* *aṯrh.tdd.ilm*	The s[hades] hastened [to his shrine], To his shrine hastened the spirits.
2–3	*[mrkbt.] / asr.* *sswm.tṣmd.* *dg[lm.tšu.]*	They hitched [the chariots], They yoked the horses, [They raised the stan]dards.
4	*tʿln.lmrkbthm.* *ti[tyn.ʿrhm]*	They mount their chariots. They co[me on their stallions.]
5	*tlkn.ym.wṯn* *aḫr.š[pšm.bṯlṯ]*	They journey a day and a second, At night[fall on the third,]
6–7	*mǵy rpum.lgrnt.* *i[lm(*or *ilnym).bqrb (*or *l)]/* *mṭʿt.*	The shades reached the threshing squares, The sp[irits] the planted fields.

7–8	*wyʿn.dnil.[mt.rpi]*	Then up spoke Daniel, [man of Rapiu,]
	yṯb.ǵzr.mt hrnmy	Replied the hero, man of the Harnemite:
		(Daniel:)
8–9	*[.rpum.] / bgrnt.*	"[The shades] are at the threshing squares,
	ilm.bqrb.m[ṭʿt.]	The spirits are at the plan[ted fields,]
10	*dtit.yspi.* *spu.q[ ]*	Those who came, let them be fed, Feed [the ancient ones (?),]
11	*[ ]tpḥ.ṯṣr.*	[ ] apples, delights (?)"
	shr	[…]

(The text breaks off. No part of the bottom portion of the tablet is preserved to allow one to estimate the length of the ongoing narrative.)

21. *CAT* 1.21 — Second Tablet

CAT 1.21.II — Side 1

		(El:)
1–2	*[ ]mrzʿy.*[1] *lk bty / [rpʾm.]*	"[Come to] my banquet. Set off to my house, O shades.
2–3	*[bb]ty.aṣḥkm.* *iqra / [km.bqrb.h]kly.*	[Into] my [hous]e I bid you I beckon [you into] my [pa]lace."
		(Narrator:)
3–4	*aṯrh.rpum/[ltdd.]* *[aṯrh].ltdd.ilnym*	To his shrine, O shades, [hasten,] [To his shrine,] hasten, O spirits.[2]
		(El:)
5–6	*[ ]mrzʿy.*	"[ ] my banquet.

	apn!nk.[3] *yrp[ ]* *[ ]km.rʿy.*	Then O shad[es] [ ] like a shepherd
6–8	*ḥt.alk / [ym.wṯn.]*	Now I shall journey, [a day and a second]
	[b]ṯlṯt.amǵy.lbt / [y]	[On] the third I shall reach [my] house.
	[.bqr]b.hkly.	[I will arrive] at my palace."
8	*wyʿn.il*[4]	Again El spoke:
9	*[mrzʿ]y.* *lk.bty.rpim*	"[Come to] my [banq]uet. Set off to my house, O shades.
10–11	*[bbty.aṣ]ḥkm.* *iqrakm / [bqrb.hk]ly.*	[Into my house I b]id you, I beckon you [into] my [pal]ace."
		(**Narrator:**)
11–12	*aṯrh.rpum / [ltdd]* *[aṯ]rh.ltdd.i[ln]y[m]*	To his shrine, O shades, [hasten,] To his sh[rine], hasten, O spi[rits.]
	]rn[	[. . .]

(The text breaks off. No part of the bottom portion of the tablet is preserved to be allow one to estimate the length of the ongoing narrative.)

CAT 1.21.V Side 2

(Only five letters of this side of the tablet are preserved.)

]b.larṣ	[ ] to the earth

22. *CAT* 1. 22 — Third Tablet

CAT 1.22 II — Side 1

(The top portion of the tablet is missing. There is no indication of how many lines preceded what is preserved below. Nor is there any clear indication whether the tablet preserved four or six columns.)

		(El:)
1–2	*[ ]r. ṯl[ṯt.amǵy.lbty.]*	"On the thi[rd I shall reach my house.]
	[bqr] / b.hkly.	[I will arrive] at my palace."
2	*[wyʿn.il]*	[Again El spoke:]
2–3	*[mrzʿy]* *lk bty.r[pʾm.]*	"[Come to my banquet.] Set off to my house, O sh[ades.]
3–4	*[bbty.aṣḥ] / km.* *iqr[akm.bqrb.hkly]*	[Into my house I bid] you, I beck[on you into my palace."]
		(Narrator:)
5–6	*aṯrh.r[pum.ltdd.]* *[aṯrh] / ltdd.il[nym]*	To his shrine, O sh[ades, hasten,] [To his shrine], hasten, O sp[irits.]
7–8	*mhr.bʿl* *[mhr.] / ʿnt.*	Warriors of Baal, [Warriors of] Anat.
		(El:)
8–10	*lk b[ty.rpʾm.]* *[bbty] / aṣḥ.km.* *i[qrakm.bqrb] / hkly.*	"Set off to [my] hou[se, O shades.] [Into my house] I bid you, I [beckon you into] my palace."
		(Narrator:)
10–11	*aṯr[h.rpum.ltdd]* *aṯrh.lt[dd.ilnym]*	To his shrine, [O shades, hasten,] To his shrine, has[ten, O spirits.]

12	*yḥpn.ḥy[ly.]*	Armed forces encircle (?) …
13–14	*šmʿ.atm [rpum]*	Listen, you [shades (?)]
	[iln]/ym.	[Pay attention, O spi]rits.
14	*lm.qd [*	…
15	*šmn.prs [*	Oil …
16	*ydr.hm.y [*	He vows
17	*ʿṣ.amr.*	…
17–18	*yuḫ[d.ksa.mlkh]*	He gras[ps the throne of his royalty,]
	nḫ!t.[5] *kḥṯ.dr[kth.]*	The dais, the seat of his dom[inion.]
		(El:)
18–20	*[bbty] / aṣḥ.rpim[.]*	["Into my house] I bade the shades,
	[iqra.ilnym] / bqrb.h[kly.]	[I beckoned the spirits] into [my pa]lace."
		(Narrator:)
20–21	*[aṯrh.rpum.] / tdd.*	[To his shrine, the shades] hastened,
	aṯrh[.tdd.ilnym]	To his shrine, [hastened the spirits.]
22	*asr.mr[kbthm]*	They hitched [their] char[iots.]
	[sswm.tṣmd.]	[They yoked the horses.]
23–24	*tʿln. lmr[kbthm.]*	They mount [their] char[iots,]
	[tityn.] / ʿrhm.	[They come on] their stallions.
24–25	*tl[kn.ym.wṯn.]*	They jour[ney a day and a second,]
	[aḫr.špšm]/bṯlṯ.	[At nightfall] on the third,
25–26	*mǵy[.rpum.lgrnt]*	[The shades] reached [the threshing squares,]
	i[ln]y[m.lmṭʿt.]	The spir[its the planted fields.]
(The text breaks off. No part of the bottom portion of the tablet		[…]

is preserved to allow one to estimate the length of the ongoing narrative.)

CAT 1.22 I Side 2

(The top portion of the tablet is missing. There is no indication of how many lines preceded what is preserved below.)

1–2	*m[ ] [ ]h.*	
2–3	*hn bnk.hn [ ]* *[ ] bnbn.aṯrk.*	Behold your son, behold ... (your) grandson [ ] your shrine;
3–4	*hn [ ] r / ydk.* *ṣǵr.tnšq.šptk.*	Behold ... your hand. The small one will kiss your lips.
4–6	*ṯm / ṯkm.bm ṯkm.* *aḫm.qym.il / blsmt.*	There, shoulder to shoulder. Brothers, attendants of El ...
6–7	*ṯm.yʿbš.šm.il.mtm* *yʿbš.brkn.šm.il.ǵzrm*	There mortals ... the name of El, ... heroes bless the name of El.
8–9	*ṯm.ṯmq.rpu.bʿl.* *mhr bʿl* *wmhr.ʿnt.*	There the shades of Baal ... Warriors of Baal, Warriors of Anat.
9–10	*ṯm.yḥpn.ḥyl / y.* *zbl.mlk.ʿllmy.*	There armed forces encircle (?), The eternal royal princes.
10–11	*km.tdd / ʿnt.ṣd.* *tštr.ʿpt.šmm*	As when Anat hastens to the hunt, sets to flight the birds of the heavens.
12–13	*ṭbḫ.alpm.ap ṣin.* *šql.ṯrm / wmri*	They slaughtered oxen; sheep as well; They felled bulls, fatlings too,

13–14	*ilm.ʿglm.dt.šnt* *imr.qmṣ.llim.*	Also rams and year old calves, They butchered lambs and even kids.
14–15	*kksp / lʿbrm.zt.* *ḫrṣ.lʿbrm.kš*	Olive oil—like silver to travelers, ... —like gold to travelers.
16–17	*dpr.ṯlḥn.bqʿl.* *bqʿl / mlkm.*	... a table set with fruit, Laid with fruit fit for kings.
17–18	*hn.ym.yṣq.yn.* *ṯmk / mrṯ.yn.srnm.*	Daylong they pour the wine, ... must-wine, fit for rulers.
18–19	*yn.bld / ǵll.* *yn.išryt.ʿnq.*	Wine, sweet and abundant, Select wine ...
19–20	*smd / lbnn.ṭl!.*[6] *mrṯ.yḫrṯ.il*	The choice wine of Lebanon, Must nurtured by El.
21–22	*hn.ym.wṯn.* *tlḥm<n>*[7]*.rpum / tštyn.*	One day passed, then a second, the shades eat, they drink;
22–24	*ṯlṯ.rbʿ.ym.* *ḫmš / ṯdṯ.ym.* *tlḥmn.rpum / tštyn.*	A third day, then a fourth; A fifth day, then a sixth; the shades eat, they drink.
24–25	*bt.ikl.bprʿ* *bṣq[.]birt.lbnn.*	In the banquet house, on the summit, ... in the heart of Lebanon
25–26	*mk.bšbʿ / [ymm.]* *[ap]nk.aliyn.bʿl*	Finally, on the seventh [day] Mighty Baal [ ]
27–28	*[ ]t.rʿh aby[* *[ ]yʿ[*	[...]

(The text breaks off. No part of the bottom portion of the tablet is preserved to allow one to estimate the length of the ongoing narrative.)

Notes

1. Assuming the equivalence of *mrzʿ* and *mrzḫ*.
2. Alternatively:

    To his shrine the shades surely hasten,
    To his shrine surely hasten the spirits.

3. The text, which reads *apank,* is most likely a scribal error.
4. Some scholars emend the text to read *<dn>il* "Danel said." It is preferable to leave the text as it stands rather than making such a drastic change (in effect removing the god El as a major participant) based on conjecture.
5. The text, which reads *nzt,* is most likely a scribal error.
6. The text, which reads *ṭṣ,* is most likely a scribal error.
7. Restoring *n,* which may have been lost by haplography (cf. line 23).

The Birth of the Gracious Gods

23. *CAT* 1.23
Translated by Theodore J. Lewis

The text is partitioned neatly into two sections. In the first section (lines 1–29) the scribe has inserted nine horizontal dividing lines, which are completely absent from the latter half of the text. Liturgical directions are common only in the first half. The mention of royalty as well as unspecified officiants suggests a ritual or sacred play (a sevenfold rite involving fire, song, and offerings seems to have been envisioned [lines 12, 14–15]). In the second half of the text (lines 30–76), ritual gives way to myth as the author chooses to place front and center the sexual activity of El; the role of a pair of maidens who become his wives; and the offspring, who are marked by a ravenous appetite. Many scholars have concluded that this text is the best example of how mythical narratives and rituals were wedded at ancient Ugarit.

The literary genre of the text has resisted classification. Many translators pick up on the bawdy language and conclude that we have a burlesque. Some even go so far as to see a New Year's festival here and/or a *hieros gamos* (sacred marriage) rite where the king and queen mentioned in line 7 play the role of the gods El and Athiratu (but notice the difficulty that there are two wives of El who give birth). Our text yields no information on whether the king and queen functioned in the role of patrons, spectators or participants.

Other scholars take a decidedly different approach, which notes a preoccupation with foodstuffs and wine especially in the latter part of the text. Some conclude that we have a vintage festival recited at harvest time, while others sense a more ominous feel to the text and conclude that we have a famine myth and ritual.

Still other scholars argue that the text's purpose is to function as a sympathetic magic ritual to cure impotence. The euphemistic use of the words "hand" and "staff" to refer to El's penis is widely acknowledged. What is debatable is its condition. Several scholars think that the expression "to be long of hand" as well as the description of El's "staff" *descending* or being *fatigued* implies that his penis is flaccid and that the actions of the two females are undertaken to excite old man El (a *deus otiosus*), who suffers from impotency. Others interpret these two key words in the opposite sense and see El as a "vigorous and prodigiously lusty old man" whose "hand" is *stretched* and *taut.* Still others would have El portrayed as spright and agile, laying aside his (walking) stick (a reference to setting aside the props of old age) so as to engage in the youthful activity of hunting.

It is hard to maintain that El is impotent in view of his ribald behavior in this text and elsewhere (cf. text 10 IV 38–39 where El brazenly brags of his sexual endowment and prowess: "Does the *yd* [a play on words meaning both "hand" and love] of El the King excite you, the love of the Bull arouse you."). This so-called old timer is repeatedly portrayed in our text as an amorous kisser who successfully impregnates two females. In addition, El has already excited the adulating and bouncing females in lines 32–33, which is hard to do if he is drooping. Nowhere else in Ugaritic myth does the creator of the gods have any problems with impotency.

That the second half of the text has to do primarily with fertility cannot be ignored. Its appeal (and hence its preservation in written form) certainly derived from its ribald character and its ability to fascinate an audience with the sexual escapades of El, the head of the pantheon, and the traits of his children, the gracious gods. The precise relation of the latter section to the ritual in lines 1–29 remains cloudy at best. The mention of bread and wine (lines 6, 71–76), vineyards (lines 9–11), fields (lines 13, 28), branches (line 25), grapes (line 26), and sown land (lines 68–69, 73) suggests an agricultural (especially viticultural) character to the ritual which was witnessed and/or performed by numerous participants (king, queen, ministrants, marshals, lute players, youthful choristers, and an assembly). El's patronage of drinking is well attested (cf. text 19).

The identities of several personages in the text are open to question. If there is a consensus among scholars regarding the identity of "Motu and Sharru" (who occurs only here [lines 8–11] in all Ugaritic literature), it would be to see a reference to Mot, the god of Death. The title Motu and Sharru would reflect a composite divine name (the use of which was known at Ugarit: e.g., Kothar and Hasis, Nikkal and Ib). The imprecation associated with Motu and Sharru (lines 9–11) has to do with viticulture, although the underlying rationale is not wholly apparent. One could infer that the author thought that the powers of death must be magically bound in some way to permit the fertility that follows.

Second, interpreters are divided about whether the reference to "Athiratu and Rahmayyu" (line 13) depicts one goddess or two. Those who favor a single deity see a compound divine name referring to the mother goddess who suckles the newborn gods in our text (lines 24, 59, 61). Those who see two goddesses refer to Rahmayyu either as the goddess Anat or a deity in her own right (although *rḥmy* is never found in any pantheon or sacrificial list; but cf. text 2 II 6).

Finally, the relation of (a) the deities Dawn and Dusk (lines 52–53) and (b) the gracious gods is uncertain and thus the text is known under varying titles: "Shahar and Shalim" and "The Birth of the Gracious and Beautiful Gods." Some scholars take great pains to show that these are separate groups of gods while others collapse the two into one because they feel that the repetitious nature of the poetry is simply a device that was not meant to be understood sequentially.

Whoever the newborn gracious gods may be, they are characterized by a ravenous appetite. The description of their gaping jaws is identical to that of the god Mot ("Death"), known for his insatiable appetite (cf. text 11 II 2–3). After a portrait of their gluttony, we find El commanding the gods to search for food in the wilderness. Some scholars read explicit motives (the exiling of disinherited kin, avoiding a famine) behind El's actions, but the text is mute regarding the deity's intent. The new gods are forced to roam the desert steppe until they eventually happen upon a nameless guardian of the sown land who gives them sustenance.

The text, which is written in a single column on both sides of the tablet, is mostly intact and in fairly good shape overall except for the usual defacement resulting from deterioration. The upper right corner of the obverse (and the corresponding lower right corner of the reverse) is missing. Thus, the right half of lines 1–5 and most of the right half of lines 71–76 are absent. The largest unreadable block due to damage occurs in the right half of lines 14–25.

Obverse

1–2	*iqra.ilm.nʿ[mm.]*	Let me invoke the gracious gods […]
	wysmm.bn.šp[ ]	Handsome lords, sons of […]
3–4	*ytnm.qrt.lʿly[ ]*	Render glory to the gods most high,
	bmdbr.špm.yd[ ]r	In the desert, the windswept heights.
5	*lrišh̆m.wyš[ ]xm*	[…] on their heads.
6	*lḥm.blḥm.ay.*	Eat such savory fare,
	wšty.bḫmr yn ay	Drink such vintage wine.
7	*šlm.mlk.šlm.mlkt.*	Hail, O King! Hail, O Queen!
	ʿrbm.wṯnnm	O ministrants and marshals.

8–9	*mt.wšr.yṯb.*	Motu and Sharru sits enthroned,
	bdh.ḫṭ.ṯkl.	A scepter of sterility in one hand,
	bdh. / ḫṭ.ulmn.	A scepter of widowhood in the other.
9–11	*yzbrnn.zbrm.gpn*	May vine-pruners prune him,
	yṣmdnn.ṣmdm.gpn.	May vine-binders bind him,
	yšql.šdmth / km gpn	May they trim his tendrils like a vine.

12	*šbʿd.yrgm.ʿl.ʿd.*	To be performed seven times with lute accompaniment,
	wʿrbm.tʿnyn	With antiphonal response by ministrants.

13	*w.šd.šd.ilm.*	"Fertile fields, fields divine,
	šd aṯrt.wrḥm<y>	The fields of Athiratu and Rahmayyu."
14–15	*ʿl.išt.šbʿd.ǵzrm g.ṭb[.]*	Seven times by fire, youthful voices
	gd.bḥlb.	a *gd* in milk,
	annḫ bḫmat /	a *annḫ* in butter
	wʿl.agn.šbʿdm.dǵṯt xx[ ]	Seven times by the firestand, inc[ense … .]

16–18	*tlkm.rḥmy.wtṣd.[ ]* *tḥgrn.ǵzr.nʿm.[ ]* *wšm.ʿrbm.yr[ ]*	Off went Rahmayyu, [Athiratu] to the hunt, Girded with a hero's grace [...] name, ministrants [...]
19–20	*mṯbt.ilm.ṯmn.* *ṯ[ ]/pamt.šbʿ[ ]*	The gods' thrones are eight, Th[eir thrones] are seven in a row.
21–22	*iqnu.šmt[ ]* *ṯn.šrm.[ ]*	Lapis-lazuli, brilliant gold [... ,] The scarlet of princes [... .]
23–24	*iqran.ilm.nʿmm[.]* *[agzr ym.bn]ym /* *ynqm.bap zd.aṯrt.[ ]*	Let me invoke the gracious gods, [Paired devourers of the day that] bore them. Who suck the teats of Athiratu's breasts.
25–26	*špš.mṣprt.dlthm[.]* *[ ]wǵnbm.*	Shapshu shines(?) on their branches, [...] their grape clusters.
26–27	*šlm.ʿrbm.ṯnnm* *hlkm.bdbḥ nʿmt*	Hail, O ministrants and marshals! Who proceed with gracious sacrifice.
28	*šd.<šd.>ilm.* *šd.aṯrt.wrḥmy*	"<Fertile fields>, fields divine, The fields of Athiratu and Rahmayyu."
29	*[š]bʿd ǵ[zr]m.g.ṭb xxx*	Seven times youthful voices [...]

A description of El's intercourse with the goddesses, who are referred to as firebrands. The words "hand" and

"staff" are used euphemistically to refer to El's phallus. The maids, who are given the option of being either the daughters or wives of El, choose the latter and give birth to the gods Dawn and Dusk.

Lower edge		
30	*[i]l[ ]y[ ].i gp.ym.* *wyṣǵd.gp.thm*	[El strides(?)] the sea's shore, He marches to the shore of the deep.
31	*[x]x[xx].il.mšṭʿltm.* *mšṭʿltm.lriš.agn*	El [takes(?)] a pair of brands, Twin brands from atop the firestand.
32–33	*hlh.tšpl.hlh.trm.* *hlh.tṣḥ.ad ad /* *whlh.tṣḥ.um.um.*	Now one bends low, another arcs high, Now one cries: "Father! Father!" Now cries the other: Mother!"
33–34	*tirkm.yd.il.kym* *wyd il.kmdb.*	El's "hand" grows long as the sea, El's "hand" as the ocean.
34–35	*ark.yd.il.kym*	El's "hand" is long as the sea,
Reverse		
	w.yd.il.kmdb.	El's "hand" as the ocean.
35–36	*yqḥ.il.mšṭʿltm* *mšṭʿltm.lriš.agn.*	El takes a pair of brands, Twin brands from atop the firestand.
36	*yqḥ.yš<t>.bbth*	He takes them into his house.
37	*il.ḥṭh.nḥt.* *il.ymnn.mṭ.ydh.*	El lowers his scepter, El is generous with the "staff" in his hand.
37–39	*yšu / yr.šmmh.* *yr.bšmm.ʿṣr.* *yḥrṭ.yšt / l pḥm.*	He lifts, he shoots skyward, He shoots a bird in the sky, He plucks and sets it on the coals.

39	*il.aṯtm.kypt.*	El charms the pair of maids.
	hm.aṯtm.tṣḥn	If the maiden pair cries out:
40	*ymt.mt.* *nḥtm.ḫṭk.* *mmnnm.mṭ ydk*	"O husband! husband! Lowered is your scepter, Generous the "staff" in your hand.
41	*h[l].ʿṣr.tḥrr.lišt.* *ṣḥrrt.lpḥmm*	Look! a bird roasted on the fire, Basted and browned on the coals."
42	*a[ṯ]tm.aṯt.il.* *aṯt.il.w.ʿlmh.*	They then would be his wives, Wives of El, his wives forever.
42–43	*whm / aṯtm.tṣḥn.*	But if the maiden pair cries out:
43–44	*y.ad.ad.* *nḥtm.ḫṭk /* *mmnnm.mṭ ydk.*	"O father! father! Lowered is your scepter, Generous the "staff" in your hand.
44–45	*hl.ʿṣr.tḥrr.lišt* *wṣḥrrt.lpḥmm.*	Look! a bird roasted on the fire, Basted and browned on the coals."
45–46	*btm.bt.il.* *bt.il / wʿlmh.*	They then would be his daughters, Daughters of El, his daughters forever.
46	*whn.aṯtm.tṣḥn.*	Lo! the maiden pair cries out:
46–47	*y.mt.mt /* *nḥtm ḫṭk.* *mmnnm.mṭ ydk.*	"O husband! husband! Lowered is your scepter, Generous the "staff" in your hand.
47–48	*hl.ʿṣr / tḥrr.lišt.* *wṣḥr<r>t.lpḥmm.*	Look! a bird roasted on the fire, Basted and browned on the coals."
48–49	*aṯtm.aṯ[t.il]* *aṯt.il.wʿlmh.*	The pair became his wives, Wives of El, his wives forever.

49–50	*yhbr.špthm.yšq /* *hn.špthm.mtqtm.* *mtqtm.klrmn[m]*	He bows down to kiss their lips, Ah! their lips are sweet, Sweet as succulent fruit.
51	*bm.nšq.whr.* *bḥbq.ḥmḥmt.*	In kissing, conception, In embracing, pregnant heat.
51–52	*tqt[nṣn w] / tldn.* *šḥr.wšlm.*	The two travail and give birth to the gods Dawn and Dusk.
		The announcement celebrating the divine births.
52	*rgm.lil.ybl.*	Word is brought to El:
52–53	*aṯ[ty] / il.ylt.*	"Paired wives of El have given birth."
	mh.ylt. *yldy.šḥr.wšl[m]*	"What did they bear?" "A pair is born, Dawn and Dusk."
54	*šu.ʿdb.lšpš.rbt.* *wlkbkbm.knm*	"Raise an offering to the Lady Sun, Thanks to the immovable stars."
		Repetition of the description of El's intercourse.
55	*yhbr.špthm.yšq.* *hn.špthm.mtqt[m.]* *[mtqtm.klrmnm]*	He bows down to kiss their lips, Ah! their lips are sweet, Sweet as succulent fruit.
56	*bm.nšq.whr.* *bḥbq.wḥ[m]ḥmt.*	In kissing, conception, In embracing, pregnant heat.
56–57	*yṯbn / yspr.lḥmš.* *lṣ[ ]šr.pḥr*	They recite again five more times, [. . .] the assembly [si]ngs(?).
57–58	*klat / tqtnṣn.wtldn.* *tld[.i]lm.nʿmm.*	Both travail and give birth, Birth to the gracious gods.

58–59	*agzr ym / bn.ym.* *ynqm.bap[.]ḏd[.št]*	Paired devourers of the day that bore them, Who suck the teats of [the Lady's (?)] breasts.

Second announcement.

59	*rgm.lil.ybl*	Word is brought to El:
60	*aṯty.il.ylt.*	"Paired wives of El have given birth."
	mḫ.ylt.	"What did they bear?"
	ilmy.nʿmm [ ][1]	"The gracious gods ...
61	*agzr ym.bn ym.*	Paired devourers of the day that bore them,
	ynqm.bap.ḏd.št.	Who suck the teats of the Lady's breasts."

A description of the ravenous appetite of the newborn gods.

61–62	*špt / larṣ.* *špt lšmm.*	One lip to earth, The other to sky.
62–63	*wyʿrb.bpḫm.* *ʿṣr.šmm /* *wdg bym.*	Then enter their mouths Birds of the sky, Fish from the sea.
63–64	*wndd.gzr[.]l<g>zr[.]* *yʿdb.uymn/ušmal.bpḫm.* *wl[.]tšbʿn.*	Rushing to eat, bite by bite, Gorging their mouths left and right, But even so, not sated.

El commands the gods to search for food in the wilderness. Eventually they happen upon the Guardian of the sown land who gives them sustenance.

64–65	*y.aṯt.itrḫ* *y bn.ašld.*	"O wives whom I wed, O sons whom I sire,

65–66	*šu.ʿdb.tk.mdbr.qdš* *ṯm.tgrgr.labnm.wl.ʿṣm.*	Raise an offering in the holy desert, There sojourn mid rock and brush."
66–67	*šbʿ.šnt / tmt.* *ṯmn.nqpt.ʿd.*	Seven years complete, Eight cycles full,
67–68	*ilm.nʿmm.ttlkn / šd.* *tṣdn.pat.mdbr.*	The gracious gods roam the steppe, They hunt the desert fringe.
68–69	*wngš.hm.nǵr / mdrʿ.* *wṣḥ.hm.ʿm.nǵr.mdrʿ.*	They approach the Guardian of the sown, They cry out to the Guardian of the sown.
69–70	*y.nǵr / nǵr.ptḥ.*	"O Guardian, Guardian, open!"
70–71	*wptḥ[.]hw.prṣ.bʿdhm* *wʿrb.hm.*	He opens a breach for them, They enter (and say:)
71–72	*hm[.iṯ l]ḥm.* *wtn / wnlḥm.*	"If [there is b]read [. . . ,] Then gi[ve] that we may eat,"
72	*hm.iṯ[ ]* *[w]tn.wnšt*	"If there is [wine. . . ,] Then give that we may drink."
73	*wʿn hm.nǵr mdrʿ[.]*	The Guardian of the sown answers,
73–74	*[ ]xt* *iṯ. yn.dʿrb.bṯk[ ]*	["There is bread for him who comes ... ,] "There is wine for him who enters[..."]
75–76	*mǵ.hw.lhn.lg.ynh[ ]* *wḥbrh.mla yn[ ]*	He approaches his flask of wine [... ,] His companion is full of wine [... .]

Notes

1. The *y* on the end of *ilmy* may be a mistake (although cf. *yldy* in line 53). Several letters occur at the end of the line, but they are unclear. Some have thought that the scribe started writing the next word (*agzr*) only to erase it when he ran out of room.

The Betrothal of Yarikh and Nikkal-Ib

24. *CAT* 1.24

Translated by David Marcus

This is a short poem of fifty lines, the first part of which recounts the myth of the betrothal of the West Semitic moon god, Yarikh ("moon"), with the Mesopotamian moon goddess, Nikkal-Ib ("great lady," "the fruit," or "radiant one"). The prelude of the first part is fragmentary. In the body of the poem, Yarikh asks Khirikhbi, the divine matchmaker, to arrange his marriage to Nikkal, and offers an enormous marriage price of silver, gold, and precious stones. Khirikhbi makes a counterproposal of two other prospective brides including Padriya, one of Baal's daughters. But Yarikh insists on Nikkal. Thereupon, the marriage price is paid, with all of Nikkal's family (father, mother, brothers, and sisters) in attendance as witnesses. The second part of the poem pertains to a human bride called PRBKHTH (vocalization unknown). It contains an ode to the *katharat*-goddesses, the patronesses of wedlock and conception, a listing of the bride's dowry, and an acclamation of the bride. It is possible that the poem was recited at marriage ceremonies to ensure for the bride the same blessing and protection by the *katharat* as was accorded the goddess Nikkal at her wedding.

Prelude

1	*a[š]r nkl wib/*	Let me sing of Nikkal-Ib
2–3	*ḫrḫb mlk qẓ* *ḫrḫb [m]/lk aǵzt.*	Khirikhbi, king of summer, Khirikhbi, king of marriage (?)
		(*The rest of the prelude is fragmentary. There is a threefold mention of the* Katharat-*goddesses, the patronesses of wedlock and conception [lines 6, 11, & 15], and a wish that the bride give birth to a child [line 7].*)
3	*bs[. . . . .]/*	
4	*yrḫ yṯkḥ [. . . . . .]/*	
5	*tld bt[. . . . . .]*	
5–6	*[lk]/ṯrt.* *lbnt. hl[l snnt]/*	To the Katharat, The radiant daughters of the new moon.

7	*hl ǵlmt* *tld b[n. . .]/*	"Behold, the young woman, Shall give birth to a child."[1]
8	*ʿnhn lydh tzd[...]/*	
9	*ptlbšrh. dm [. . . . . .]/*	
10	*wyn kmtrḫt[. . . . . .]*	
11	*šmʿ ilht kṯr[t. . . . . .]/*	The Katharat-goddesses heard....
12	*nh lydh tzdn[. . . . . .]/*	
13	*lad[nh. . . . . .]/*	
14	*dgn tt[. . . . . .]/*	
15	*ʿ. lkṯrt <bnt>* *hl[l sn]nt/*	The Katharat, the radiant daughters Of the new moon,
		Yarikh asks Khirikhbi, the match-maker, to arrange his marriage to Nikkal, offering his marriage price and promising to be a good husband.
16–17	*[y]lak yrḫ n[yr] šmm* *[ʿm]/ ḫr[ḫ]b mlk qẓ.*	Yarikh, the luminary of the sky, Sends word to Khirikhbi, king of summer:
17–19	*tn nkl [y]/rḫ ytrḫ.* *ib tʿrbm b[bh]/th.*	"Get me Nikkal! Yarikh would wed her, Let Ib enter his home!
19–23	*watn mhrh la/bh.*	Then I will give to her father, as her marriage price,
	alp ksp. *wrbt ḫ/rṣ.*	One thousand shekels of silver, And ten thousand shekels of gold.
	išlḥ ẓhrm iq/nim.	And I will send jewels of pure lapis-lazuli.
	atn šdh krm[m]/ *šd ddh ḥrnq[m]*	I will make her field like a vineyard, The field of her love like an orchard (?)."[2]

Khirikhbi makes a counteroffer.

Lines	Text	Translation
23–26	*[w]/yʿn ḫrḫb mlk qẓ* *[l]/ nʿmn [i]lm* *lḫt[n]/m. bʿl*	Khirikhbi, king of summer, responds: "O favorite of El, O brother-in-law of Baal!
26–27	*trḫ pdry b[t ar]/* *aqrbk abh bʿ[l]/*	Wed Padriya, daughter of Light! I will introduce you to her father Baal.
28–30	*yǵtr. ʿṯtr* *t/rḫ lk ybrdmy. b[t]/* *bh lbu yʿrr.*	If Ashtar ... , Then wed Yaparudmay, daughter of ... ! The lion will stir up (?)."

Yarikh's insistence on Nikkal.

Lines	Text	Translation
30–32	*w[yʿn/ yrḫ nyr šmm* *wnʿ[n]/ ʿmn nkl ḫtny*	But Yarikh, the luminary of the sky, replies: "Now! look here! My marriage must be with Nikkal!"

The bride-price is paid.

Lines	Text	Translation
32–33	*[aḫ]r/ nkl yrḫ ytrḫ.*	Then Yarikh pays the bride-price for Nikkal.
33–37	*adnh/ yšt mṣb. mznm* *umh/ kp mznm.* *iḫh yṯʿr/ mšrrm.* *aḫtth la/bn mznm.*	Her father sets up the balance stand, Her mother positions the trays of the scales, Her brothers ready the standard weights, Her sisters ready the ingots.

Concluding hymn

Lines	Text	Translation
37–39	*nkl wib/ dašr.* *ar yrḫ.* *wy/rḫ yark*	Oh, Nikkal-Ib, whom I sing. May Yarikh shine bright, May Yarikh shine on you.

....

Epilogue

40–42	*[ašr ilht kt̲rt*	Let me sing of the Katharat-goddesses,
	bn]/t hll. snnt.	The radiant daughters of the new moon,
	«bnt h/ll» bʿl gml.	The lord of the sickle,
42–45	*yrdt/ bʿrgzm.*	Who descend with ʿrgz-plants,
	bgbz tdmʿ/ llay.	. . .
	ʿm lẓpn [i]/l d̲pid.	With Kindly El Benign.
45–47	*hn bpy sp/rhn.*	See, their number is on my mouth,
	bšpty mn/thn	Their counting is on my lips.[3]
47–48	*t̲lḫh wmlgh*	Let her parting gifts and dowry,
	y/t̲tqt ʿmh	Be weighed out (?) for her.
48–50	*bqʿt/tqʿt ʿm prbḫt̲/*	Bursts (?) of handclapping for PRBKHTH,
	dmqt ṣġrt kt̲rt	The fairest and youngest of the Katharat.[4]

Notes

1. This line has often been compared with Isa 7:14, "Look, the young woman is with child and about to give birth to a son."

2. Referring to a wife as a field to be cultivated was common in the ancient Near East. A popular proverb read, "a woman without a husband is like an uncultivated field."

3. It is unclear whether the number refers to the preceding Katharat, or to the following marriage gifts.

4. The human bride PRBKHTH is here compared metaphorically to one of the Katharat.

Photograph of CAT 1.100 by Wayne Pitard and Theodore Lewis,
West Semitic Research
Courtesy Department of Antiquities, Syria

The Mare and Horon

25. *CAT* 1.100

Translated by Simon B. Parker

Even though this text is completely preserved and has been the subject of numerous studies, no completely satisfying interpretation of the whole has yet appeared. This is explained in part by the lack of any congeneric text, and in part by the fact that several individual words and lines are susceptible of more than one interpretation, none entirely convincing in some cases.

What is clear is that the mother of horses asks her mother, Shapsh, the sun goddess, to take a message to a series of deities. (The sun goddess, whose daily journey takes her over the world and through the underworld, is ideally suited to convey messages to the various homes of the gods.) The precise nature of this message is disputed, but it certainly refers to a spell or incantation against the venomous bite of the viper. I take it to be a request for such a spell, that the mother of horses can then make available to an exorcist, who will then be able to remove the poison. In the case of the first eleven requests, no permanent disposal of the poison is achieved—the exorcist only binds and feeds the viper. The twelfth appeal is to the deity Horon, whose creatures are being bereaved, presumably as a result of snakebite. Horon goes to a town called Arashshikh (otherwise known as the Hurrian name of the River Tigris) and there himself disposes of the venom, using materials whose names suggest words meaning "dispel."] He then proceeds to "the house of the spell," in which "she"—presumably the original goddess, the mother of horses—has now locked herself. He demands entry, and she successfully bargains for the snakes, now rendered harmless, as an appropriate gift. Thus she finally gets what she may have sought all along.

The narrative refers to a ritual in lines 65–67, and the twelvefold repetition in lines 2–60 suggests that the narrative itself may have been used in a ritual of some kind. While the text hints at relations with snake charming and snake goddesses, those relations are uncertain.

1	*um.pḥl.pḥlt.*	The mother of stallion and mare,[1]
	bt.ʿn.bt.abn.	Daughter of spring, daughter of stone,
	bt.šmm.wthm/	Daughter of Heavens and Deep,

2	*qrit.lšpš.umh.*	Is calling to Shapsh, her mother:
2–3	*špš.um.ql.bl.* *ʿm/il.mbk nhrm.* *bʿdt.thmtm/*	"Shapsh, mother, carry my cry To El at the source of the Rivers, At the confluence of the Deeps,
4–5	*mnt.nṯk.nḥš.* *šmrr.nḥš/ʿqšr.*	For a spell for a viper's bite, For a sloughing viper's venom.[2]
5–6	*lnh.mlḫš abd.* *lnh.ydy/ḥmt.*	Let the exorcist banish the bane, Expel from it the poison."
6	*hlm.yṯq.nḥš.* *yšlḥm.<nḥš>3ʿqšr/*	But he only binds the viper, Feeds the sloughing viper,
7	*yʿdb.ksa.wyṯb/*	Arranges a chair and sits.

(Without the first verse [tricolon], this passage is repeated nine more times, each stanza beginning, after a scored line: *tqru.lšpš.umh.* According to a note in the margin, one of the stanzas was omitted and is to be inserted, for a total of eleven stanzas. Otherwise, apart from occasional scribal errors, the text is identical in each stanza except for the colon stating the name and residence of the deity to whom the message is carried. These read as follows:)

(Without the first verse [tricolon], this passage is repeated nine more times, each stanza beginning, after a scored line: "She calls to Shapsh, her mother." *According to a note in the margin, one of the stanzas was omitted and is to be inserted. Otherwise, apart from occasional scribal errors, the text is identical in each stanza except for the lines stating the name and residence of the deity to whom the message is carried. These read as follows:)*

		(Second stanza)
9	*ʿm.bʿl.mrym.ṣpn.*	To Baal on the Heights of Zaphon
		(Third stanza)
14–15	*ʿm/dgn.ttlh.*	To Dagan in Tuttul

		(Fourth stanza)
19–20	*ʿm!/ʿnt wʿ[.]ṯtrt inbbh.*	To Anat in INBB
		(Fifth stanza)
25–26	*ʿm/yrḫ.lrgth.*	To Yarikh in RGT
		(Sixth stanza)
30–31	*ʿm/ršp.bbth.*	To Rashap in Bibit
		(Seventh stanza)
78	*ʿm ʿṯtrt.mrh* (This in the stanza to be inserted following *ršp*, according to the marginal note.)	To Athtart in Mari (This is in the stanza to be inserted following Resheph, according to the marginal note.)
		(Eighth stanza)
35–36	*ʿm/ẓẓ.wkmṯ.ḫryth.*	To SS and Chemosh in HRYT
		(Ninth stanza)
40–41	*ʿm/mlk.ʿṯtrth.*	To Milk in Athtart
		(Tenth stanza)
45–46	*ʿm.kṯr.wḫss.kptrh.*	To Kothar and Khasis in Caphtor
		(Eleventh stanza)
51–52	*ʿm/šḥr.wšlm šmmh.*	To Shahar and Shalim in the Heavens[4]
	(A twelfth stanza follows the same pattern but stops short of the last verse [tricolon] as follows.)	*(A twelfth stanza follows the same pattern, but stops short of the last verse [tricolon] as follows.)*

57	*tqra.lšpš.umh.*	She calls to Shapsh, her mother:
57–58	*špš.um.ql.bl/* *ʿm.ḥrn.mṣdh.*	"Shapsh, mother, carry my voice To Horon in MSD,
58–59	*mnt.nṯk nḥš* *šmrr.nḥš.ʿqšr.*	For a spell for a viper's bite, For a sloughing viper's venom.

59–60	*lnh.mlḫš/abd.* *lnh.ydy.ḥmt.*	Let the exorcist banish the bane, Expel from it the poison."

61–62	*bḥrn.pnm.trǵn{w}.* *wtṯkl/bnwth*	Horon's face turns dark; His creatures are deprived of their young.
62	*ykr.ʿr.dqdm/*	He … the city of the east.[5]
63–64	*idk.pnm.lytn.* *tk aršḫ.rbt/* *waršḫ.ṯrrt.*	Then he sets his face Toward Arashshikh the Great, Toward Arashshikh the Little.
64–65	*ydy.bʿṣm.ʿrʿr/* *wbšḥt.ʿṣ.mt.*	From the trees, he drives out the tamarisk, From the bushes, the tree of death.
65–67	*ʿrʿrm.ynʿrn![6]h/* *ssnm.ysynh.* *ʿdtm.yʿdynh.* *yb/ltm.yblnh.*	With the tamarisk he scatters it, With the cluster of dates he clears it out, With the swirl he swills it, With the channel he discharges it.[7]
67–68	*mǵy.ḥrn.lbth.* *w/yštql.lḥẓrh.*	Horon arrives at his house, And comes to his court.
68–69	*tlu.ḥ<m>t.km.nḫl/* *tplg.km.plg/*	The poison peters out like a stream, Dissipates like a ditch.[8]

70–71	*bʿdh.bhtm.mnt.* *bʿdh.bhtm.sgrt/* *bʿdh.ʿdbt.ṯlṯ.*	Behind her, the house of the spell— Behind her, she's closed the house, Behind her, she's slipped the bolt.[9]
71–72	*ptḥ.bt.mnt/* *ptḥ.bt.wuba.* *hkl.wištql/*	"Open the house of the spell, Open the house—I would enter,, The palace—I would come."
73–74	*tn.{km.} nḥšm.yḥr<n?>*	"Give me { } vipers, O Hor(on),

	tn.<nḫšm.>km/mḫry. *wbn.bṯn.itnny/*[11]	Give <vipers> as my gift,[10] The serpent's brood as my present."
75–76	*ytt.nḫšm.mḫrk.* *bn.bṯn/itnnk/*	"I give vipers as your gift, The serpent's brood as your present."[12]

Notes

1. Or "the stallion's mother, the mare."

2. Snakes are particulary poisonous after sloughing.

3. Restored on the basis of the following stanzas.

4. Some of the places associated with the various deities are unknown. Some, however, are known as cult centers of the deity (so Tuttul, Mari, Athtart), or—from various myths—as their mythological residences (so the heights of Zaphon, INBB, Caphtor, the Heavens). The mythological residences may also be real locations: Mt. Zaphon is north of Ugarit and Caphtor is Crete.

5. Or "the ancient city."

6. The tablet reads *a*.

7. "It" evidently refers to the poison. My translation attempts an English counterpart to the play on the sound of the verb and the noun in the Ugaritic of each of these four cola.

8. The images are apparently of a wadi that dries up and an irrigation channel which divides into smaller channels until the water supply is exhausted.

9. Literally, "arranged the bronze"—presumably an idiom.

10. The word for "gift"—*mḫr*—is commonly used of a marriage gift. Cf. the previous text and Exod 22:16–17 (Heb 15–16).

11. The emendations yield a common form of tricolon, to which the following bicolon is a direct response. A slighter emendation yields:

tn.km.<mḫry.>nḫšm.
yḫr.tn.km/mḫry.
wbn.bṯn.itnny/
"Give as <my gift> vipers,
Give a noxious lizard as my gift,
The serpent's brood as my present."

But this introduces between the parallel "vipers" and "serpent's brood" a new creature ("noxious lizard"), which is then ignored in the following response. Similarly del Olmo Lete 1992: 248 n. 116.

12. The three speeches are evidently by Horon, the mother of horses, and Horon.

26. *CAT* 1.96

Translated by Mark S. Smith

This text is remarkable because it narrates a scene unique in ancient Near Eastern literature: the protagonist eats the flesh and drinks the blood of his or her "brother" in lines 4–5. The protagonist is the major interpretive issue. For decades scholars have regarded the text's very first word as a reference to Anat (*ʿnt*), either by reading *ʿnt* or by emendation. Accordingly, the text has been compared with Dionysiac rites of sparagmos (the tearing apart of a live victim), Orphic orgies, Egyptian impregnation texts, the Indian goddess Kali devouring Shiva, incest cannibalism or warrior cannibalism (by which warriors ingest the strength of their victims),[1] or a love song.[2] In any case, the text seems to describe Anat's consumption of Baal, as long as the first word is read as, or emended to, *ʿnt*. This view would also accord to some degree with Anat's savage character known from 9 II 4–30 and *CAT* 1.13.

A further problem involves the relationship between lines 1–5 and 6–13, an issue that few commentators have addressed. Lines 1–5 may represent Anat's intense mourning for her deceased brother as in 12 II[3] and lines 6–13 her subsequent purification as in 9 II. Lines 6–13 may describe some sort of movement from spring to spring (Oldenburg 1969: 79–80), perhaps implying a series of ritual washings at different springs. Anat's warfare in 9 II may in part be comparable to 26: her consumption of enemies is followed by an act of washing and anointing with oil. Washing in both instances signifies the removal of impurity derived from warfare or, more specifically, contact with a corpse. In either case, such washing and anointing "may be traced to a purificatory rite which was used to prepare for the change in status" (Pardee 1977: 17). This narrative perhaps then drew on and adapted material known from traditional themes of Anat's discovery of Baal's corpse in 12 II and her savage feasting, known from texts involving the West Semitic warfare "ban" called *ḥrm* (9 II 4–30; *CAT* 1.13; *KAI* 181; and Isaiah 34; see Smith 1995).

Anat's ingestion of her brother in lines 4–5 seems to involve a phenomenon more complicated than mourning. Relating Anat's ingestion of her brother in lines 4–5 to the mention of springs in lines 6–13, Caquot suggests that a nature myth lies behind this text (Caquot, Sznycer, and Herdner 1974: 87). He argues that the text represents Anat, the spring, absorbing the substance of her brother, the rainwater. Astour (1963: 20; 1988) criticizes this approach both for assuming that *ʿn* ("spring") is the etymology of Anat's name,[4] and for explaining Anat's consumption of Baal's blood without explaining as well her consumption of his flesh. Astour's two criticisms do not disqualify Caquot's proposal. A secondary or folk etymology may have associated Anat's name with *ʿn,* thereby offering a connection between Anat's action in lines 1–5 and her visits to the springs in lines 5–13. Moreover, it is unnecessary to equate Baal's blood with rainwater in order to explain this text as a nature myth. Instead, Anat's cannibalism of both his flesh and blood may constitute her incorporation of his power over rainwater. In accordance with Caquot's approach, Messer suggests that the motif of Anat's warfare cannibalism may represent a means of expressing the natural reality of waters from above appearing below in springs.[5]

The various interpretations of Anat in this text have lessened in probability, now that the reading of the goddess's name in line 1 has been challenged and another interpretation of the text has been proposed. Lewis (1996) has definitively shown that the first word is not *ʿnt* but *ʿnn,* which is adopted also in *CAT.* Assuming the reading *ʿnn,* del Olmo Lete (1992), anticipated by Lichtenstein (1979: 236 n. 392), plausibly proposes that the text is not a narrative describing Anat but an incantation against the evil eye which travels to and from various places.[6] Different aspects of this interpretation have yet to be resolved: Is the evil eye said elsewhere to devour its "brother"? Moreover, the text, at least the first part, hardly appears to belong to the genre of incantations.

The interpretation of *ʿnn* in line 1 as a textual mistake for the name of Anat remains plausible. Indeed, Anat does have a brother; she does engage in consumption of others and she is associated with springs. Despite the coherence of this view, any attempt to read Anat in this text remains tentative. Because of the interpretational ambiguity, the translation below offers both possiblities.

	Transliteration[7]	Translation
		Anat/The Eye Consumes Her Brother
1–3	*ʿnn*[8]*.hlkt.wšnwt/*	Anat/the Eye went and admired[9]
	tp.aḫh.	The beauty of her brother,[10]
	wnʿm.aḫh/kysmsm.	Indeed, her brother's loveliness,[11] handsome as he is.

3–5	*tspi.širh*[12]*/l.blḥrb.*	She eats his flesh without a knife,
	tšt.dmh/lbl.ks.	She drinks his blood without a cup.[13]
		Anat Visits Springs (?)[14]
5–6	*tpnn.ʿn/bṯy.*	She faces the spring of sex (?),[15]
	ʿnbṯt.tpnn	The spring of sex (?) she faces:
7–8	*ʿn.mḫr.*	The spring of the market,
	ʿn.pḫr/	The spring of the assembly,
	ʿn.ṯǵr.	The spring of the gate.
8–11	*ʿnṯǵr/lṯǵr.ṯṯb.*	To the spring of the gate from the gate she turns,
	ʿn.[16]*pḫr/lpḫr.ṯṯb.*	To the spring of assembly from the assembly she turns,
	ʿn.mḫr/lmḫr ṯṯb	To the spring of market from the market she turns,
11–13	*ʿn.bṯy/lbṯy.ṯṯb.*	To the spring of sex (?) from the place of sex (?) she turns,
	ʿ[n.1[17]*bṯt]/lbṯt.[ṯṯb]*[18]	To the spring of sex (?) from the place of sex (?) [she turns.]

Notes

1. For these suggestions, see Lewis 1996: 117. For the proposal that this text involves an inversion of warfare cannibalism, add Cazelles 1969 and Smith 1995 (cf. *Iliad* 22:338–60, esp. 346–48). Cazelles suggests that Anat strengthens herself by devouring her defeated warrior-brother.

2. Lipiński 1965: 45–73; de Moor 1987: 109–10. For criticism of Lipiński's approach, see Lichtenstein 1979: 236 n. 392; Day 1991: 329 n. 15. Walls (1992: 213) notes that the content of lines 4–5 would be unprecedented for a love song.

3. So most recently Walls 1992: 214.

4. Opinions on the etymology of Anat's name differ.

5. E. Messer, personal communication, cited with permission. I wish to thank Dr. Messer for discussing this text with me.

6. For others considering this approach to the text, see Lewis 1996: 119 n. 16. For the evil eye in a number of different cultures, see the essays in Maloney 1976.

7. The back of the tablet contains a scribal exercise. See *CAT* for further information and bibliography.

8. Emend to *ʿnt* (the name of the goddess, Anat)? See the discussion in the introduction.

9. The word *šnwt* is a matter of philological dispute. The least colorful and otherwise attested form in Ugaritic is the verb of motion, *šnt,* "I depart," in 9 V 33 (and reconstructed in the parallel text, 7 III 18); both verbs are "final weak." This interpretation of *šnwt* would also fit with the verb *hlkt.* Other suggestions include Virolleaud's "regardant," and in favor of this view, Caquot (1974: 207) cites Soqotri and Mehri *sini* and Shauri *sene,* "to see." Astour (1988: 15–16) compares Arabic *sana* in the meaning "to admire" (most tentatively adopted here). Pope (1977a: 358) presumes Syriac *šnâ,* "be insane, frenzied." For these options offered for this word and for others below, see Astour 1963, 1988; Caquot in Caquot, de Tarragon, and Cunchillos 1989: 42–44; and Walls 1992: 210–14.

10. Walls (1992: 211) takes *nʿm* as a verb completing this line ("and he was lovely"), but this word is otherwise unattested as a verb in Ugaritic. Walls's suggestion would provide, however, for a greater balance of lines.

11. Albright (1968: 132) and Pope (1977: 358; cf. 1994: 161, 372) take *tp, nʿm* and *ysmsm* as terms for Baal's physical appearance, but Walls (1992: 213 n. 44) plausibly understands *tp* as the 3 fem. sg. G-stem prefix form for **phy,* "to look" (on this root, see Coote 1974). The second view provides reasonable sense with the direct objects, although Astour's and Pope's interpretations of *šnwt* (see n. 9) also resolve this difficulty. Less likely is the proposal of Astour (1988: 16) to take *tp* and *nʿm* as musical words, although it is philologically defensible. The implied picture of Baal playing music (?) followed by Anat's consuming him may seem unlikely; she would appear to consume a deceased Baal.

12. The final letter is read by all, but it is not clearly visible in either Lewis 1996 (cover photograph) or in West Semitic Research Project photographs.

13. The two prepositional phrases may not be literal, but "metaphorical, expressing hurried or ravenous consumption" (Lewis 1996: 117).

14. If *ʿn* were to refer to "the eye" and not "spring," then it would be the subject of the clauses in lines 6–13. The translation here assumes that Anat is the subject. The structure assumed in this translation derives from Greenfield (1965: 16–18) and Lichtenstein (1979: 237). The latter notes that *tpnn ʿn bṯy//ʿn bṯt tpnn* in lines 5–6 form an envelope with *ʿn bṯy lbṯy ṯṯb//ʿn [bṯt] lbṯt ṯ[ṯb]* in lines 11–13. The first half of the structure is governed by *tpnn,* while each clause in the second half uses *ṯṯb.* Furthermore, the five nouns in lines 5b–8a appear in reverse order in lines 8b–13. These five words may be words for places (see n. 15).

15. The words, *bṯt* and *bṯy,* remain extremely problematic; they may be the same word with two different forms of the Ugaritic final feminine ending (see Layton 1990: 241–45). Elsewhere *bṯt* is usually taken as "shame" (10 III 19, 21; cf. 7 IV 5). In 10 III 19, 21 the word is applied to a feast that apparently includes sexual relations (cf. BH *bōšet* referring to illicit sexual activity in 1 Sam 20:30 and Micah 1:11; *mĕbūšāw* for genitals in Deut 25:11). If *bṯt* and *bṯy* were words for a location in 26 and mean "shame," one might speculate that they refer to a setting reminis-

cent of 10 III 19 and 21 (a place of sexual relations?), but such an interpretation is offered only most tentatively. Comparison with Akkadian *būšu*, "goods," has been proposed as well, and perhaps a place for (buying?) goods could be involved. Alternatively, if *ʿn* means "eye" throughout lines 6–13, *bṯt* and *bṯy* as well as *mḫr, pḫr* and *tǵr* may be persons and not places (so de Moor 1987: 109–10).

16. The word divider is generally read, but it is not clear in either Lewis 1996 (cover photograph) or in West Semitic Research Project photographs.

17. CTA reads *ʿn*, but only the first letter is visible in Lewis 1996 (cover photograph).

18. The last two lines of the text are not preserved according to Virolleaud (1960). *CAT* reads traces of a two wedges at the beginning of what would be line 14. Parts of wedges are evident from Lewis 1996 (cover photograph).

Concordances

WAW	*CTA*	*CAT/KTU*	**RS**
1	14	1.14	2.[003] + 3.324 + 3.344 + 3.414
2	15	1.15	3.343 + 3.345
3	16	1.16	3.325 + 3.342 + 3.408
4	17	1.17	2.[004]
5	18	1.18	3.340
6	19	1.19	3.322 + 3.349 + 3.366
7	1	1.1	3.361
8	2	1.2	3.367 + 3.346
9	3	1.3	2.[014] + 3.363
10	4	1.4	2.[008] + 3.341 + 3.347
11	5	1.5	2.[022] + 3.[565]
12	6	1.6	2.[009] + 5.155
13	-	1.133	24.293
14	8	1.8	3.364
15	10	1.10	3.362 + 5.181
16	11	1.11	3.319
17	12	1.12	2.[012]
18	-	1.83	16.266
19	-	1.114	24.258
20	20	1.20	3.348
21	21	1.21	2.[019] + 5.155
22	22	1.22	2.[024]
23	23	1.23	2.002
24	24	1.24	5.194

25	-	1.100	24.244
26	-	1.96	22.225

(Note: the numbers of the texts in BDFSN correspond to those in *CAT/KTU*. BDFSN's use of 00-, 10-, etc. before these numbers serves to distinguish the text as copied from *KTU* and subsequent collations and does not affect the basic identification of the text in BDFSN by its *CAT/KTU* number.)

CAT/KTU	WAW
1	7
2	8
3	9
4	10
5	11
6	12
8	14
10	15
11	16
12	17
14	1
15	2
16	3
17	4
18	5
19	6
20	20
21	21
22	22
23	23
24	24
83	18
96	26
100	25
114	19
133	13

Bibliography

Aartun, K.

1991 *Studien zur ugaritischen Lexikographie. Teil I: Bäume, Tiere, Gerüche, Götterepitheta, Götternamen, Verbalbegriffe.* Wiesbaden: Otto Harrassowitz.

Aitken, K. T.

1990 *The Aqhat Narrative: A Study in the Narrative Structure and Composition of an Ugaritic Tale.* Journal of Semitic Studies Monograph 13. Manchester: University of Manchester.

Albright, W. F.

1934 "The North-Canaanite Poems of Alʾêyân Baʿal and the 'Gracious Gods.'" *Journal of the Palestine Oriental Society* 14: 133–40.

1968 *Yahweh and the Gods of Canaan: A Historical Analysis of Two Contrasting Faiths.* Reprinted: Winona Lake, IN, Eisenbrauns, n.d.

1969 *Archaeology and the Religion of Israel.* 5th ed. Garden City, NY: Anchor Books.

Amir, D.

1975 "The Image of the King in the Ugaritic Epics and in the Bible." In Hebrew. M.A. thesis, Hebrew University of Jerusalem.

Astour, M. C.

1963 "Un texte d'Ugarit récemment découvert et ses rapports avec l'origine des cultes bachiques grec." *Revue de l'Histoire des Religions* 164: 1–15.

1968 "Two Ugaritic Serpent Charms." *Journal of Near Eastern Studies* 27: 13–36.

1973 "A North Mesopotamian Locale of the Keret Epic?" *UF* 5: 29–39.

1988 "Remarks on KTU 1.96." *Studi Epigrafici e Linguistici* 5 (= *Cananea Selecta: Festschrift für Oswald Loretz zum 60. Geburtstag*): 13–24.

Badre, L., P. Bordreuil, J. Mudarres, L.'Ajjan, and R. Vitale

1976 "Notes ougaritiques I: Keret." *Syria* 53: 95–125.

Bernhardt, K.
1955–56 "Anmerkungen zur Interpretation des KRT-Textes von Ras Schamra-Ugarit." *Wissenschaftliche Zeitschrift der Ernst Moritz Arndt-Universität Greifswald, Gesellschaftliche und Sprachwissenschaftliche Reihe* 5: 101–21.

Bordreuil, P.
1989 "La citadelle sainte du Mont Nanou." *Syria* 66: 275–79.

Bordreuil, P., and D. Pardee
1993 "Le combat de *Baᶜlu* avec *Yammu* d'après les textes ougaritiques." *Mari: Annales de Recherches Interdisciplinaires* 7: 63–70.

Caquot, A.
1958 "Le dieu 'Athtar et les textes de Ras Shamra.'" *Syria* 35: 45–60.
1974 "Notes de lexicographie ougaritique." Pp. 203–8 in *Actes du premier congrès international delinguistique sémitique et chamito-sémitique: Paris 16–19 juillet 1969*. Ed. A. Caquot and D. Cohen. Janua Linguarum, Series Practica, 159. The Hague/Paris: Mouton.
1979 "La littérature ugaritique." Cols. 1361–1417 in *Supplément au Dictionnaire de la Bible*, vol 9. Ed. H. Cazelles and A. Feuillet. Paris: Letouzey & Ané.
1985 "Une nouvelle interprétation de KTU 1.19 I 1–19." *Studi Epigrafici e Linguistici* 2: 93–114.
1987 "Notes philologiques sur la légende ougaritique de Danel et d'Aqhat." *Semitica* 37: 5–16.

Caquot, A., J.-M. de Tarragon, and J.-L. Cunchillos
1989 *Textes Ougaritiques. Tome II, Textes Religieux, Rituels, Correspondance*. Littératures Anciennes du Proche-Orient 14. Paris: Les Editions du Cerf.

Caquot, A., M. Sznycer, and A. Herdner
1974 *Textes Ougaritiques. Tome I. Mythes et légendes*. Littératures Anciennes du Proche-Orient 7. Paris: Les Editions du Cerf.

Cartledge, T. W.
1992 *Vows in the Hebrew Bible and the Ancient Near East*. Journal for the Study of the Old Testament Supplement 147. Sheffield: Sheffield Academic Press.

Cassuto, U.
1975 *Biblical & Oriental Studies 2: Bible and Ancient Oriental Texts*. Trans. I. Abrahams. Jerusalem: Magnes.

Cathcart, K. J., and W. G. E. Watson
1980 "Weathering a Wake: A Cure for a Carousal. A Revised Translation of *Ugaritica V* text 1." *Proceedings of the Irish Biblical Association* 4: 35–58.

Cazelles, H.
1969 "Essai sur le pouvoir de la divinité à Ugarit et en Israël." Pp. 25–44

in *Ugaritica VI*. Mission de Ras Shamra XVII. Paris: Mission archéologique de Ras Shamra/Geuthner.

Clear, J.

1976 *Ugaritic Texts in Translation*. 2nd ed. Seattle: J. Clear.

Clifford, R. J.

1984 "Cosmogonies in the Ugaritic Texts and in the Bible." *Orientalia* 53: 183–201.

Considine, P.

1969 "The Theme of Divine Wrath in Ancient East Mediterranean Literature." *Studi micenei ed egeo-anatolici* 8: 85–159.

Coogan, M. D.

1978 *Stories From Ancient Canaan*. Philadelphia: Westminster.

Cooper, A.

1981 "Divine Names and Epithets in the Ugaritic Texts (with introduction and selected comments by Marvin H. Pope)." Pp. 333– 469 in *Ras Shamra Parallels: The Texts from Ugarit and the Hebrew Bible*. Vol. III Ed. S. Rummel. Analecta Orientalia 51. Rome: Pontificium Institutum Biblicum.

1988 "Two Exegetical Notes on Aqhat." *UF* 20: 19–26.

Coote, R. B.

1974 "Ugaritic *PH(Y)*, 'see'," *UF* 6: 1–5.

Cross, F. M.

1973 *Canaanite Myth and Hebrew Epic: The History of the Religion of Ancient Israel*. Cambridge: Harvard University Press.

Cutler, B., and J. Macdonald

1982 "On the Origin of the Ugaritic Text KTU 1.23." *UF* 14: 33–50.

Day, J.

1985 *God's Conflict with the Dragon and the Sea: Echoes of a Canaanite Myth in the Old Testament*. University of Cambridge Oriental Publications 35. Cambridge: University of Cambridge.

Day, P. L.

1991 "Why is Anat a Warrior and Hunter?" Pp. 141–46, 329–32 in *The Bible and the Politics of Exegesis: Essays in Honor of Norman K. Gottwald on His Sixty-Fifth Birthday*. Ed. D. Jobling, P. L. Day, and G. T. Sheppard. Cleveland, OH: Pilgrim Press.

1992 "Anat: Ugarit's 'Mistress of the Animals.'" *Journal of Near Eastern Studies* 51: 181–90.

DeGuglielmo, A. A.

1955 "Sacrifice in the Ugaritic Texts." *Catholic Biblical Quarterly* 17: 76–96.

del Olmo Lete, G.

1965 "La conquista de Jerico y la leyenda ugaritica de Krt." *Sefarad* 25: 3–15.

1981 *Mitos y leyendas de Canaan segun la tradicion de Ugarit*. Madrid: Ediciones Christiandad.

1984 "Antecedentes cananeos (ugaríticos) de formas literarias hebreo-biblicas." Pp. 83–114 in *Simposio Biblico Español (Salamanca, 1982)*. Ed. N. Fernandez Marcos et al. Madrid: Universidad Complutense.

1992a *La Religión Cananea según la Liturgia de Ugarit. Estudio Textual.* Barcelona: Editorial Ausa.

1992b "Un conjuro ugarítico contra el 'mal ojo' (KTU 1.96)," *Anuario de filologia* 15: 7–16.

Dietrich, M., and O. Loretz

1980a "Die Bannung von Schlangengift (KTU 1.100 und KTU 1.107: 7b–13a. 19b–20)." *UF* 12: 153–70.

1980b "Der Ausmarch des Heeres im Keret-Epos (KTU 1.14 II 27b–III 1// IV9b–31)." *UF* 12: 193–97.

1980c "Das Porträt einer Königin in KTU 1.14 I 12–15. Zur ugaritischen Lexikographie (XVIII)." *UF* 12: 199–204.

1986 "Kerets Krankheit und Amtsunfähigkeit (KTU 1.16 VI 30–38. 43–54b)." *UF* 17: 123–27.

Dietrich, M., O. Loretz, and J. Sanmartín

1974 "Kūn-Š und Škn im Ugaritischen." *UF* 6: 47–53.

1975 "Der Stichometrische Aufbau von RS 24. 258." *UF* 7: 109–14.

Dijkstra, M.

1979 "Some Reflections on the Legend of Aqhat." *UF* 11: 199–210.

1983 "Contributions to the Reconstruction of the Myth of Baᶜal." *UF* 15: 25–31.

1986 "Once Again: The Closing Lines of the Baᶜal Cycle." *UF* 17: 147–52

1988 "The Legend of Danel and The Rephaim." *UF* 20: 35–52.

Dijkstra, M., and J. C. de Moor

1975 "Problematical Passages in the Legend of Aqhâtu." *UF* 7: 171-215.

Dobrusin, D. L.

1981 "The Third Masculine Plural of the Prefixed Form of the Verb in Ugaritic." *Journal of the Ancient Near Eastern Society of Columbia University* 13: 5-14.

Dossin, G.

1980 "Ugarit, Homère et la culture mésopotamienne." *Annales Archéologiques Arabes Syriennes* 29-30: 207-11.

Driver, G. R.

1949 "Ugaritic and Hebrew Problems." *Archiv Orientalni* 17, Part I: 153-57.

1956 *Canaanite Myths and Legends*. Edinburgh: T. & T. Clark.

Durand, J. M.

1993 "Le mythologème du combat entre le dieu de l'orage et la mer en Mésopotamie." *Mari: Annales de Recherches interdisciplinaires* 7: 41-61.

Emerton, J. A.

1969 "The Meaning of the Root 'MZL' in Ugaritic." *Journal of Semitic Studies* 14: 22-33.

Fensham, F. C.

1969a "The Obliteration of the Family as Motif in the Near Eastern Literature." *Annali dell 'Istituto Universitario Orientale di Napoli* 19: 191-99.

1969b "The Son of a Handmaid in Northwest Semitic." *Vetus Testamentum* 19: 312-21.

Fenton, T. L.

1969 "Ugaritica-Biblica." *UF* 1: 65-70.

Finkel, J.

1954 "The Expedition of the Ugaritian King Keret in the Light of Jewish and Kindred Traditions." *Proceedings of the American Academy for Jewish Research* 23: 1-28.

1955 "A Mathematical Conundrum in the Ugaritic Keret Poem." *Hebrew Union College Annual* 26: 109-49.

Fisher, L. R.

1975 "Literary Genres in the Ugaritic Texts." Pp. 131–52 in *Ras Shamra Parallels Vol. 2*. Ed. Loren R. Fisher. *Analecta Orientalia* 50. Rome: Pontifical Biblical Institute.

Freilich, D. F.

1992 "Ili-malku the ṯʿy." *Studi Epigrafici e Linguistici* 9: 21–26.

Gaster, T. H.

1946 "A Canaanite Ritual Drama. The Spring Festival at Ugarit." *Journal of the American Oriental Society* 66: 49–76.

1947 "The Canaanite Epic of Keret." *Jewish Quarterly Review* 37: 285–93.

1952 *The Oldest Stories in the World*. New York: Viking.

1966 *Thespis: Ritual, Myth, and Drama in the Ancient Near East*. Rev. ed. New York: Harper & Row.

Gibson, J. C. L.

1975 "Myth, Legend and Folklore in the Ugaritic Keret and Aqhat Texts." *Vetus Testamentum Supplements* 28: 60–68.

1978 *Canaanite Myths & Legends*. 2nd ed. Edinburgh: T. & T. Clark.

1984 "The Theology of the Ugaritic Baal Cycle." *Orientalia* 53: 202–19.

Ginsberg, H. L.

1935 "Notes on 'The Birth of the Gracious and Beautiful Gods.'" *Journal of the Royal Asiatic Society*: 45–72.

1946 *The Legend of King Keret*. Bulletin of the American Schools of Oriental Research Supplementary Studies 2–3. New Haven: American Schools of Oriental Research.

1969 "Ugaritic Myths, Epics, and Legends." Pp. 129–55 in *Ancient Near Eastern Texts Relating to the Old Testament*. 3d ed. Ed. James B. Pritchard. Princeton: Princeton University Press.

1973 "Ugaritico-Phoenicia." *Journal of the Ancient Near Eastern Society of Columbia University* 5: 131–47.

Good, R. M.
1982 "Metaphorical Gleanings from Ugarit." *Journal of Jewish Studies* 33: 55–59.
1984 "Some Ugaritic Terms Relating to Draught and Riding Animals." *UF* 16: 77–81.
Gordon, C. H.
1955 "Homer and the Bible: The Origin and Character of East Mediterranean Literature." *Hebrew Union College Annual* 26: 43–108.
1965 *Ugaritic Textbook.* Analecta Orientalia 38. Rome: Pontifical Biblical Institute.
1977 "Poetic Legends and Myths from Ugarit." *Berytus* 25: 5–133.
Grabbe, L. L.
1976 "The Seasonal Pattern and the Baal Cycle." *UF* 8: 57–63.
Gray, J.
1964 *The Krt Text in the Literature of Ras Shamra*. 2d ed. Leiden: E. J. Brill.
1965 *The Legacy of Canaan. The Ras Shamra Texts and Their Relevance to the Old Testament*. 2d ed. Vetus Testamentum Supplement 5. Leiden: E. J. Brill.
Greenfield, J. C.
1964 "Ugaritic *mdl* and Its Cognates." *Biblica* 45: 527–34.
1965 "Studies in West Semitic Inscriptions. I: Stylistic Aspects of the Sefire Treaty Inscriptions." *Acta Orientalia* 29: 1–18.
1969 "Some Glosses on the Keret Epic." *Eretz-Israel* 9: 60*–65*.
Greenstein, E. L.
1982a "The Snaring of Sea in the Baal Epic." *MAARAV* 3: 195–216.
1982b "'To Grasp the Hem' in Ugaritic Literature." *Vetus Testamentum* 32: 217–18.
Handy, L. K.
1994 *Among the Host of Heaven: The Syro-Palestinian Pantheon as Bureaucracy.* Winona Lake, IN: Eisenbrauns.
Healey, J. F.
1984 "Burning the Corn: New Light on the Killing of Motu." *Orientalia* 34: 248–51.
Hendel, R. S.
1987 *The Epic of the Patriarch: The Jacob Cycle and the Narrative Traditions of Canaan and Israel*. Harvard Semitic Monographs 42. Atlanta: Scholars Press.
Hens-Piazza, G.
1992 "Repetition and Rhetoric in Canaanite Epic: A Close Reading of KTU 1.14 III 20–49." *UF* 24: 103–12.
Herdner, A.
1963 *Corpus des tablettes en cunéiformes alphabétiques découvertes à Ras Shamra-Ugarit de 1929 à 1939*. Mission de Ras Shamra 10. Paris: Imprimerie Nationale.

1974 "La légende de Keret." Pp. 503–74 in *Textes ougaritiques,* Tome 1: *Mythes et légendes.* By André Caquot, Maurice Sznycer, & Andrée Herdner. Paris: Editions du Cerf.

Herrmann, W.

1968 *Yariḫ und Nikkal und der Preis der Kuṯarāt-Göttinen: Ein kultisch-magischer Text aus Ras Schamra.* Beiheft zur Zeitschrift für die alttestamentliche Wissenschaft 106. Berlin: Töpelmann.

Hoffner, H. A., Jr.

1990 *Hittite Myths.* Ed. G. M. Beckman. Writings from the Ancient World. Atlanta: Scholars Press.

Irvin, D.

1978 *Mytharion: A Comparison of Tales from the Old Testament and the Ancient Near East.* Alter Orient und Altes Testament 32. Neukirchen-Vluyn: Neukirchener Verlag.

Izre'el, S.

1974 "The Symptoms of King KRT's Illness." *UF* 6: 446–48.

Jacobs, I.

1977 "Elements of Near-Eastern Mythology in Rabbinic Aggadah." *Journal of Jewish Studies* 28: 1–11.

Janowski, B.

1980 "Erwägungen zur vorgeschichte des israelitischen *šelamîm*-Opfers." *UF* 12: 231–59.

Kapelrud, A. S.

1979 "Baᶜal, Schöpfung und Chaos." *UF* 11: 407–12.

1980 "The Relationship between El and Baal in the Ras Shamra Texts." Pp. 79–85 in *The Bible World: Essays in Honor of Cyrus H. Gordon.* Ed. Gary A. Rendsburg et al. New York: Ktav.

Kinet, D.

1978 "Theologische Reflexion im ugaritischen Baᶜal-Zyklus." *Biblische Zeitschrift* 22: 236–44.

Kleven, T.

1988 "Kingship in Ugarit." (KTU 1.16 I: 1–23.) Pp. 29–53 in *Ascribe to the Lord: Biblical and Other Studies in Memory of Peter C. Craigie.* Journal for the Study of the Old Testament Supplement 67. Sheffield: Sheffield Academic Press.

Kloos, C. J. L.

1986 *Yhwh's Combat with the Sea: A Canaanite Tradition in the Religion of Ancient Israel.* Amsterdam: van Oorschot; Leiden: Brill.

Knoppers, G. N.

1994 "Dissonance and Disaster in the Legend of Kirta." *Journal of the American Oriental Society* 114: 572–82.

Kottsieper, I.

1984 "KTU 1.100—Versuch einer Deutung.." *UF* 16: 97–110.

Landy, F.
1981 *The Tale of AQHAT*. London: Menard.

Langhe, R. de
1946 "Het Ugarietisch Keretgedicht: Legende, Mythus of Mysteriëspel?" *Miscellanea historica in honorem Albert de Meyer = Receuil de Travaux d'Histoire et de Philosophie* 3/22: 92–108.

Layton, S.
1990 *Archaic Features of Canaanite Personal Names in the Hebrew Bible*. Harvard Semitic Monographs 47. Atlanta: Scholars Press.

Leslau, W.
1987 *Comparative Dictionary of Geʿez (Classical Ethiopic)*. Wiesbaden: Harrassowitz.

Levine, B. A., and J. M. de Tarragon
1984 "Dead Kings and Rephaim: The Patrons of the Ugaritic Dynasty." *Journal of the American Oriental Society* 104: 649–59.
1988 "'Shapshu Cries out in Heaven': Dealing with Snake-Bites at Ugarit (KTU 1.100, 1.107)." *Revue Biblique* 95: 481–518.
1993 "The King Proclaims the Day: Ugaritic Rites for the Vintage (KTU 1.41//1.87)." *Revue Biblique* 100: 76–115.

Lewis, T. J.
1989 *Cults of the Dead in Ancient Israel and Ugarit*. Harvard Semitic Monographs 39. Atlanta: Scholars Press.
1996 "Toward a Literary Translation of the Rapiuma Texts." In *Ugarit, Religion and Culture. Proceedings of the International Colloquium on Ugarit, religion and culture. Edinburgh, July 1994. Essays presented in honour of John C. L. Gibson*. Ugaritisch-Biblische Literatur 12. Ed. N. Wyatt, W. G. E. Watson, and J. B. Lloyd. Münster: Ugarit-Verlag.
1996 "The Goddess Anat Disappears." *Biblical Archaeologist* 59: 115–21. With cover photograph.

L'Heureux, C. E.
1979 *Rank Among the Canaanite Gods*. Harvard Semitic Monographs 21. Missoula, MT: Scholars Press.

Lichtenstein, M. H.
1968 "The Banquet Motif in Keret and in Proverbs 9." *Journal of the Ancient Near Eastern Society of Columbia University* 1: 19–31.
1970 "A Note on the Text of 1 Keret." *Journal of the Ancient Near Eastern Society of Columbia University* 2: 94–100.
1979 "Episodic Structure in the Ugaritic Keret Legend: Comparative Studies in Compositional Technique." Ph.D. dissertation, Columbia University.
1987 "Rite and Writ in an Ugaritic Legend: Ritual and Literary Elements in the Curing of King Keret." Unpublished manuscript.

Lipiński, E.
1965 "Les conceptions et couches merveilleuses de 'Anath.'" *Syria* 42: 45–73.
1986 "Fertility Cult in Ancient Israel." Pp. 207–16 in *Archaeology and Fertility Cult in the Ancient Mediterranean*. Ed. A. Bonanno. Amsterdam: Grüner.

Liverani, Mario
1970 "L'epica ugaritica nel suo contesto storico e letterario." Pp. 859– 69 in *La poesia epica e la sua formazione*. Accademia Nazionale dei Lincei, Quaderno 139.

Lloyd, J. B.
1990 "The Banquet Theme in Ugaritic Narrative." *UF* 22: 169–93.

Loewenstamm, S. E.
1965 "The Seven Day-Unit in Ugaritic Epic Literature." *Israel Exploration Journal* 15: 121–33.
1969 "Eine lehrhafte Ugaritische Trinkburleske." *UF* 1: 71–77.
1992 "On the Theology of the Keret-Epic." Pp. 185–200 in *From Babylon to Canaan: Studies in the Bible and Its Oriental Background*. Jerusalem: Magnes Press.

Maloney, C., ed.
1976 *The Evil Eye*. New York: Columbia University.

Marcus, D.
1973 Review of J. C. de Moor, *New Year with Canaanites and Israelites*. *Journal of the American Oriental Society* 93: 589–91.

Margalit, B.
1976 "Studia Ugaritica II: Studies in *Krt* and *Aqht*." *UF* 8: 137–92.
1980 *A Matter of 'Life' and 'Death': A Study of the Baal-Mot Epic (CTA 4–5–6)*. Alter Orient und Altes Testament 206. Kevelaer: Butzon & Bercker; Neukirchen-Vluyn: Neukirchener Verlag.
1981 "Excursus: The Creation of *Š*ʿ*tqt* (CTA/KTU 16:V:23–30)." *UF* 13: 142–44.
1989 *The Ugaritic Poem of Aqhat*. Berlin: de Gruyter.
1995 K-R-T Studies. *UF* 27: 215–315.

Margulis, B.
1970 "A New Ugaritic Farce (Ras Shamra 24.258)." *UF* 2: 131–38.

Maróth, M.
1973 "Bemerkungen zum ugaritischen Text *KRT*." *Acta Orientalia* 27: 301–7.

Merrill, A. L.
1968 "The House of Keret: A Study of the Keret Legend." *Svensk Exegetist Årsbok* 33: 5–17.

Miller, P. D.
1970 "Animal Names as Designations in Ugaritic and Hebrew." *UF* 2: 177–86.

1988 "Prayer and Sacrifice in Ugarit and Israel." Pp. 139–55 in *Text and Context: Old Testament and Semitic Studies for F. C. Fensham*. Ed. W. Claassen. Journal for the Study of the Old Testament Supplement 48. Sheffield: Sheffield Academic Press.

Moor, J. C. de

1969 "Studies in the New Alphabetic Texts from Ras Shamra I." *UF* 1: 167–75.

1971 *The Seasonal Pattern in the Ugaritic Myth of Baᶜlu According to the Version of Ilimilku*. Alter Orient und Altes Testament 16. Kevelaer: Butzon & Bercker; Neukirchen-Vluyn: Neukirchener Verlag.

1972 *New Year with Canaanite and Israelites*. Part Two: *The Canaanite Sources*. Kampen: Kok.

1980 "El, the Creator." Pp. 171–87 in *The Bible World: Essays in Honor of Cyrus H. Gordon*. Ed. Gary A. Rendsburg et al. New York: Ktav.

1987 *An Anthology of Religious Texts from Ugarit*. Nisaba 16. Leiden: Brill.

1994 "Ugarit and the Origin of Job." Pp. 225–57 in *Ugarit and the Bible: Proceedings of the International Symposium on Ugarit and the Bible, Manchester, September 1992*. Münster: Ugarit-Verlag.

Moor, J. C. de, and K. Spronk

1982a "Problematic Passages in the Legend of Kirtu (I)." *UF* 14: 153–71.

1982b "Problematic Passages in the Legend of Kirtu (II)." *UF* 14: 173–90.

Mosca, P.

1986 "Ugarit and Daniel 7: A Missing Link." *Biblica* 67: 496–517.

Müller, H. P.

1969 "Magisch-mantische Weisheit und die Gestalt Daniels." *UF* 1: 79–94.

O'Connor, D. J.

1989 "The Keret Legend and the Prologue-Epilogue of Job." *Irish Theological Quarterly* 55: 1–6.

O'Connor, M. P.

1989 "Semitic *mgn and Its Supposed Sanskrit Origin." *Journal of the American Oriental Society* 109: 25–32.

Oldenburg, U.

1969 *The Conflict between El and Baᶜal in Canaanite Religion*. Leiden: Brill.

Pardee, D.

1973 "A Note on the Root *ᶜtq* in CTA 16 I 2, 5. (UT 125, KRT II)." *UF* 5: 229–34.

1977 "A New Ugaritic Letter." *Bibliotheca Orientalis* 34: 3–20.

1978 "A Philological and Prosodic Analysis of the Ugaritic Serpent Incantation *UT* 607." *Journal of the Ancient Near Eastern Society of Columbia University* 10: 73–108.

1980 "The New Canaanite Myths and Legends." *Bibliotheca Orientalis* 37: 269–91.

1983 "Visiting Ditanu: The Text of RS 24.272." *UF* 15: 127–40.

1984 "Will the Dragon Never be Muzzled?" *UF* 16: 251–55.

1986 "Ugaritic." *Archiv für Orientforschung* 33: 117–47.

1988a *Ugaritic and Hebrew Poetic Parallelism: A Trial Cut* (ʿnt *I and Proverbs 2*). Vetus Testamentum Supplements 39. Leiden: Brill.

1988b *Les Textes Para-mythologiques de la 24e Campagne (1961)*. Ras Shamra – Ougarit 4. Paris: Editions Recherche sur les Civilizations.

Parker, S. B.

1976 "The Marriage Blessing in Israelite and Ugaritic Literature." *Journal of Biblical Literature* 95: 23–30.

1977 "The Historical Compostion of *Krt* and the Cult of El." *Zeitschrift für die alttestamentliche Wissenschaft* 89: 161–75.

1979 "The Vow in Ugaritic and Israelite Narrative Literature." *UF* 11: 693–700.

1989a *The Pre-Biblical Narrative Tradition: Essays on the Ugaritic Poems* Keret *and* Aqhat. Resources for Biblical Study 24. Atlanta: Scholars Press.

1989b "KTU 1.16 III, the Myth of the Absent God and 1 Kings 18." *UF* 21: 283–96.

1995 "The Literatures of Canaan, Ancient Israel, and Phoenicia: An Overview." Pp. 2399–2410 in *Civilizations of the Ancient Near East*, ed. J. M. Sasson, 4 vols. New York: Scribner's.

Pedersen, J.

1939–40 "Die Krt Legende." *Berytus* 6: 63–105.

Peterson, A. R.

1994 "Where Did Schaeffer Find the Clay Tablets of the Ugaritic Baal-Cycle?" *Scandinavian Journal of the Old Testament* 8: 45–60.

Pitard, W. T.

1992 "A New Edition of the 'Rāpi'ūma' Texts: *KTU* 1.20–22." *Bulletin of the American Schools of Oriental Research* 285 (Feb. 1992): 33–77.

Polak, F.

1992 "Some Aspects of Literary Design in the Ancient Near Eastern Epic." Pp. 135–46 in *kīnattūtu ša darāti: Raphael Kutscher Memorial Volume*. Ed. Anson F. Rainey. Tel Aviv: Tel Aviv University/ Institute of Archaeology.

Pope, M. H.

1955 *El in the Ugaritic Texts*. Leiden: E. J. Brill.

1971 "The Scene on the Drinking Mug from Ugarit." Pp. 393–405 in *Near Eastern Studies in Honor of William Foxwell Albright*. Ed. H. Goedicke. Baltimore/London: John Hopkins, 1971. Reprinted in M. H. Pope 1994, pp. 17–27.

1972 "A Divine Banquet at Ugarit." Pp. 170–203 in *The Use of the Old Testament in the New and Other Essays. Studies in Honor of Wm. F. Stinespring*. Ed. by J. M. Efird. Durham, NC: Duke University Press. Reprinted in Pope 1994, pp. 153–80.

1977a *The Song of Songs*. Anchor Bible 7C. Garden City, NY: Doubleday.

1977b "Notes on the Rephaim Texts from Ugarit." Pp. 165–177 in *Essays on the Ancient Near East in Memory of Jacob Joel Finklestein*. Ed. M. Ellis. Hamden, CT: Archon. Reprinted in Pope 1994, pp. 185–224.

1979 "Ups and Down in El's Amours," *UF* 11: 701–708. Reprinted in Pope 1994, pp. 29–39.

1981 "The Cult of the Dead at Ugarit." Pp. 159–79 in *Ugarit in Retrospect*. Ed. Gordon D. Young. Winona Lake, IN: Eisenbrauns. Reprinted in Pope 1994, pp. 225–50.

1989 "The Status of El at Ugarit." *UF* 19: 219–29. Reprinted in Pope 1994, pp. 47–61.

1994 *Probative Pontificating in Ugaritic and Biblical Literature: Collected Essays*. Ed. M. S. Smith. Ugaritisch-Biblische Literatur 10. Münster: Ugarit-Verlag.

Rainey, A. F.

1974 "The Ugaritic Texts in Ugaritica 5." *Journal of the American Oriental Society* 94: 184–94.

Ratner, R., and B. Zuckerman

1986 "'A Kid in Milk'?: New Photographs of *KTU* 1.23, Line 14." *Hebrew Union College Annual* 57: 15–60.

Renfroe, F.

1992 *Arabic-Ugaritic Lexical Studies*. Abhandlungen zur Literatur Alt-Syrien-Palästinas 5. Münster: Ugarit-Verlag.

Röllig, W.

1978 "Die ugaritische Literatur." Pp. 255–71 in *Altorientalische Literaturen*. Neues Handbuch der Literaturwissenschaft 1. Ed. Wolfgang Röllig. Wiesbaden: Akademische Verlaggesellschaft.

Rüger, H. P.

1969 "Zu RS 24. 258." *UF* 1: 203–6.

Rummel, S.

1981 "Narrative Structures in the Ugaritic Texts." Pp. 221–332 in *Ras Shamra Parallels Vol. 3*. Ed. S. Rummel. Analecta Orientalia 51. Rome: Pontifical Biblical Institute.

Saliba, G. A.

1972 "A Cure for King Keret (IIK, col. vi, 1–13)." *Journal of the American Oriental Society* 92: 107–10.

Sapin, J.

1983 "Quelques systèmes socio-politiques en Syrie au 2e millenaire avant J-C. et leur évolution historique d'après des documents religieux (Légendes, rituels, sanctuaires)." *UF* 15: 157–90.

Sasson, J. M.

1972 "Flora, Fauna and Minerals." Pp. 383–452 in *Ras Shamra Parallels Vol I*. Ed. Loren R. Fisher. Analecta Orientalia 49. Rome: Pontifical Biblical Institute.

Sauren, H., and G. Kestemont
1971 "Keret, roi de Ḫubur." *UF* 3: 181–221.
Schloen, J. D.
1993 "The Exile of Disinherited Kin in KTU 1.12 and KTU 1.23." *Journal of Near Eastern Studies* 52: 209–20.
Schmidt, B. B.
1994 *Israel's Beneficent Dead*. Tübingen: J. C. B. Mohr.
Selms. A. van
1954 *Marriage and Family Life in Ugaritic Literature*. London: Luzac.
Seow, C. L.
1984 "The Syro-Palestinian Context of Solomon's Dream." *Harvard Theological Review* 77: 141–52.
1989 *Myth, Drama, and the Politics of David's Dance*. Harvard Semitic Monographs 44. Atlanta: Scholars Press.
Smith, M. S.
1984 "The Magic of Kothar, the Ugaritic Craftsman God, in KTU 1.6 VI 49–50." *Revue Biblique* 91: 377–80.
1990 *The Early History of God: Yahweh and the Other Deities in Ancient Israel*. San Francisco: Harper & Row.
1994a "Mythology and Myth-making in Ugaritic and Israelite Literatures." Pp. 293–341 in *Ugarit and the Bible: Proceedings of the International Symposium on Ugarit and the Bible. Manchester, September 1992*. Ed. G. J. Brooke, A. H. W. Curtis and J. F. Healey. Ugaritisch-Biblische Literatur 11. Münster: Ugarit-Verlag.
1994b *The Ugaritic Baʿal Cycle: Volume I: Introduction with Text, Translation and Commentary of KTU 1.1–1.2*. Vetus Testamentum Supplements 55. Leiden: Brill.
1995 "Anat's Warfare Cannibalism and the West Semitic Ban." Pp. 368–86 in *The Pitcher is Broken: Memorial Essays for Gösta W. Ahlström*. Ed. S. W. Holloway and L. K. Handy. Journal for the Study of the Old Testament Supplement Series 190. Sheffield: Sheffield Academic Press.
Spronk, K.
1986 *Beatific Afterlife in Ancient Israel and in the Ancient Near East*. Alter Orient und Altes Testament 219. Kevelaer: Butzon & Bercker; Neukirchen: Neukirchener Verlag.
Stolz, F.
1982 "Funcktionen und Bedeutungsbereiche des ugaritischen Ba'almythos." Pp. 83–118 in *Funktionen und Leistungen des Mythos: Drei altorientalische Beispiele*. Ed. J. Assman et al. Orbis Biblicus et Orientalis 48. Freiburg: Universitätsverlag; Göttingen: Vandenhoeck & Ruprecht.
Talmon, S.
1992 "The 'Topped Triad': A Biblical Literary Convention and the

'Ascending Numerical' Pattern." *Maarav* 8 (=*Studies in Memory of Stanley Gevirtz Part II*): 181–98.

Tropper, J.

1989 *Nekromantie*. Neukirchen-Vluyn: Neukirchener Verlag.

Tsumura, D. T.

1984 "The Problem of Childlessness in the Royal Epic of Ugarit: An Analysis of KRT [KTU 1.14:I]: 1–25." *Bulletin of the Middle Eastern Culture Center of Japan* 1: 11–20.

Veldhuis, N.

1991 *A cow of Sin*. Library of Oriental Texts 2. Groningen: Styx Publications.

Verreet, E.

1987 "Der Keret-Prolog." *UF* 19: 317–35.

Virolleaud, C.

1933 "La naissance des dieux gracieux et beaux, poème phénicien de Ras Shamra." *Syria* 14: 128–51.

1936 *La légende de Keret, roi des Sidoniens*. Mission de Ras Shamra 2. Paris: Imprimerie Nationale.

1939 "La légende du roi Kérèt, d'aprés de nouveaux documents." Pp. 755–62 in *Mélanges syriens offerts à Monsieur René Dussaud par ses amis et ses élèves*. Paris: Paul Geuthner.

1941a "Le roi Kéret et son fils (II K). Part 1." *Syria* 22: 105–36.

1941b "Le roi Kéret et son fils (II K). Part 2." *Syria* 22: 197–217.

1942–43a "Le roi Kéret et son fils (II K). Part 3." *Syria* 23: 1–20.

1942–43b "Le mariage du roi Kéret (III K)." *Syria* 23: 137–72.

1942–45 "Le mariage du roi Kéret d'après les tablettes de Ras-Shamra." *Revue des Etudes Sémitiques*: 50–58.

1960 "Un nouvel épisode du mythe ugaritique de Baal." *Comptes rendus des seances de l'académie des inscriptions et belles-lettres*: 180–86.

Walcot, P.

1969 "The Comparative Study of Ugaritic and Greek Literatures." *UF* 1: 111–18.

Walls, N. H.

1992 *The Goddess Anat in Ugaritic Myth*. Society of Biblical Literature Dissertation Series 135. Atlanta: Scholars Press.

Watson, W. G. E.

1976a "Puzzling Passages in the Tale of Aqhat." *UF* 8: 371–78.

1976b "A Suppliant Surprised (CTA 16 I 41b–53a)." *Journal of the Ancient Near Eastern Society of Columbia University* 8: 105–11.

1989 "What does Ugaritic *gmn* mean?" *Aula Orientalis* 7: 129–31.

1990 "Comments on KTU 1.114: 29'–31'." *Aula Orientalis* 8: 265–67.

Westermann, C.
1980 *The Promises to the Fathers*. Trans. David E. Green. Philadelphia: Fortress Press.

Wiggins, S.
1993 *A Reassessment of 'Asherah'*. Alter Orient und Altes Testament 235. Kevelaer: Butzon & Bercker; Neukirchen: Neukirchener Verlag.

Wyatt, N.
1977 "The Identity of *Mt wŠr*." *UF* 9: 379–81.
1983 "A Suggested Historical Context of the Keret Story." *UF* 15: 316–18.

Xella, P.
1973 *Il mito di Šḥr e Šlm: Saggio sulla mitologia ugaritica*. Studi Semitici 44. Roma: Istituto di Studi del Vicino Oriente.
1984 "Eblaita *mu-ḫu* SAG ed ugaritico *mḫ riš*." *Studi Epigrafici e Linguistici* 1: 27–33.
1976 *Problemi del Mito nel Vicino Oriente Antico*. Annali del'Istituto Orientale di Napoli Supplement 7.

Yon, M., D. Pardee, and P. Bordreuil
1992 "Ugarit." Pp. 695–721 in vol. 6 of *The Anchor Bible Dictionary*. Ed. D. N. Freedman. 6 vols. New York: Doubleday.

Glossary

Abiluma. The "Town of Prince Yarikh," near the place where Aqhat was killed. One of three towns that Daniel curses after burying Aqhat's remains.

Amurru. Either the coastal kingdom of the Late Bronze Age located to the south of Ugarit or the eastern region of Jebel Bishri. The Baal Cycle mentions it for its abundance of animals.

Anat (Anath). A goddess of war, daughter of El and sister of Baal. Full of concern for her brother, she is often depicted as being violent and obstinate toward others. Her epithet, "Anat the Girl" or "Adolescent Anat," reflects her status as a young adolescent who has not borne children and who here operates outside the authority of father or husband. She sometimes appears in the form of a bird.

Aqhat. The son of Daniel and protagonist of the story which bears his name. He is killed due to Anat's desire for his bow. His most common epithet is "Aqhat the Hero."

Arsay. One of three women who are referred to as Baal's "daughters" and "brides." Her name means "Earthy" or "Underworldly," perhaps related to Baal's descent into the underworld. Her most common epithet is "Daughter of the Wide World (?)."

Asherah. See **Athirat.**

Astarte (Athtart). Goddess of war (as known especially from New Kingdom Egyptian texts). She is often paired with Anat. Her epithets include the "Name of (or: named with) Baal" (reflecting the two deities' close relationship).

Athirat (Asherah). The consort of El and the mother of the gods, who are sometimes called "the (seventy) sons of Athirat." Asherah is attested in the Hebrew Bible (2 Kgs 21:7; 23:4), in the Kuntillet ʿAjrud inscriptions in the phrase "Yahweh and his Asherah," and in inscriptions from Tel Miqne-Ekron. Her epithets include: "Creatress of the Gods," "Mother of the Gods," and "Lady Athirat of the Sea." In a particular manifestations she is "Asherah of Tyre" (or the Tyrians) or "the Goddess of Sidon" (or the Sidonians). Variant forms of her name appear in Akkadian, Egyptian, and Hittite sources.

Athtar. An astral god and Athirat's son, who is nominated to replace Baal as king in the Baal Cycle. His full title is "Athtar the Strong."

Attenu. Teacher of the scribe Ilimalku and the chief of priests mentioned in the colophons at the end of the Baal Cycle and the first tablet of the Aqhat narrative.

Ayyamarri. One of two weapons, along with Yagarrish, made by Kothar-wa-Khasis for Baal to use in his fight against Yamm. The name means literally "may he expel all."

Baal. "Lord," the Canaanite storm god and lord of the sky who resides on Mount Saphon. His proper name is Haddu. He is depicted as a warrior and his weapons are thunder (his voice) and lightning. His major battles are with Yamm and Mot. He also provides rain and fertility. Although El is the patriarch of the pantheon, Baal plays the largest role in the Ugaritic narratives. His epithets include: "Dagon's Son" (he is not the son of El and Asherah, but refers to El as his father), "Prince Baal of the Earth," "Mighty Baal," "Mightiest of Warriors," "Rider of the Clouds," and "Most High." Many of the motifs associated with Baal are used to describe Yahweh in the Hebrew Bible.

Bibit. A place associated with Rashap in text 25.

Byblos. A cosmopolitan city during the Bronze Age. It is located on the coast of Lebanon about twenty miles north of Beirut. It was a principal seaport and one of the most important Phoenician cities in later periods.

Caphtor. See **Kaphtor.**

Chemosh. Familiar from the Bible as the god of the Moabites, he is now known from the third millennium on in Syria and appears to have chthonic associations.

Dagan (Dagon). Although prominent in Syrian religion from the third millennium on, he has no major role in the Ugaritic narratives, appearing chiefly in Baal's title "the Son of Dagan." Later, he appears in the Bible as the god of the Philistines.

Danatiya. The wife of Daniel in the Aqhat narrative. Her fuller name is "Danatiya the Lady."

Daniel. The father of Aqhat and Paghit in the Aqhat narrative. His epithets include the following: "Man of Rapiu," "the Hero," "Man of the Harnemite."

Dawn (Shahar). A minor god who is the sibling of Dusk. Their birth is recounted in text 23.

Death. See **Mot.**

Desire. Anat's opponent whom she defeats in text 9, also called "Beloved of El."

Ditana (Ditanu). An ancient ancestor of Kirta, a leader among the shades of the dead.

Dusk (Shalim). A minor god who is the sibling of Dawn. Their birth is recounted in text 23.

Eaters. Extraordinary beings whose birth is recounted, along with that of the Tearers, in text 17.

El. The patriarch of the gods and the patron of kings. (The word "El" is also the common noun for god.) He is depicted as an old, wise man with a grey beard. His epithets include the following: "Father of Humanity," "Father," "Bull El," "Creator of Creatures," "the King," "the Father of Years," and "Beneficent El the Benign." Many of the motifs associated with El are used to describe Yahweh in the Hebrew Bible.

Fire. Anat's opponent whom she defeats in text 9, also called "Bitch of El."

Flame. Anat's opponent whom she defeats in text 9, also called "Daughter of El."

Gapn. One of Baal's messengers who is paired with Ugar. His name means "vine," perhaps a reflection of the agricultural fertility produced by Baal's rains.

Habaya. A minor figure in text 19 who scolds El for his drunkenness. He has the epithet "He of two horns and a tail."

Hadd (Hadad). The Semitic storm god who controls elements of storms (rain, thunder, and lightning) and, therefore, fertility. He is usually referred to by his title, "Baal" ("Lord").

Hargub. The father of the birds in the Aqhat narrative whose belly is torn open in Daniel's search for his son's remains.

Hasis. See **Kothar.**

Hell. A modern translation for the underworld, which is not a fiery place of the devil, but a deep pit located beneath the earth. It serves as home to the dead and is the realm of Mot, the god of Death.

Horon. An underworld deity. His name is invoked in curses against enemies in Ugaritic narrative poems, against snakebites in text 25, and against demons elsewhere.

Huraya (Lady Huraya). The wife of Kirta and daughter of King Pabuli whom Kirta takes in marriage after negotiations with Pabuli. Her epithet is "The Fair One."

Ilhau. Kirta's second-born son.

Ilimilku (Ilimalku). A well-known scribe at Ugarit. His name appears in the colophons at the end of the Kirta narrative and Baal Cycle.

Ilish. The herald god; the herald of Baal's house.

INBB. Anat's home, mentioned in parallelism with UGR.

ITHM. A deity mentioned with SHGR in the Baal Cycle and in a god-list. Based on the association with SHGR, this minor deity may be regarded as a patron of some aspect of agricultural fertility.

Kaphtor. Crete. One of Kothar's two homes reflecting the association of both with metallurgy.

Katharat. Goddesses of conception in Aqhat and patrons of wedlock and conception in text 24. Their most common epithet is "the radiant daughters of the (new) moon."

Khirikhbi. The divine matchmaker in text 24. He is called the "King of Summer" and the "King of Marriage."

Khubur. The town in which Kirta lived and the capital city of his kingdom.

Kirta. The protagonist of the Kirta narrative. He is the king of Khubur. His epithets include the following: "Pleasant, Lad of El"; "Scion of El"; "Kirta the Noble"; "Devotee of El"; "Son of the Gentle and Holy One."

KNRT. The place where Daniel buries Aqhat's remains; it is paired with MDGT.

Kothar (and Khasis). The artisan(s) of the gods who produced Aqhat's bow, Baal's palace, and furniture for Athirat. The names mean "skilled and wise." Also called Hayyan.

Lebanon. A coastal mountain range running from north to south in modern Syria and Lebanon. It was famous for its cedars.

Litan. A cosmic enemy of Baal, mentioned as Leviathan in the Hebrew Bible (Isa 27:1; Ps 74:14; Job 3:8; 40:25). His epithets include the following: "the Fleeing Serpent," "the Twisting Serpent," "Potentate with Seven Heads."

MDGT. The place where Daniel buries Aqhat's remains, paired with KNRT.

Memphis. A city in Egypt, residence of the Egyptian artisan god, Ptah. The Baal Cycle and Aqhat mention it as one of Kothar's two homes.

Milk. A minor god mentioned in text 25, associated with Athtart (place name).

Mot. The god of death and the underworld, one of Baal's two major rivals in the Baal Cycle, in which he temporarily gains power over Baal. His name means simply "Death." His epithets include "Beloved of El."

Mount KNKNY. A mountain at the entrance to the underworld.

Mount KS. The mountain containing El's dwelling.

Mount LL. The mountain where the Ugaritic pantheon meets under the leadership of El. This mountain has been identified with Mount KS, the mountain of El's home, but this equation is uncertain.

Mount Nani. Mt. Anti-Casius.

Mount Saphon (Mount Zaphon). A mountain north of Ugarit where Baal resides. It is known in Akkadian and Hittite sources as Mount Hazzi, in classical sources as Mons Casius, and today as Jebel al-Aqra . See illustration.

Mount THRMG. A mountain at the entrance to the underworld, at the edge of the earth.

Mount TRGZZ. A mountain at the entrance to the underworld, at the edge of the earth.

MRRT TGHLL BNR. A town near the place where Aqhat was killed. It is one of three towns which Daniel curses after burying Aqhat's remains.

Nahar. An epithet of Yamm meaning "River," characteristically occurring in the expression "Judge River."

Nikkal. The Mesopotamian moon goddess. Her epithets include the following: "Great Lady," "the Fruit," and "Radiant One." In text 24 she marries Yarikh, the West Semitic moon god.

Niqmadd. A king of Ugarit in the mid-fourteenth century B.C.E. His name appears in the colophons at the end of the Kirta narrative and Baal Cycle.

Pabuli. The king of Udum, a city that Kirta attacks. Kirta takes Pabuli's daughter Huraya as his wife.

Paghit. The daughter of Daniel and sister of Aqhat, who sets out to avenge Aqhat's death in the Aqhat narrative. Her epithets include the following: "Bearer of Water," "Collector of Dew from the Fleece," and "Who knows the Course of the Stars."

Pidray. One of three women referred to as Baal's "daughters" and "brides." The meaning of her name is debated. She also has the title "Daughter of Light," perhaps a reflection of her meteorological kinship with Baal.

QR-MYM. A town near the place where Aqhat was killed. It is one of three towns that Daniel curses after burying Aqhat's remains.

Qudsh wa-Amrar. Athirat's servant. His double name may mean "Holy and Blessed." The second element may reflect the name Amurru, that of an Amorite god attested as the consort of Ashratu, the cuneiform equivalent of Athirat. He bears the title "Fisher of Athirat," reflecting Athirat's association with the sea.

Rahmay. A minor goddess mentioned in the Kirta narrative.

Rashap. The winged god of pestilence (cf. the biblical Resheph).

Rebel. Anat's opponent whom she defeats in text 9, also called "Calf of El."

Rephaim. The "shades" or inhabitants of the underworld. The Rephaim (Rapiuma), who are the focus of texts 20-22, are also mentioned in the Hebrew Bible, where they appear both as the dead and a race of giants.

RGT. A place associated with Yarikh in text 25.

Samal. The mother of the birds in the Aqhat narrative, in whose belly Aqhat's remains are finally found.

Sapan. See **Mount Saphon.**

Sea. See **Yamm.**

Shades. See **Rephaim.**

Shapsh. The sun goddess. The name means simply "Sun." She bears the title "Divine Lamp." She communicates El's will to other deities in her travels through both the world and the underworld.

Shataqat. A divine being created by El to heal Kirta from his illness. Her name means literally "The female who causes (the illness) to pass." Her epithets include the following: "Remover of Illness," "Dispeller of Disease."

SHGR. A deity mentioned together with ITHM in the Baal Cycle and in a god-list. The deity's name may reflect an association with the offspring of animals.

Sidon. A Phoenician coastal city associated with Asherah and paired with Tyre in the Kirta narrative.

Siryan. Inland mountains running from north to south east of the Lebanon range; also known as the Anti-Lebanon.

Tallay. One of three women referred to as Baal's "daughters" and "brides." She is called the "Daughter of Rain."

Tearers. Extraordinary beings whose birth is recounted, along with the Eaters, in text 17.

Thitmanit ("Octavia"). Kirta's eighth child. Her name means literally "the Eighth."

THRMN. Part of Niqmaddu's title (a place or divine name?) mentioned in the colophon at the end of the Baal Cycle.

Tunnan. One of the cosmic enemies which Anat claims to have defeated.

The Hebrew Bible mentions this figure as one of Yahweh's foes (Job 3:8), and a group of Yahweh's enemies, also known by this name, reside in the cosmic waters (Job 38:8; Pss 74:13; 89:10).

Tuttul. The cultic center of the god Dagan; mentioned in text 25.

Tyre. A Phoenician coastal city associated with Asherah and paired with Sidon in the Kirta narrative.

Udum. City of King Pabuli, which he claims as a gift from El, but which Kirta attacks in the Kirta narrative.

Ugar. One of Baal's two messengers, paired with Gapn. His name means "field," perhaps a reflection of the agricultural fertility produced by Baal's rains.

Yagarrish. One of two weapons, along with Ayyamarri, made by Kothar for Baal's fight against Yamm. The name means literally "may he drive."

Yaman. A region renowned for its abundance of wild oxen according to the Baal Cycle; its location is uncertain.

Yamm. One of Baal's two great rivals. The name means simply "Sea." (See also Nahar.) His full title is "Prince Yamm." Like Mot, he is called "Beloved of El." He is mentioned in the Hebrew Bible as Yahweh's enemy (Ps 74:13; Job 7:12; 26:12; 38:8).

Yarikh. The West Semitic moon god.

Yassib. Kirta's firstborn son. His name literally means "he who erects (his father's mortuary stele after his death)."

YDᶜ-YLHN. One of Athirat's sons nominated to be king of the pantheon during Baal's absence in the Baal Cycle. His name seems to mean "knowledgeable sage" or the like.

YRGB. Part of Niqmaddu's title (a place or divine name?) mentioned in the colophon at the end of the Baal Cycle.

YTPN. The "Sutean Warrior" who helps Anat in her plot to kill Aqhat.

Zaphon. See Mount Saphon.

Indexes

1. Deities and Other Extraordinary Beings

2. Personal Names

3. Places

4. Subjects

5. References to the Bible and Pseudepigrapha